KOHUT'S LEGACY

Contributions to Self Psychology

KOHUT'S LEGACY

Contributions
to Self Psychology

Edited by

Paul E. Stepansky and Arnold Goldberg

 THE ANALYTIC PRESS
1984

Distributed by
LAWRENCE ERLBAUM ASSOCIATES, PUBLISHERS
Hillsdale, New Jersey   London

The Analytic Press

Distributed solely by

Lawrence Erlbaum Associates, Inc., Publishers
365 Broadway
Hillsdale, New Jersey 07642

Library of Congress Cataloging in Publication Data
Main entry under title:

Kohut's legacy.

   Bibliography: p.
   Includes indexes.
   1. Psychoanalysis.   2. Self.   3. Kohut, Heinz.
I. Stepansky, Paul E.   II. Goldberg, Arnold, 1929–
RC506.K654   1984   150.19′5   84-4192
ISBN 0-88163-016-0

Printed in the United States of America
10 9 8 7 6 5 4 3 2 1

Contents

Contributors

Gerald Adler, M.D.—Training and Supervising Analyst, Boston Psychoanalytic Society and Institute; Director of Medical Student Education in Psychiatry, Massachusetts General Hospital.

Michael Franz Basch, M.D.—Faculty, Training and Supervising Analyst, Chicago Institute for Psychoanalysis; Professor of Psychiatry, Rush Medical College.

Bernard Brandchaft, M.D.—Training and Supervising Analyst, Los Angeles Psychoanalytic Society and Institute; Assistant Clinical Professor of Psychiatry, UCLA School of Medicine.

Frank M. Lachmann, Ph.D.—Faculty, Senior Supervisor and Training Analyst, Postgraduate Center for Mental Health, New York.

Joan A. Lang, M.D.—Assistant Clinical Professor of Psychiatry, UCLA School of Medicine.

Lars B. Lofgren, M.D.—Training and Supervising Analyst, Los Angeles Institute for Psychoanalytic Studies; Associate Professor of Psychiatry, UCLA School of Medicine.

Andrew P. Morrison, M.D.—Assistant Professor of Psychiatry, Harvard University Medical School at the Massachusetts Mental Health Center; Member, Boston Psychoanalytic Society and Institute.

Hyman L. Muslin, M.D.—Professor of Psychiatry, Abraham Lincoln School of Medicine, University of Illinois; Faculty, Continuing Education Division, Chicago Institute for Psychoanalysis.

Anna Ornstein, M.D.—Professor of Child Psychiatry, College of Medicine, University of Cincinnati; Faculty, Cincinnati Psychoanalytic Institute.

Kurt A. Schlesinger, M.D.—Associate Professor of Psychiatry, University of California at San Francisco; Faculty, San Francisco Psychoanalytic Institute.

Estelle Shane, Ph.D—Director, Center for Early Education, Los Angeles; Research Clinical Associate, Los Angeles Psychoanalytic Society and Institute.

Robert D. Stolorow, Ph.D.—Professor of Psychology, Albert Einstein College of Medicine Campus, Yeshiva University; Training and Supervising Analyst, Institute of the National Psychological Association for Psychoanalysis.

Paul H. Tolpin, M.D.—Faculty, Training and Supervising Analyst, Chicago Institute for Psychoanalysis; Associate Attending, Michael Reese Hospital Medical Center.

Ernest S. Wolf, M.D.—Faculty, Training and Supervising Analyst, Chicago Institute for Psychoanalysis; Assistant Professor of Psychiatry, Northwestern University Medical School.

Acknowledgment

The editors are indebted to Nicholas Cariello for his valuable collaborative assistance in organizing this volume. The contributors are indebted to him for his superb developmental line editing of their manuscripts. We have a superior book for his efforts.

Preface

THE DEBATE SURROUNDING the historical meaning and clinical implications of psychoanalytic self psychology continues unabated in the aftermath of Heinz Kohut's death. But the debate, in itself, pays homage to Kohut: The fact that self psychology has mobilized the introspective potential of the psychoanalytic profession writ large bears testimony to the catalytic importance of Kohut's work to analysts of various theoretical persuasions. In the aftermath of Kohut, in other words, it has become increasingly incumbent on *any* analyst professing theoretical credibility to reflect with heightened sensitivity on *how* he observes *what* he observes, and on what he can or cannot do—empathically, interpretively, or otherwise—with the yield of his observations. Self psychology has revivified psychoanalysis, even as it has promoted new points of contact between analysis and the wider scientific community.

A related point about Kohut's legacy should also be made. To the extent that analysts of all theoretical persuasions now wrestle with the fundamental questions highlighted by Kohut's work, they, perforce, cultivate historical sensibilities which, before Kohut, complacently lay fallow. To consider simultaneously the ranging theoretical compass and the time-bound limitations of classical psychoanalytic theory, to confront at one and the same time the significant clinical potentialities and the circumscribed clinical parameters inhering in the classical psychoanalytic method, to reflect critically on how psychoanalysts "cure" their patients and on just what types of patients they can presume to have cured—to discuss such matters in a spirit of open-minded inquiry is to engage in a kind of Socratic broadening that invariably benefits all participants to the dialogue and, one would hope, all their patients as well.

By way of demonstrating the continuing centrality of self psychology, by way of exemplifying the enriching legacy of Heinz Kohut, we have assembled in this volume noteworthy contributions to the 1981 Berkeley Self Psychology Conference and the 1982 Atlanta Self Psychology Conference, respectively.

Our contributors address themselves to a variety of issues: to
the developmental and epistemological moorings of self psychology, to the refinement of its theoretical presentation, and
to the range of its clinical and nonclinical applications. Collectively, these papers highlight important questions about psychoanalysis that must be addressed in the aftermath of Kohut's
death. At the same time, they offer the type of critical emenda-
tions to, and elaborations of, self psychology that must be forthcoming if Kohut's work is to remain a wellspring of psychoanalytic innovation in the years ahead.

By way of prologue to the collection, we offer Michael
Basch's thoughtful assessment of the selfobject theory of motivation within the history of psychoanalysis. Basch makes a per-
suasive case for the evolutionary character of self psychology,
contending that Kohut's inductive receptiveness to his clinical
data and undogmatic estimation of theory are thoroughly
"Freudian" in substance and spirit. His reminder that Freud's
central achievement consisted in "raising the scientific interpretation of psychological manifestations to its own universe
of discourse" not only provides the context for adjudging
Kohut's clinical breakthroughs, but serves as the methodological watchword of the chapters to follow.

The papers in Section II probe the theoretical implications
of Kohut's work from the standpoint of the dual unity of self
and selfobject. Basch's historically informed exposition of these
terms highlights both the clinical circumstances out of which
they evolved and the scientific advances which accrue from
their utilization as psychoanalytic explanatory constructs. The
following chapters by Joan Lang and Andrew Morrison provide ample testimony to the fact that self-psychologically informed theorizing in the spirit of Kohut need hardly conform
to the letter of Kohut. They bear out Basch's claim that the self-
psychological orientation militates against the dogmatic pro-
clivities of "doctrinal psychoanalysis," opening the door to new
discoveries in the spirit of Kohut's own pioneering advances.
Lang points to a genuine lacuna in self psychology—the failure
to demarcate with sufficient precision the constituents of the
"feminine" self—and provides some pertinent suggestions for
filling it in. Morrison's probing analysis of shame excavates and

integrates Kohut's scattered remarks on this phenomenon, only to propose a significant revision of the self-psychological perspective on this complex affect.

Section III offers a number of perceptive commentaries on the therapeutic yield that follows from the self-psychological focus on self and selfobject. The first two chapters are substantive contributions to the timely nosological problem of the "borderline" diagnosis; they demonstrate the range of self-psychological interpretive strategies that may be brought to bear on a specific clinical issue. Bernard Brandchaft and Robert Stolorow propose that the very notion of a borderline character structure is fallacious, insofar as borderline phenomena necessarily presuppose the "archaic intersubjective context" of a therapist and a patient in a self-selfobject relationship; self psychology, they argue, provides the "observer" with an intersubjective focus whereby borderline phenomena can be profitably *reformulated* as dynamic self disorders. Gerald Adler, for his part, invokes a self-psychological referent to *sustain* the viability of the borderline diagnosis and to differentiate, both diagnostically and prognostically, borderline patients from patients with more tractable "narcissistic personality disorders." Ernest Wolf concerns himself with the transferential and countertransferential implications of working with such difficult patients; he explores "disruptions" in the treatment of self disorders which follow from the analyst's inability to monitor infallibly the analysand's selfobject requirements. Taking the selfobject concept beyond the purview of psychoanalytic treatment per se, Basch comments perceptively on the relevance of the selfobject to any type of effective psychotherapy. His remarks are complemented nicely by Anna Ornstein's brief, albeit compelling, illustration of how a nonanalytic transaction can be illuminated by the invocation of a self-psychological perspective incorporating the selfobject concept.

In Section IV, we proceed to a series of illuminating extensions of the self-psychological viewpoint to phenomena "beyond the bounds of the basic rule," to borrow Kohut's expression. Estelle Shane demonstrates the relevance of self-psychological formulations to the diagnosis and pedagogical management of children with learning disabilities; of special note is her self-psychological rendering of data derived from educational research concerning the learning disabled. Lars Lofgren applies the insights of self psychology to the dynamic transactions typifying Wilfred Bion's Tavistock study groups; by implication, his chapter points to the relevance of the self-psychological viewpoint to an understanding of dynamic group therapy in general. Hyman Muslin demonstrates the explanatory power of self psychology in the *explication de texte* of Shakespearean tragedy, in this case, *Othello*. On a more expansive note, Kurt Schlesinger ends the volume with a moving odyssey into his personal past. For Schlesinger, self psychology does not provide an explanatory handle for deciphering meaning; instead, it supplies an existential focus for achieving meaning and, hence, mastery within the subjective contours of life history.

It is fitting that we end the volume with Schlesinger's contribution to the psychology of creativity for, taken together, the papers in this volume indicate that Kohut's work itself remains a potent catalyst for psychoanalysts aspiring to creativity in their professional lives. His is a creative legacy that has infused the dialogue among analysts with new vitality and animation; it presents analysts with insights that are valuable precisely because they circumscribe with sensitivity and, often, poignancy, those fundamental issues of theory and therapy about which insight is most urgently required. In offering this collection of contributions to self psychology, we seek to do justice to Kohut's legacy in its rich two-sidedness—as a body of clinical and theoretical wisdom that has permanently enriched psychoanalysis at the same time as it invites continuing refinement and emendation.

That Kohut's work has generated lively controversy among analysts is, by now, apparent to friend, foe, and bystander alike. But that this revitalizing controversy is itself predicated on the magnitude of Kohut's personal achievement is a fact that certain "opponents" of self psychology would rather leave unsaid. With this collection, we vouchsafe this achievement by demonstrating its continuing fruitful yield at the level of theory, clinical practice, and application.

PROLOGUE: SELF PSYCHOLOGY IN PERSPECTIVE

1 The Selfobject Theory of Motivation and the History of Psychoanalysis

Michael Franz Basch, M.D.

SOME MONTHS AGO I was asked to be a member of a panel dealing with the centrality of the oedipal conflict for psychoanalysis. Urging me to join them, my caller told me that the organizers of the panel were especially eager to have a Kohutian represented in the discussion. No such animal exists, I told him; I and others like me who study and take very seriously the implications of Kohut's contributions to psychoanalysis form no monolithic movement of the sort implied by the term "Kohutian." I am certainly proud to be identified as a student of Kohut's, but if I am to be on your panel you will hear my ideas. I do not speak for his other students and they do not speak for me, and Kohut's work speaks for itself.

Shortly thereafter, I received a letter from one of the other organizers welcoming me to a panel on current views on the role of the oedipal constellation in *neurosogenesis*, and the suggestion that we should all keep our presentations clinically grounded so as not to drift too far from the topic. This time I wrote suggesting that they had better find someone else, since I felt I had nothing to say about this topic that had not been said already and said very well by Sigmund Freud. The centrality of the Oedipus complex for psychoanalysis as a whole has become a controversial issue, and Kohut's work addresses it directly and indirectly; as far as I know, however, when it comes to the formation of the psychoneuroses, that is, for neurosogenesis, there is no argument but that the vicissitudes of the oedipal phase and the resulting conflict are central for the pathology that must be analyzed. Kohut certainly states that quite clearly in *The Restoration of the Self* (1977), and I would have nothing to add. As far as keeping my presentation clinically grounded, here too I would be at a loss as to what I might contribute. Some fifteen or so years ago I did have one case of a psychoneurotic patient of the sort Freud described, and by following Freud's papers on technique to the letter I watched the patient do exactly what Freud predicted she would do. A classic transference neurosis developed, was interpreted and resolved, and a grateful patient left symptom free with, as Freud (1923) put it, the ego in the position it would have been in had her pathology not originally interfered with its development. What more is there to say? Send me a patient with a psychoneurosis today and I, like any other properly trained psychoanalyst, will have that marvelous and dramatic experience of once more "being Freud," that is, seeing before my eyes what Freud himself saw, and corroborating the brilliance of his insight into the psychoneuroses.

Let me be frank to the point of bluntness. When we so-called Kohutians are asked to participate in national psychoanalytic meetings it is as representatives of an alien movement, a dissident school, and it soon becomes clear that there are those who feel they must defend psychoanalysis against this anti-analytic heresy, this anti-Freudian conspiracy. Whence this conviction that Kohut, and by implication his students, "don't believe in the Oedipus complex," or "don't analyze the oedipal conflict," or "gratify rather than interpret"? Where does the notion come from that Heinz Kohut wanted to do anything besides advance traditional psychoanalysis? Read again Ornstein's summary and appreciation of Kohut as teacher, clinician, and author in the introduction to *The Search for the Self* (Kohut, 1978). Was there anyone more deeply immersed in, more knowledgeable about, or more sincerely dedicated to Freud's work than Heinz Kohut? As Kohut himself said in his last public address at Berkeley, for years he was "Mr. Psychoanalysis." What is it now about Kohut's work that agitates some of our colleagues so?

I would like to suggest that given the history of the development of psychoanalysis as a branch of science, the distortion to which Kohut's work has been and is subjected is not a new but, rather, a repetitive and predictable phenomenon, whose explanation lies not in Kohut's work per se, but in the confusion about the nature of psychoanalysis, a confusion that Freud inadvertently built into his theory long before psychoanalysis as such came to be, and that has always handicapped its scientific development and practice.

Perhaps the most important stumbling block to progress in psychoanalysis is a misunderstanding as to the nature and purpose of theory. All science originates not in induction or deduction, but in what Aristotle called abduction, that is, in the formulation of hypotheses that are subject to practical testing and then altered in keeping with what experiment and experience teach the investigator about those hypotheses. A theory or a concept is an organizing framework that enables us to think about a particular subject. Without a theory all is noise and confusion. A theory orients us, tells us what we should see so we may look for it, and what we should hear so we may listen for it. A theory tells us what is to be figure and what is to be background, what we should pay attention to and what may be disregarded. Only with the map provided by theory can we begin to find our way in a new and different situation. A *scientific* theory is one that is organized and promulgated formally and subject to direct or indirect experimentation that will confirm or disprove its hypotheses. Paradoxical as it sounds, the ultimate goal of scientific work is to disprove the theory which first made it possible, because in doing so a more accurate and more encompassing framework is erected, one which in turn, as long as that branch of science is viable, will eventually be replaced by a conceptual framework that is even more serviceable, accurate, and/or beautiful. No scientific theory is ever absolute or immutable; that psychological position of certainty comes with belief and belongs to the category of religion, whose theory is dogmatic, not scientific, and where it is a foregone conclusion that counterfactual discoveries will be rationalized or disavowed so that theory always triumphs.

When Freud began his work with psychoneurotic patients the theoretical framework that explained neuroses and guided

Freud in his initial clinical experience was the one developed by his teacher Jean-Martin Charcot. Charcot demonstrated that a neurotic symptom, which had been considered a form of malingering or worse, was a legitimate medical phenomenon that represented an involuntary reaction to a forgotten emotional stress of an earlier time. Since no brain lesion could be found that would account for this sequence, the only other cause that was imaginable at that time was a physiological one. Charcot postulated a hereditary weakness of the brain that made it impossible for the neurotic's cerebrum to handle the discharge of emotions consciously, while the inadequate attempt of the lower centers to cope with that task without the benefit of consciousness, i.e., reason, resulted in the otherwise meaningless neurotic symptoms. After working with psychoneurotic patients using the hypnotic method, Freud took the position that the high intelligence of neurotic patients spoke against brain weakness being responsible for their difficulties and that, as a neurologist, he saw no reason why the absence of consciousness meant that there could have been no cerebral contribution, i.e., reason, to forming neurotic symptoms; in other words, Freud postulated the possibility of unconscious (not-conscious) thought. Freud disputed the notion that neurotic symptoms were meaningless, demonstrating clinically that they represented a purposeful, though not conscious compromise between the urge for the implementation of an idea, usually a sexual wish, and the moral barriers that made even its acknowledgment unacceptable. Here we see that Freud had gone beyond the theory that enabled him to begin his clinical investigation of the psychoneuroses. If neurotic illness had psychological causes, rather than anatomical or physiological ones, then it was pointless to continue to look to neuroanatomy and neurophysiology for either an explanation of the origin or the definitive treatment of the neuroses. Psychological causes and cures, rather than physical ones, had to be found. Freud saw that the conflicts that make for neuroses represented developmental, not physiological mishaps. The future neurotic had as a child been overstimulated, either in reality or in fantasy, and could not cope with the excitement generated in this manner; that is, being too immature physically and mentally, he neither mastered the excitement himself nor could turn to adults who might have helped him to do so. This situation obtained because the parents to whom the child might have turned for help were the source of the actual or fantasied stimulation which, as Freud had learned to his surprise, was blatantly sexual in nature. He soon realized that the sexuality of children was not an aberrant development in the life of the future neurotic, but an aspect of everyone's childhood. From his patients Freud learned to stop his incessant probing for the psychologically traumatic event and to let the patient reveal his inner life in his own way. Hypnotic investigation gave way to open-ended association. Left more to their own devices, patients told of dreams they had had and Freud was struck by the similarity of the structure of the dream and the structure of a neurotic symptom. He learned that the similarity was due to the fact that the content of both symptom and dream was not organized along logical lines but, like a rebus or a charade, could be understood in terms of analogy and metaphor. Appropriately translated, the symbolic configurations gave added evidence for the existence of an active, unconscious mental life in all people, a mental life dominated not by the exigencies of reality nor dictated by society, but by the egocentric wishes and entitlements of childhood.

Equally important was Freud's discovery that given the unstructured atmosphere of his consulting room, patients did not simply remember the past but attempted to reenact it, making the analyst the target of past wishes and fears—transferring to him with all the original intensity the positive and negative passions of their earlier life.

All these discoveries furthered the hermeneutic capacity of the analyst and enabled Freud to learn more and more about human motivation—why we do what we do, and why we do it when we do it—in both health and disease (Basch, 1983).

As I mentioned before, the difference between a scientific theory and a cherished belief lies in the fact that a scientific theory can be, at least potentially, falsified by experiment. So far we have been talking about the clinical theory of psychoanalysis. Every generalization made by Freud on this level is derived from clinical experience and can be tested and potentially falsified by the psychoanalytic method. This is not so for the general psychology that Freud tried to build on and around his work with neurotic patients. Freud always believed in Hughling Jackson's concept that psychopathology was an inverse recapitulation of normal development. It was assumed that, like in a reel of film played backwards, you could see the earlier stages that an individual had traversed in development as his pathology disinhibited higher centers and permitted earlier behavior to reemerge. Freud felt that his insight into neurotic pathology had given him a picture of how normal development took place. He seems to have reasoned somewhat like this: The vicissitudes of infantile sexuality are fundamental for the development of neuroses. Dreams and errors of everyday life show that infantile sexuality is universal. Therefore, development as reconstructed in the analysis of neurotic patients is the equivalent of and mirrors the early development of all people, the neuroses showing in bold relief what is ordinarily hidden from view by the resolution of the oedipal conflict in normal individuals. Similarly: neurotic development reflects infantile (childlike) thinking and does not follow the rules of everyday adult logic. Dreams and errors of everyday life show the same type of organization. Therefore, we have discovered the primary process, the earliest form in which the brain or mind attempts to adapt itself to the problems of life.

In retrospect, such conclusions are, of course, non sequiturs. The insight into development offered by an analytic study of the neuroses does not in itself offer a guarantee that *all* of infantile development or all that is significant about early development is now understood. Nor is it to be taken for granted that the ability to decode the results of an earlier logical manner of ordering stimuli has put us in touch with the earliest or "primary" process of thought. Nevertheless, erroneous though it was, such reasoning transformed what had been learned about the developmental vicissitudes of the psychoneurotic into the psychoanalytic theory of development. The oedipal conflict discovered by Freud as focal for psychoneurotic pathology became the focus for development generally. The resolution of the Oedipus complex, which made neurotic symptomatology unnecessary and let the erstwhile neurotic integrate *sexuality* with the rest of his life, now became thought of as the gateway to *maturity* for everyone. The resolution of sexual conflict became the goal of all development, and the capacity for heterosexually achieved orgastic satisfaction came to be equated with the capacity for meaningful adulthood. The vicissitudes of infantile sexuality had become the indicators of development in psychoanalysis. Maturation consisted of a progression from oral, to anal, to phallic sexuality, culminating in the Oedipus conflict, whose resolution then paved the way for genital primacy in adulthood. So was the psychoanalytic theory of development born—not a theory of the development of the neuroses, which Freud was entitled to postulate on the basis of his findings—but a theory of development that he believed held true for all human beings. In other words, to take this thesis to its logical conclusion, we are all basically neurotic, though all of us do not have neurotic symptoms.

This descriptive explanation of the laws that were postulated as governing development was joined with a causal explanatory theory or metapsychology that purported to account for the interacting forces responsible for mental life.

When Freud first began to study the neuroses and long before psychoanalysis evolved, he postulated somatic instincts to account for the driven quality of behavior. Hormones had just been discovered, and Freud pictured instincts as glandular secretions that entered the bloodstream and upon reaching the brain became converted into ideas that strove for fulfillment through externally directed behavior. How this transformation took place he could not imagine; he later called it the mysterious leap between body and mind. The primacy of the sexual drive in the motivation of neurotic behavior was extrapolated to serve, initially accompanied by the self-protective drive and later by the aggressive drive, as the basis for all human motivation. Sexuality provided, as Freud was later to write to Jung, the biological base for psychoanalysis necessary if doctors were to accept his work as truly scientific (McGuire, 1974). The instincts were then employed to power a hypothetical mental apparatus, essentially a neurological model (a "brain mythology," as Andersson [1962] has called it), which was thought to be instrumental in generating thoughts and emotions. With the postulation of the instinct theory and the mental apparatus

Freud undid much of what he had accomplished in raising the scientific interpretation of psychological manifestations to its own universe of discourse, and reverted to biological reductionism in his search for a causal explanation for his clinical findings. His biological causal hypotheses came to be imbricated and confused with the law-like hypotheses for understanding human motivation that were derived directly from the psychoanalytic method. This conflation led to a situation in which to question the validity of the instinct theory as an explanation for all human behavior was mistakenly equated with abandoning the psychoanalytic method, or questioning the validity of Freud's discovery of the universality of infantile sexuality. Although a nonsequitur, this misunderstanding created a tension between clinical findings and theoretical formulations that has been, to this day, the bane of psychoanalysis as a scientific endeavor.

Ferenczi was perhaps the first analyst to report that there were patients whose pathology he could not satisfactorily explain, at least in its entirely, in terms of the vicissitudes of the oedipal phase, and whose problems did not respond to interpretations that focused on psychosexual conflict. Kohut has helped us to understand why this was so. Patients like those described by Ferenczi do not develop problems because of overstimulation and premature sexual excitement, but, rather, because they were emotionally neglected and/or misunderstood. Such patients have as children been understimulated rather than overstimulated and, instead of defending themselves against an instinctual overload, are struggling with an inability to deal appropriately with their emotional needs. For these patients it is not the unconscious thought of forbidden erotic love that generates anxiety, but the anticipation of reexperiencing the devastating, potentially disintegrating disappointment of early empathic failures if they dare once again to reach for emotional fulfillment.

Beginning with Ferenczi, there have always been analysts who did exactly what Freud did when he first encountered neurotic patients. That is, they let their patients lead the way and tried to follow as best they could. But, when these analysts have brought what they found to the attention of their colleagues for further consideration, they learned that they no longer had Freud's privilege of experimenting, revising, and reformulating explanatory theory whenever clinical evidence pointed to that necessity. Ferenczi and others like him soon found that if their results did not fit the formula that the study of the neuroses had led analysts to anticipate, then their work was simply considered to be unanalytic, their findings the result of either poor technique and/or their unconscious resistance to psychoanalysis and to the universality of infantile sexuality.

What had been an open system—a system whose output is influenced and modified by the information it receives—had become a closed and predetermined one. No matter who the patient, it was a foregone conclusion that his difficulties, whatever their nature, would ultimately be found to be due to some variant of the oedipal conflict whose eventual interpretation and resolution would provide the definitive cure. The theory of infantile sexuality had been transformed from a scientific hypothesis into a shibboleth and adherence to it made into a test of loyalty to the movement and its leader.

Patients who refused to fit on the procrustean bed of the oedipal conflict were simply considered to be unanalyzable; but that didn't stop these patients from demanding help, or analysts from trying to help them with Freud's methods. Many analysts then, and still today, simply modified their techniques and kept their innovations to themselves and out of their publications. Others left or were forced out of organized psychoanalysis. As these individuals amalgamated Freud's technique with their own modifications, many schools of dynamic psychotherapy began to evolve emphasizing this or that aspect of development that Freud's instinct theory could not encompass. But there have also been in each generation of psychoanalysts some who carried forward the work of reexamination and reformulation that Ferenczi began. Considering themselves to be following and expanding Freud's insights, they refused to leave organized psychoanalysis and struggled, usually against heavy opposition, to gain a hearing.

Beginning with Ferenczi and continuing in the work of analysts like Balint, Bowlby, Erikson, Fairbairn, Guntrip, Kohut, Kahler, Winnicott, and others, an implicitly contrary view about human development is to be found, namely, one that suggests that the human infant is not essentially asocial, and that maturation is not based on an adversary relationship, but on a cooperative one, and, furthermore, that development is not based in the first instance on instinctual frustration and conflict, but on the anticipation of a harmonious interplay between instinctually potentiated genetic patterns and the releasor mechanisms for that potential embodied in the caregiver's empathic response to the infant's affective communications. As I described last year at the Berkeley conference (see Chapter 2) and in a previous publication (1975), advances made by biology and psychology in the study of instinct, and what has been learned about development in infancy and childhood in the last forty years seem to bear out the correctness of this contention. The scientific evidence from other fields that speaks against a theory of mental functioning based on Freud's conceptualization of instinct or drive as force impelling to discharge was ably summarized and discussed by Holt (1976). In psychoanalysis the systematic clinical exposition that instinctual conflict is a secondary rather than a primary form of psychopathology is to be found in Kohut's *The Restoration of the Self* (1977). All this implies that instinctual conflict is only one of many forms of developmental failure with which analysts must be prepared to deal.

If we are to understand Kohut's work and its significance, we must look at it in the context of this ongoing struggle in organized psychoanalysis. A struggle between those who believe that Freud's method of investigation defines psychoanalysis as a science, and are willing to follow where it leads them, and those who believe psychoanalysis is defined and limited by the doctrines that Freud adduced from 19th-century biology and neurology to provide a causal explanatory theory for what the hermeneutic examination of neurotic symptoms had revealed to him.

But even while we view Kohut's work as part of a continuum that is as old as psychoanalysis, we should not overlook the unique contribution that he made. Freud himself had already commented that all patients to some extent, and some patients to a very great extent, require a "belated upbringing" or

Nacherziehung, an extra-analytic, educational effort on the part of the analyst to help them repair defects or arrests in their character (Freud, 1919; Basch, 1981). Kohut was the first to show, using the classical psychoanalytic method, that this was not so. He demonstrated that the sense of entitlement and other characterological defects in patients with narcissistic personality disorders could be investigated and resolved through interpretation without resorting to extra-analytic measures. If, as with neurotic patients, one accepts the patient's character symptoms as defenses worthy of investigation and avoids prejudging them as attempts to act out sexual or aggressive fantasies, then one remobilizes transference wishes for the helpful and/or admirable parent who the patient believes could help him feel secure, beloved, and competent. Kohut went on to document that, contrary to what had been the practice, these wishes need not be indulged, it was not necessary to provide the patient with an extra-analytic emotional or educational experience, it was enough to interpret them. Insight enabled the patient to mature, and reshape his attitudes and behavior accordingly, proving once again the truth of Freud's dictum to the effect that if we do the analysis the synthesis will take care of itself. Kohut had expanded traditional analysis to include a group of patients heretofore thought for the most part to be unanalyzable (Kohut, 1971). But since he also demonstrated that the analysis of their transferences did not culminate in the working through of oedipal fantasies, and that the development of self-esteem rather than the resolution of psychosexual conflict heralded the end of the analysis, predictably, his work became the focus for the ever-present struggle within psychoanalysis to which I have referred.

We should not forget that the instinct theory was pure speculation on Freud's part and had nothing to do with anything actually uncovered through the psychoanalytic method. That Freud's and our patients, indeed all human beings, feel "driven" to engage in one or another kind of behavior is open to introspection and empathy and is grist for the psychoanalytic mill, but this does not validate Freud's hypothetical causal explanation for those observations. Freud himself made it explicitly clear that his theories about drives and instincts were *biological* speculations that he adduced to explain his clinical findings. As he said, these ideas were imposed upon rather than derived from psychoanalytic observations (Freud, 1915). He acknowledged that these hypotheses were vague and unsatisfactory at best, and he referred to the instinct theory as the "mythology" of psychoanalysis. Freud anticipated that eventually his libido theory would have a proper organic foundation, and only in the absence of a definitive theory of instincts did he feel justified in speculating about the biological on the basis of his psychological findings (Freud, 1914). Freud's reservations were well-founded. In the years after his death, the evidence has continued to accumulate from other branches of psychology, from biology, from neurophysiology, from physics, and from new fields such as cybernetics, linguistics, communication science, and semantics, that the hypotheses that Freud had formulated to explain development and the functioning of the brain or mental apparatus were in error and that experimentally validatable alternative explanations are now at hand (see Chapter 2). There has been for some time awareness of these findings in psychoanalysis, but, rather than undertaking the necessary task of revision, analysts, when they are not defending its explanatory value, have taken the position that metapsychology is simply an elegant set of *metaphors* devised to describe and generalize clinical findings. Biologists have found that instincts are genetic blueprints for information processing rather than forces demanding an outlet; neurophysiologists tell us that the brain is not an energy-discharging organ; infant observation shows that human babies are not asocial, impulse-ridden creatures, and so on, but all this does not matter to us supposedly. We are only borrowing the vocabulary of force and energy for our own purposes, and who is to say we may not do so? It is not the words but the clinical experience they express that is important. What we see here, as I mentioned earlier, is the fallacy of neglecting the influence exerted on those clinical findings by the theories implicit in the words we use. Our freely hovering attention is not that free; it covers only a limited area because it has to be anchored somewhere. Our theories provide those points for attachment and we observe only within the limits prescribed by that theory.

To convince ourselves of this we need only look again at the first analysis of Mr. Z. (1979), or at the case of Miss F. in *The Analysis of the Self* (1971), to see how even a master clinician like Heinz Kohut, who always emphasized the primacy of clinical experience, was nevertheless programmed by traditional psychoanalytic instinct theory into not hearing what his patients had to say and into attributing to them in his interpretations feelings and motives that they did not have. That is, until he repeated Freud's feat and broke through the confines of the theory that he had been taught, as Freud, using Charcot's hypnotic method, went beyond Charcot's explanation for the neuroses.

At first Kohut believed he was making only a clinical contribution, applying the psychoanalytic method of empathy and introspection to narcissistic personality disorders. Then he recognized that a separate line of development was implied by his findings, and only after years of further clinical work did he come to recognize and finally to accept that his findings necessitated postulation of a single theory of development organized around the maturation of the self that encompassed but transcended Freud's instinct theory.

Freud first liberated himself from biological reductionism only to become enmeshed in it again. Kohut, through the discovery and formulation of the selfobject theory of human motivation, has put psychoanalysis back on the right track. Kohut would never let himself be provoked or seduced into leaving the main body of psychoanalysis; he knew very well that that is where his work belonged. Thanks to his persistence and willingness to suffer what he had to in order to maintain those ties, the once evident pressure to separate from the parent body is pretty much a thing of the past. What we must do now is resist ideological separation, the pressure to make us into "Kohutians." I dare say Kohut was, to say the least, the leading Freudian of his generation, and we are all better Freudians for his work.

In the aftermath of Kohut's death, it is incumbent on us not merely to pay tribute to his achievements, but to work together to see that what he began will continue to be the cutting edge of psychoanalysis and psychoanalytic psychotherapy. History is

Janus-faced. Tomorrow, today will be history. Nor is history only made by people like Heinz Kohut, those giants whose achievements are permanently recorded. In years to come, those of us who call ourselves his students, no matter how small each of our respective parts may be, will have shaped the history of psychoanalysis that future generations will be studying. Each of us will have played his or her part well or badly, but we will all have played a part.

We are in a time of transition. The reformulation of psychoanalytic theory and practice sparked by Kohut's work now represents the mainstream of psychoanalysis. It is important for those of us who are committed to furthering the evolution of psychoanalysis along the lines that Kohut envisioned to speak up and emphasize this point as often as we are challenged, and to be prepared to pay whatever personal, economic, or political price will be exacted for our stand by the powers that be. Rather than taking a defensive position vis-à-vis those analysts who mistakenly believe that their often personally motivated defense of theoretical rigidity is a defense of psychoanalysis, we must assert that we do Freud neither honor nor service by perpetuating or compounding his mistakes. Nor do we advance psychoanalysis by declaring Freud's thoughts, because they were *his* thoughts, to be *eo ipse* correct and immutable, thereby transmuting psychoanalysis from science to faith.

The opposition to Kohut's discoveries is essentially similar to that aroused when other analysts in the past have brought forward evidence that Freud's biological formulations were not adequate to what clinical practice was uncovering. But as more and more analysts become familiar through their own analyses with the necessity for and technique of dealing with early self-object failures in their own development, through the analysis of the grandiose and idealizing aspects of their respective transferences, Kohut's contributions will be seen to be not in competition with Freud's discoveries in the area of psychoneurotic transferences, but complementing and enhancing those discoveries.

If we carry out the task that the privilege of being the first to benefit from Heinz Kohut's work imposes upon us, future generations will be able to continue what we began in a less difficult atmosphere than the one in which we often find ourselves at present. I believe that the more thorough and more accurate our grasp of our history, the more likely we are to succeed in this endeavor.

REFERENCES

Andersson, O. (1962). *Studies in the Prehistory of Psychoanalysis.* Stockholm: Svenska Bokförlaget/Norstedts.

Basch, M. F. (1975). Toward a theory that encompasses depression: A revision of existing causal hypotheses in psychoanalysis. In *Depression and Human Existence,* eds. E. J. Anthony & T. Benedek. Boston: Little, Brown & Co.

———— (1981). Selfobject disorders and psychoanalytic theory: A historical perspective. *J. Amer. Psychoanal. Assn.,* 29:337–351.

———— (1983). Some theoretical and methodological implications of self psychology. In *The Future of Psychoanalysis,* ed. A. Goldberg. New York: International Universities Press.

Freud, S. (1914). On narcissism: An introduction. *S.E.,* 14.

———— (1915). Instincts and their vicissitudes. *S.E.,* 14.

———— (1919). Lines of advance in psycho-analytic therapy. *S.E.,* 17.

———— (1923). The ego and the id. *S.E.,* 19.

Holt, R. R. (1976). Drive or wish? A reconsideration of the psychoanalytic theory of motivation. In *Psychology Versus Metapsychology: Psychoanalytic Essays in Memory of George S. Klein,* eds. M. M. Gill & P. S. Holzman. *Psychological Issues,* Monograph 36. New York: International Universities Press.

Kohut, H. (1971). *The Analysis of the Self.* New York: International Universities Press.

———— (1977). *The Restoration of the Self.* New York: International Universities Press.

———— (1978). *The Search for the Self,* ed. P. Ornstein, New York: International Universities Press.

———— (1979). The two analyses of Mr. Z. *Int. J. Psycho-Anal.,* 60:3–27.

McGuire, W., ed. (1974). *The Freud/Jung Letters.* New Jersey: Princeton University Press.

SELF AND SELFOBJECT: NEW DIMENSIONS IN PSYCHOANALYTIC THEORY

2 Selfobjects and Selfobject Transference: Theoretical Implications

Michael Franz Basch, M.D.

THE CONTRIBUTION TO PSYCHOANALYSIS that we call self psychology was born out of a not uncommon psychoanalytic therapeutic impasse. Narcissistic personality disorders have, since the days of Freud, been a frustrating thorn in the body analytic. Patients with these disorders were hampered by a sense of entitlement that seemingly prevented them from understanding and benefiting from interpretations directed at helping them recognize that behind their incessant demanding and complaining lay aggressive and libidinal impulses directed at the analyst, impulses they were afraid to face. These patients rejected interpretations with telling scorn; they had suffered, and now they demanded compensation—the love and understanding they had deserved and been cheated of throughout their lives. As Freud regretfully acknowledged years ago, as analysts we are helpless when confronted with patients who require gratification instead of insight—as he put it, who will accept only the logic of soup with dumplings for arguments. In many instances when patients like this entered analytic treatment they often left dissatisfied, or the analyst decided they were unanalyzable and either dismissed them or settled for more superficial therapeutic results. Not uncommonly, the persistence of the analyst and the patient's need for the analyst's good will, approval, love, and continued attention resulted in a compromise in which the patient eventually acquiesced to the analyst's interpretations, accepting them as the price that had to be paid for being able to continue the relationship. It was the latter situation that led to the not infrequent interminable analyses, or to the allegedly fully analyzed patient who was not much better subjectively or objectively after years of acquiring "insight" into his supposed "neurotic" core conflict than he had been.

Why did we persist, one might ask, in an enterprise that was so painful for all concerned and of so little avail? From the best of motives. For we believed we knew, based on Freud's analysis of psychoneurotic patients, that reasonably healthy development depended on the sublimation of psychic energies derived from sexual and aggressive instincts—an adaptation that was opposed by a human nature bent on direct and instantaneous gratification. The result was instinctual conflict, that is, a conflict between nature and culture in which, not surprisingly, and more often than not, nature triumphed. In the case of the neurotic individual, patient and analyst could see this sequence unfold as the transference neurosis was formed and then interpreted. The narcissistic patient, however, could not give us the cooperation of the more mature neurotic patient, for his symptoms were not like a foreign body in an otherwise healthy character, a foreign body that analyst and patient could look at together. Instead, the narcissistic patient had responded to instinctual pressures with a retreat into immaturity. Such a patient was not the victim of a struggle between id and ego, but suffered from an ego *defect,* so that asking him to look at himself was like asking someone to pull himself up by his own bootstraps. That is to say, if he had had the capacity for self-observation he wouldn't have been sick to begin with. All that seemed to be left was to try to help the patient see what the analyst already knew lurked behind and was responsible for his regressive symptoms, in the hope that there was sufficient remaining objectivity on the part of the patient to join with the analyst in forming a so-called therapeutic split (Sterba, 1934) between inner experience and its observation. This is what Kohut tried to do with Miss F., the critical case for the development of self psychology described in *The Analysis of the Self*

(1971). Initially Kohut did his best to persuade Miss F. that he was for her an instinctual object, a target for her libidinal impulses. Fortunately Miss F. continued to behave like an obstreperous, not an obedient child, insisting that the analyst did not have the meaning for her that he was so sure he did have.

Self psychology exists today because Kohut was ultimately able to empathize with what was happening to the patient in the analysis and interpret that to her, rather than continue to insist that he knew a priori from his past experience as an analyst and his long immersion in Freud's theoretical writings, what she must be reliving.

The important therapeutic innovation that Kohut introduced here was that he did not deviate from the psychoanalytic method in his treatment of these patients. He did not resort to the belated attempt at upbringing that Freud said such patients needed, and, in not doing so, did not settle for the improvement that a non-analytic learning experience could have given (Basch, 1981). Nor did he, as some analysts had tried to do in these cases, directly gratify wishes by role playing the good, understanding parent or friend that these patients so desperately needed. Instead, he dealt with Miss F.'s demands, complaints, and fears by interpreting what these seemed to say about her and her past relationships.

In this way Kohut continued to use his capacity for empathy in the interest of interpretation and never fell into the error of neglecting the rule of abstinence (Basch, 1981). (Unlike some who choose to misunderstand him, Kohut never mistook empathy for sympathy [Basch, 1983a].) But this achievement, essential as it was, was just the first step in the analytic process.

The ability to be empathic with, rather than rejecting of the patient is in and of itself not yet curative. This is a point about self psychology that is often misunderstood. Interpretation based on empathy with what Miss F. was trying to express, rather than interpretation based on what Freud's theory dictated she should have been saying, only removed the resistance to the development of the analytic transference and, essential though that was, was only the first step in a treatment with analytic goals. Once the patient saw that she would be understood, the unconscious hopes, wishes, and fears that had received defensive, distorted expression through the development of the narcissistic character became more directly available in the transference and could then be clarified and interpreted for and with her in the interest of arriving at a valid genetic reconstruction of her developmental history. In other words, as in the case of the neurotic patient, the analyst's initial interpretations, by conveying intellectual and emotional readiness to deal with the patient as he found her, enabled the patient's wish for improvement and health to ally itself with the analyst so that the so-called therapeutic split could take place. In the case of Miss F. and others like her, however, this did not lead to abandonment of a regressive position followed by mobilization of aggressive and libidinal impulses in their analyzable form. Instead, what emerged was an increasingly clear picture of how these patients had been thwarted in their development, especially when it came to the formation of a concept of self that was reasonably secure and flexible. In the transference they displayed clearly their need to have the analyst serve as part of a dyadic mother-infant or father-child system in which their capacities for maturation in the affect-charged realm of parent-child relationships would be fostered in an age-appropriate manner.

Kohut found himself engaged in analytic work that went beyond and deeper than what Freud had declared to be the limits of analytic intervention, penis envy in the female and castration anxiety in the male. The transference of narcissistic patients led to reconstruction of relationships that antedated self and object differentiation. In these situations, as Kohut established retrospectively, the child seems to need the parent as an extension of his own system, without the parent having an existence of his own—the kind of relationship recaptured in the wish-fulfilling fairy tale of Alladin; as you will recall, Alladin could summon a genie to do his bidding, and, once his needs were gratified, send the all-powerful, obliging spirit back to its abode where it rested in suspended animation until he needed it once more. The analytic evidence indicated that, unlike the neurotic, the narcissistic patient had not gone beyond this stage in his capacity for relationships. On the emotional level, the analyst as an individual in his own right did not exist for the patient, while the latter used, or tried to use the analyst in the transference purely as an impersonal need-fulfilling force. It was this heretofore ununderstood developmental vicissitude that made these patients so difficult to deal with. As long as the analyst did not recognize that the patient was not in retreat from an oedipal transference but was trying to mobilize a form of transference that had to be dealt with as such, the patient and the analyst were at loggerheads, the analyst making ineffectual interpretations postulated on the assumption of resistance to oedipal feelings, while the patient could do nothing but repeat over and over in symbolic and displaced form the unconscious, inchoate demands stirred up in and by the analytic relationship.

Kohut was now able to explore these transferences and found that they could be subdivided into grandiose and idealizing forms: mirroring or grandiose if the patient required support in and acknowledgment for his attempts at active mastery of the world, idealizing insofar as he needed, in some form, the soothing or meaningfulness that comes from being part of a larger unit. Together he called these selfobject transferences, differentiating them from object-instinctual transferences, and indicating that they represented aspects of the development of the self, a maturational line different from that leading to sublimation of the instincts and to object love. Indeed, he found that the interpretation and resolution of the selfobject transference did not lead to formation and resolution of an oedipal transference and then to object love, but to a maturation in the area of ambition and ideals that left the patient free in a sufficiently significant sector of his personality to lead a life that was satisfying and meaningful to him or her.

I have elsewhere (1983b, 1981a) described what this achievement meant for psychoanalysis as a science. But when *The Analysis of the Self* was first published twelve years ago, the verdict of the elder statesmen of psychoanalysis was: "clever, but not psychoanalysis." Psychoanalysis by definition centered on the resolution of instinctual conflict, this work did not, therefore, and so on. Nevertheless, Kohut's work was put to the test by analysts all over the world who, recognizing in his case material those situations in which their own best efforts too had failed and, having nothing to lose, studied and applied his insights and technical suggestions. The results were such that more and more analysts not only used Kohut's work in their own practices, but taught his approach to their students and began to make contributions to the literature based on what has come to be known as the approach of self psychology in psychoanalysis. Though widespread utilization of his work did not lead to what might be called "official" recognition of Kohut's achievement, it did necessitate a change in the "Establishment's" attitude. Where before his approach was acknowledged as novel but condemned as unanalytic, now his emphasis on interpretation guided by empathy for the patient's situation was considered to be paradigmatic for all analysis, and, *mirabile dictu*, no longer new. It turned out that analysts had been doing this all the time, and better to boot! Actually one could say with Polonius that here their bait of falsehood had caught, if not a carp, at least a minnow of truth. The older analysts came out of the closet, so to speak, and acknowledged that the talented ones among them had permitted themselves a leeway in the transactions with their patients that they had not previously been willing to acknowledge openly. So perhaps Kohut's approach was after all of general interest to psychoanalysts, and one could even admit publicly that in the analysis of narcissistic personalities Kohut's technique might have the most to offer. Now all that was needed to restore him and his work to the supposed mainstream of psychoanalysis was a withdrawal of the theoretical heresy that maturation could take place other than through the resolution of an oedipal conflict. But such a rapprochement was not to be. Kohut had not stood still. Based on the reconstructions in his clinical work he had, reluctantly, being a theoretical conservative, been forced to accept the evidence that there were not two or more lines of maturation as he had originally thought, but only the one illustrated by the selfobject transference. He concluded not only that the oedipal phase is not central for all development, but that it is not necessarily a time when permanent internal conflict is generated; rather, it is a time of particular mirroring and idealizing needs that, if appropriately met by the parents as selfobjects, result in healthy growth of self-esteem and the possibility of establishing what analysts have called "object love." In other words, the sexualization of normal assertiveness and competitiveness, which forms the basis for neurotic conflict, is the result of selfobject failure at this particular phase of maturation and does not represent the average expected course of human development, as Freud had thought it did.

It is a mistake to think that the outcome of healthy oedipal development is that the selfobject relationship of the child to his parents is *replaced* by object love. The oedipal phase of psychosexual development coincides with a phase of affective/cognitive maturation that enables the child to reflect on his experience in a more objective manner, potentially permitting the relationship between self and other to be viewed differently than before. The oedipal child is faced with the potential realization that his egocentric view of the universe is not shared by others. If, with the help of appropriate selfobject relationships, he is, to use Piaget's terminology, able to assimilate the oedipal lession, i.e., change his goals and with that his self-concept, he is able to accept without a sense of permanent loss the fact that his selfobjects are selves in their own right and have needs that at any given time may disregard or even be in opposition to his own. This does not mean that his selfobject needs—the need for communication that validates his worth—disappear; instead, it raises these needs to a different level and opens up a particular maturational path. An individual who has accepted the oedipal disappointment, who, to again use Piaget's terms, has decentered on both the emotional as well as on the logical level, may come to recognize and understand that the selfobject needs of others are as significant and as worthy of respect as are his own. If then it comes to pass that such a person in fulfilling another's selfobject needs also fulfills his own, we have the situation that psychoanalysts term object love. Object love and genitality are not synonymous. One can direct object love not only to spouse or lover, but also to parents, children, friends, or abstract ideals. It is the presence of a decentered relationship, not the quality of orgasm, that testifies to object love. It should be stressed again that object love is not a replacement for selfobject relationships, but only one form of their maturation. Let us look now at the pathological rather than at the normal oedipal phase.

If a child whose selfobject relations have previously been satisfactory finds no empathy for the assertive, creative, and competitive trends normally manifested in the oedipal period, he will be traumatized when confronted by experiences that demand that he relinquish his egocentric position. Prototypically, but not necessarily, this occurs through witnessing or reexperiencing the primal scene in some form. The child, unable to ignore the evidence that brings his relative insignificance home to him, but with no support for his threatened self-esteem, is in an untenable position. Rather than a maturation of the self and selfobject needs, there is, under these circumstances, a developmental arrest and repression of the phase-appropriate wishes in a primitive, distorted sexualized form. This lays the groundwork for neurotic conflict when and if repression is later undermined by the demands of adolescent and adult sexuality.

By now equally familiar to analysts are those patients who have suffered significant early selfobject failure, so that the stresses of the oedipal phase do not determine the nature of future pathology. In these cases the defense that Freud called disavowal, which antedates repression (Basch, 1967; 1983c), operates to create an unconscious deception of the self. As a result, egocentricity is only partially relinquished. An intellectual, superficial accommodation to the reality of his relative lack of power and significance, and his less than central position in the world is made by the child while, as far as the self is concerned, the earlier sense of narcissistic urgency holds sway. The resulting behavior is a seeming accommodation to the demands of maturity which, when analytically examined, turns out to be only manipulation in the interest of continued narcissistic entitlement. These are the patients who have traditionally been labeled narcissistic characters or narcissistic personality disorders. In such cases successful psychoanalytic treatment, as Kohut and others have shown, results in a lessening of narcissistic vulnerability and the maturation of the means by which the patient's particular selfobject needs may be reasonably fulfilled. The issue here is not object love but other forms of object relationship.

Whereas before *The Restoration of the Self* (1977), Kohut had only proposed an extension of psychoanalytic technique and an addition to Freud's theory of development, now he in effect proposed that analytic evidence pointed to the necessity of revising Freud's notions of development and, incidentally, but not unimportantly, Freud's view of the nature of man.

What Kohut suggests is that man is not born to conflict, that he is not of necessity in an adversary relationship with his parents or with his culture, and that his development is not determined or predetermined by drives or instincts as psychoanalysis has understood them. The removal of the hyphen between "self" and "object" in *The Search for the Self* (Kohut, 1978) signifies that the term "selfobject" is no longer the antithesis of instinctual object, nor tied to any particular form of pathology, but is shorthand for a hypothesis about development generally, a hypothesis based on psychoanalytic reconstruction.

The question that, in my experience, is now most frequently asked is "What happens to the drives in self psychology?" Often the tone in which it is put clearly intimates that Kohut has done something terrible from which the analytic community should be protected. Although the critics of self psychology seem to think that they are instantly refuting the potential validity of Kohut's discoveries when they ask such questions, we should, rather than feeling defensive, ask those who criticize self psychology on this basis why they remain so ill-informed about the lack of scientific standing of the very constructs by which they presume to measure and evaluate Kohut's clinical work and the concept of development based on it.

Freud himself made it clear that his theories about drives and instincts were *biological* speculations that he adduced to explain his clinical findings. It is also true, however, that when Freud found them useful, the initially tentative nature of extra-analytic speculations tended to be forgotten, as if repeated usage had made these hypotheses more factual (Basch, 1976b). So it was with the theories of instinct and drive. The answer to: "What has self psychology done to the psychoanalytic theory of instinct?" is: "This question is meaningless." There can be no *psychoanalytic* theory of somatic instinct or biological drive, only a theory of instinct and drive brought *to* psychoanalysis from the appropriate branch of science for whatever light it might shed on the data regarding the meaning of human behavior as uncovered by the psychoanalytic method, a method, as Kohut (1959) has pointed out, that does not belong to the physical sciences, but is one of exploring unconscious mental life through introspection and empathy.

Science has made significant advances since Freud first lamented the paucity of reliable information regarding man's instinctual life. Not only biology, but ethology and control theory, neither of which had formal existence in Freud's day, have to a great degree clarified the issues involved, and permit us to reevaluate Freud's speculations in this area.

A number of Freud's assumptions about development and motivation have been radically altered since cybernetics and control theory replaced mechanistic discharge theories as explanations for the vicissitudes of the behavior of living systems. The notion that the motives for or the meaning of thought and behavior depend upon an energic force of libidinal or aggressive nature, in neutral or unneutralized form, has been repeatedly and tellingly rejected by biologists, neurophysiologists, and physicists, as documented in the psychoanalytic literature by Kubie (1963), Holt (1965), Rosenblatt and Thickstun (1970), Peterfreund (1971), and others (Basch, 1976b). The brain, similar to a thermostat that controls the activity of a furnace, governs or steers the organism through a hierarchy of error-correcting feedback cycles that compare a particular perceptual set with the conditions that prevail, and, if the two do not match, puts in motion that behavior that will be most likely to achieve the desired congruence of set and reality. "Instinct" is the term we apply to those feedback patterns or portions of feedback patterns that are inherited. The more primitive the organism, the more its behavior is tightly controlled by instinct. As one goes up in the hierarchy of the animal kingdom, instinctual behavior becomes more and more a *general* blueprint, rather than a specific, predetermined routine. This permits these animals to set a hierarchy of goals depending on their relative importance for survival, to respond to a variety of information, and to develop all sorts of adaptive behavior patterns that will fulfill those goals. In other words, the more advanced the animal the more there is room for learning. Freud (1915) was correct when he initially postulated that there were two broad groups of instincts, those designed for self-preservation and those meant to insure the perpetuation of the species. The more advanced, or perhaps in the interest of modesty we should say, the more complex, the animal, the more instincts achieve this end by influencing and fostering the learning process (Gould and Gould, 1981). In mammals, learning is primarily motivated by affect. Affect is not, as Freud thought it was, simply the conscious manifestation of instinct. Rather, as Darwin already realized, affect is a relatively independent control system for behavior. Affective reactions, as I have described in some detail elsewhere (1976a; 1983a), are mediated by the subcortical brain and by the autonomic nervous system. Basically they represent a reaction to the frequency and intensity of sensory stimulation. Affects are general, nonspecific reactions, and free an animal from dependence on a narrowly limited environment by enabling it to evaluate and then adapt to new and different situations in which it may find itself. Experience registered in the cortex combines with the subcortical affective reaction to modify and refine an animal's response through learning appropriate reactions to given situations, and altering them when necessary. For instance, instead of responding with fight or flight to a particular spatial configuration—the sort of external releasor of instinctual behavior that activates insects, birds, and fish—mammals (although not totally without external releasor responses) for the most part react to the affect aroused by the activity of what is encountered. Clearly this is more economical, and gives mammals the opportunity for more sophisticated learning and adaptation.

Instincts do not drive, they enable the organism and the species to survive through an inherited blueprint that resides in the signal-processing, information-generating neural network that guides behavior. Instincts, as Tomkins (1962–1963) points out, tend to react to deficits, influencing the affect system to favor that behavior that will make up for whatever is missing to maintain the optimal equilibrium for a particular animal at a given time. By thinking of affect as only the conscious manifestation of instinctual drive, Freud telescoped two different levels of biological organization: the instinctual blueprint for survival that underlies all behavior, and the affects, an advanced control mechanism that serves as an inner releasor for inherited and learned behavior patterns. It should be understood that instinct encompasses a great number of control mechanisms that seek to insure self-preservation, affect being only one of these. What analysts mean by "drive" is "motivation," and motivation is not an energic matter, as Freud thought it was. In the more primitive phyla, like insects and fish, the motivation for behavior comes from the external releasor, the sensory feature to which the animal is programmed to respond. In higher animals, including man, the immediate motivation for behavior is the inner releasor, the affective reaction recruited by a particular event (Tomkins, 1962–1963, 1970, 1980). The sense of "drivenness" that we experience is a manifestation of the degree of affect aroused.

Although there can be no psychoanalytic theory of instincts, now at least it is possible to replace Freud's initial speculations regarding self-preservation and the perpetuation of the species in a scientific manner. Even with this, however, we are not yet finished with the biological, for, as we know, Freud proposed a second dual-instinct theory based on his analysis of adults suffering from psychoneuroses. In this latter instinct theory, self-preservation is replaced by the instinct of aggression, and the instinct for the propagation of the species is replaced by the sexual instinct.

Perhaps the only significant ethologist to subscribe to an aggressive instinct is Lorenz (1966), but his view has been overwhelmingly rejected on the basis of evidence showing that aggression, unlike hunger, is not an independent motivational force. No predictable periodicity for aggression has been reported, no metabolic changes accompany the absence of aggression, as would occur with the absence of food, water, or air; and, though one needs to eat, drink, and breathe, there is no need to attack if there is no provocative stimulus (Scott, 1958). Within family groups of primates, shortages of food or water, or the absence of a sexual outlet, do not routinely lead to aggression, indeed may result in cooperative sharing. Aggression is most reliably produced by bringing a stranger, an intruder, into a particular group. Aggression is a defensive behavior, a response to disorganization; aggression is affectively triggered, and is in the interest of self-preservation. Therefore, aggression is a tool and not a basic instinctual need as Freud believed it was. Furthermore, the practice in psychoanalysis of lumping assertion, competitiveness, and mastery under the rubric of aggression and tension reduction is an unwarranted use of metaphor based on the terminology of physics (Arnold, 1960).

Apparently some of the same arguments that are raised in objection to the notion of an aggressive drive hold true in the case of sexuality. Holt (1976) cites the work of Frank Beach, whom he calls the most distinguished authority on the sexual behavior of animals, to the effect that the male of the species in the mating season is not driven by an accumulation of sexual excitation that needs to be discharged. Rather, it is the presence of a suitable partner that stimulates the affect of excitement and amplifies the sexual urge. For instance, it has been shown in animal experiments that the male, having been given unrestricted opportunity to copulate with the female, comes to a point where he ceases to have sexual intercourse. The tension reduction theory would attribute this to discharge of accumulated libido. Yet when a new receptive female is introduced to the male at that point, though supposedly drained of sexual tension, he is immediately moved to have sexual relations again, showing that sexuality is a matter of interest. The presence or absence of affect, not of sexual energy, is at stake here. This and other findings indicate that genital sexuality is better thought of as an appetite, and is stimulus-bound, rather than a tension-accumulating drive seeking discharge. The feeling of genital drivenness that may be experienced by the human male or female in the absence of a suitable partner is accounted for by the human capacity for symbolic representation which can serve as a perpetual stimulus to the affect of interest and excitement regardless of external circumstances.

Drive theory as advanced by psychoanalysis is not in keeping with the facts now known about motivation in other animals and in humans. Not surprisingly, the concept of human development based on that theory has also been found wanting.

The human infant is not, as Freud had thought, simply a captive of its physical needs, driven by physiological necessity into a relationship with its caretaker; and hunger is not the basis for the attachment of the infant to his mother (Bowlby, 1969). Observations and experiments have demonstrated (Basch, 1977) that the human infant is a *human* infant right from the start, and not the premature, unformed, stimulus-avoiding creature that Freud imagined it to be. From the beginning infants are stimulus-hungry, show a readiness and a demonstrable preference for human communication, and, given the opportunity, respond with a complete range of affect to their environment.

It is self-evident that in humans birth and the separation of the infant from the placenta does not make for physical independence, and that his or her survival depends for many years on the appropriate nurturing and protecting activities of caretaking adults. What until recently was not so clear was that the humanness of human beings is not automatically guaranteed in an infant given good physical care. Since Spitz (1946) made his observations on the depression that develops in infants bereft of maternal stimulation, we have become increasingly aware that in human beings self-preservation requires psychological nourishment as well as physiological support. Infant observation relative to psychological development dovetails with Kohut's psychoanalytic observations regarding the selfobject and the selfobject transference.

Of all animals we are the most culture-dependent because neither our self-preservative nor our species-perpetuating behavior is governed by tightly coupled, inherited feedback cycles. As the study of severely neglected children, so-called feral or wolf children, who managed to survive and exist for a time on a subhuman level, has established, the lack of adequate human communication at the appropriate time in development permanently precludes the affective use of symbols, including language (Freedman, 1981, 1982). This shows that human communication is the *sine qua non* for human development, and that infants are born message processors: consumers and purveyors of affect-laden information. As we shall see, it is this instinctual need that forms the basis for the selfobject transference seen in psychoanalysis.

Man's capacity for symbolic representation and reflection, the functions that make possible abstractions like "self" and "other," is not present in the first two years of life. Insofar as the infant's self exists as an idea it is a product of the mother's mental life; the child, as Kohut points out, has only a virtual self in the mind of the parents. The mother and other adults responsible for and responsive to the child provide not just for his physical functions, but for the psychological ones that he cannot as yet provide for himself. Most important among these is the response to and the stimulation of the child's affective reactions. Unlike other animals in whom affect, the subcortical and autonomic response to stimulation, is closely coupled with particular perceptions, man has much greater latitude in the degree and quality of affect he assigns to various experiences, especially the interactions with his fellow man. When a concept of self becomes a possibility for the child, he has already been permanently influenced by the affectively toned learning experiences that he has encoded in the early sensorimotor transactions with his parents and other caretakers. These affectively weighted information-processing feedback cycles, so-called perceptual sets, which form the basis of self, serve as a sieve through which future experience is strained. What meaning we attribute to what happens to and around us in later life is to a great extent governed by these transactions of our early years when others had to bring the world to us, had to function psychologically in our stead, had to serve, as Kohut puts it, as selfobjects.

We must not assume, however, that the selfobject relationships of infancy are a one-way street. It is the infant's complex response to his mother's communications that keeps the "conversation" going. In the early months the eyes are the primary channel for signal interchange between mother and child. Freedman's (1979) study of blind newborns has shown that because these babies do not respond to visual stimulation directed toward them, their mothers tend to withdraw from the transaction; as a result, the incidence of autism among blind children is much higher than it is in the general population. If, however, the diagnosis of blindness is made early enough, and if the mother is taught how to stimulate her baby in ways meaningful to it, then the blind infant will, in turn, respond to her, the dialogue will be restored, and the danger of autism will be avoided. The infant's instinctual response to the needs of his parent is what triggers the parent's empathy for the child, and that, in turn, fosters the child's further development. In this way biology and psychology are joined through affective communication. I can think of no better example than the consequences of the failure of communication between the blind infant and his mother to illustrate the validity of Kohut's thesis that the self is not a static structure, but an ongoing process that requires appropriate selfobject relationships throughout life. Motherhood does not become a viable part of the self concept in the act of giving birth, or through hormonal stimulation, but through the ongoing selfobject transactions between a mother and her baby. The same can be said of any significant relationship, including of course that between psychoanalyst and analysand.

Kohut's conclusions regarding the self based on his psychoanalytic work are buttressed also by the work of Bowlby (1969), who has shown that the basic psychological need of infants and children is attachment to and response from the caretaker. Rather than the sexual instinct leading to attachment, it is attachment that eventually leads to sexual behavior, and *per contra,* as Harlow and Harlow (1962, 1972) have shown in primate studies, it is the failure of age-appropriate opportunity for attachment and play that leads to inadequate and aberrant sexual behavior in adulthood. Mahler's data regarding separation and individuation (Mahler, Pine, and Bergmann, 1975) demonstrate clearly how the growing child negotiates the selfobject relationship with his mother. With advancing cognitive development the child, now able to symbolize his experience and eventually to reflect upon it, becomes increasingly able to maintain the necessary communication with his mother at a distance—at first periodically renewing physical contact to reinforce the now internalized symbolic relationship, eventually trusting the efficacy of their communication sufficiently to become relatively independent of physical proximity in sustaining the internalized selfobject. As we know from clinical experience, the less trust in the relationship with the mother, the less able the child is to become physically independent—school phobias are only one dramatic example of this situation. As

Kohut has pointed out, the need for selfobject relationships is not a phase to be surmounted with maturity. Individuation, or the growth of the self, does not mean that there is less need for selfobjects. What changes is the form and the level of abstraction on which the selfobject relationships are conducted.

Having refuted the notion that self psychology takes anything away from psychoanalytic theory, I would like to say a few words about the converse. What has self psychology done *for* psychoanalytic theory?

Self psychology opens the door to the reunion of psychoanalysis with other sciences and potentially ends the isolation that has been forced on psychoanalysis as it clung to an increasingly untenable concept of human development and human nature. Unlike a psychoanalytic theory based on a 19th-century concept of instinctual drive, self psychology complements and does not contradict the findings made by science since that time. So I would answer my question by saying that self psychology has, in principle at least, restored psychoanalytic theory to scientific respectability.

Furthermore, self psychology, because it is not caught up in misleading biological reductionism, has already permitted psychoanalysis to make new contributions to the study of the humanities—to history, sociology, and to literature, for example. So far the influence of psychoanalysis on Western civilization has not been negligible. Freud's insights into the existence and significance of unconscious thought have greatly influenced every conceivable aspect of our daily lives. It may not be insignificant for our future that psychoanalysis, as a result of Kohut's reformulation of the transference, has arrived at a different picture of the nature of man than did Freud. That man is not a creature of conflict, doomed from the outset by his nature, but, instead, limited in the fulfillment of his potential, individually and collectively, only by the limits of his capacity for empathy, has obvious implications.

I would like to close by explaining why, though I use them, I do not like the terms selfobject transference and self psychology. Words tend to be imbued with a power of their own, and create pseudo-realities if one is not careful. What other psychoanalytic transferences are there besides the selfobject transference? There is no point in talking of a libidinal and an aggressive transference once the concept of drive and psychic energy has been vitiated. Rather than setting up or perpetuating a false dichotomy between one kind of transference and another, it would be more instructive to describe the level of selfobject relationships involved in any given transference situation.

For essentially the same reason I do not care for the appellation "self psychology." First of all, no psychoanalytic theory can generate a total psychology. We have been through that in psychoanalysis and it should be pretty obvious by now that insofar as we are a science, our future lies in being a branch of psychology, contributing to the greater whole the theory of motivation that it so badly needs and that only we can supply, while depending on our colleagues to bring to us the theories of cognition, learning, memory, perception, and so on that we cannot generate from our data base.

Secondly, I do not like the term self psychology because it is redundant: A psychoanalytic psychology can only deal with self.

Thirdly, I do not like the term self-psychology because it is now used to separate Kohut's work from so-called classic or traditional analysis—and for "classic" or "traditional" read "Freudian." This is a false distinction. As I have documented at length elsewhere (1981a), Kohut's work is classic analysis in the Freudian tradition. Where he explicitly or implicitly disagrees with Freud, it is in areas, as this paper demonstrates, that are not psychoanalytic ones. If one must have a dichotomy, I would suggest that it be one between analysis governed by doctrine, "doctrinal psychoanalysis," and that governed by the psychoanalytic method, "scientific psychoanalysis." Analysis governed by doctrine can by definition never discover anything new. The outcome is already determined, because whatever the patient may say or do the explanation will be known in advance to be in terms of an oedipal conflict and its vicissitudes. There is comfort of a sort in such prescience, but in repudiating the possibility that its postulates may be empirically falsified, such an enterprise cuts itself off from science and should be thought of as dogma. Scientific psychoanalysis, a psychoanalysis based on

Freud's method rather than on dogmatic considerations, is less certain, but leaves the door open for discoveries that are potentially of interest to scientists. Kohut's work falls into this latter category. It represents a step in the normal, expected evolution of our field. Therefore, I do not see why we need a special term like self psychology to designate Kohut's contribution; as far as I am concerned his discovery of the selfobject transference and its vicissitudes should simply be called psychoanalysis.

REFERENCES

Arnold, M. B. (1960). *Emotion and Personality*, Vols. I & II. New York: Columbia University Press.

Basch, M. F. (1967). Disavowal (unpublished manuscript).

_____ (1976a). The concept of affect: A re-examination. *J. Amer. Psychoanal. Assn.*, 24:759–777.

_____ (1976b). Theory formation in Chapter VII: A critique. *J. Amer. Psychoanal. Assn.*, 24:61–100.

_____ (1977). Developmental psychology and explanatory theory in psychoanalysis. *The Annual of Psychoanalysis*, 5:229–263.

_____ (1981). Selfobject disorders and psychoanalytic theory: A historical perspective. *J. Amer. Psychoanal. Assn.*, 29:337–351.

_____ (1983a). Empathic understanding: A review of the concept and some theoretical considerations. *J. Amer. Psychoanal. Assn.*, 31:101–126.

_____ (1983b). Some theoretical and methodological implications of self psychology. In *The Future of Psychoanalysis*, ed. A. Goldberg. New York: International Universities Press.

_____ (1983c). The perception of reality and the disavowal of meaning. *The Annual of Psychoanalysis*, 11:125–154.

Bowlby, J. (1969). *Attachment: Attachment and Loss*, Vol. I. New York: Basic Books.

Freedman, D. A. (1979). The sensory deprivations. *Bull. Menn. Clin.*, 43:29–68.

_____ (1981). The effect of sensory and other deficits in children on their experience of people. *J. Amer. Psychoanal. Assn.*, 29:831–867.

_____ (1982). Of instincts and instinctual drives: Some developmental considerations. *Psychoanal. Inquiry*, 2:153–167.

Freud, S. (1915). Instincts and their vicissitudes. *S.E.*, 14.

Gould, J. L., & Gould, C. G. (1981). The instinct to learn. *Science*, 81:2, 44–50.

Harlow, M. F., & Harlow, M. K. (1962). Social deprivation in monkeys. *Sci. Amer.*, 207:136–146.

—— & —— (1972). The language of love. In *Communication and Affect*, eds. T. Aloway et al., New York: Academic Press.

Holt, R. R. (1965). A review of some of Freud's biological assumptions and their influence on his theories. In *Psychoanalysis and Current Biological Thought*, eds. N. S. Greenfield & W. C. Lewis. Madison: University of Wisconsin Press.

—— (1976), Drive or wish? A reconsideration of the psychoanalytic theory of motivation. In *Psychology Versus Metapsychology: Psychoanalytic Essays in Memory of George S. Klein. Psychological Issues*, Monograph 36. New York: International Universities Press.

Kohut, H. (1959). Introspection, empathy and psychoanalysis. In *The Search for the Self*, ed. P. Ornstein. New York: International Universities Press, 1978.

—— (1971). *The Analysis of the Self*. New York: International Universities Press.

—— (1977). *The Restoration of the Self*. New York: International Universities Press.

—— (1978). *The Search for the Self*, ed. P. Ornstein. New York: International Universities Press.

Kubie, L. S. (1963). Panel: The concept of psychic energy, reporter A. H. Modell. *J. Amer. Psychoanal. Assn.*, 11:605–611.

Lorenz, K. (1966). *On Aggression*. New York: Harcourt, Brace & World.

Mahler, M., Pine, F., & Bergmann, A. (1975). *The Psychological Birth of the Human Infant*, New York: Basic Books.

Peterfreund, E. (1971). *Information, Systems and Psychoanalysis. Psychological Issues*, Monograph 25/26. New York: International Universities Press.

Rosenblatt, A. D., & Thickstun, J. T. (1970). A study of the concept of psychic energy. *Int. J. Psycho-Anal.*, 51:265–278.

Scott, J. P. (1958). *Aggression*. Chicago: University of Chicago Press.

Spitz, R. A. (1946). Hospitalism: A follow-up report on investigation described in Volume 1, 1945. *The Psychoanalytic Study of the Child*, 2:113–118.

Sterba, R. (1934). The fate of the ego in analytic therapy. *Int. J. Psycho-Anal.*, 15:117–126.

Tomkins, S. S. (1962–1963). *Affect, Imagery, Consciousness*, Vols. I & II. New York: Springer.

———— (1970). Affects as the primary motivational system. In *Feelings and Emotions*, ed. M. B. Arnold. New York: Academic Press.

———— (1980). Affects as amplification: Some modification in theory. In *Emotions: Theory Research and Experience*, eds. R. Plutchik & H. Kellerman. New York: Academic Press.

3 Varieties of Selfobject Experience

Discussion of "Selfobjects and Selfobject Transference: Theoretical Implications," by Michael Franz Basch

Robert D. Stolorow, Ph.D.

OVER THE PAST several years, Michael Basch has been engaged in a series of illuminating studies establishing links between current developments in psychoanalytic thought and the research findings and prevailing theoretical ideas of contemporary behavioral and biological science. Through these important studies, if I have correctly understood their purpose, he has hoped to restore to psychoanalysis the scientific credibility it has lacked as a result of its uncritical retention of outdated metapsychological doctrine derived from 19th-century physiology—a kind of intellectual developmental arrest. I am especially pleased to have the opportunity to discuss a paper in which Dr. Basch has extended his scholarship to the concept of selfobject, because I regard this as the single most important idea—indeed, the foundational construct—upon which the theoretical framework of the psychoanalytic psychology of the self ultimately rests.

In the first half of his paper, Basch provides us with an overview of the evolution of the concept of selfobject in the clinical and theoretical work of Heinz Kohut. I feel no need to comment on this part of the paper, except to say that I admired its clarity and succinctness, and that I especially appreciated the creative synthesis of Freudian, Piagetian, and self-psychological concepts in Basch's formulation of the developmental tasks of the oedipal period.

Four issues raised in the second half of the paper will serve as starting points for some further reflections on the nature of psychoanalytic theory and the selfobject concept: first, the question of the scientific status of Freud's instinct theory; second, the central motivational importance of affect and the need for a more adequate psychoanalytic theory of affect; and third and fourth, Basch's objections to the terms "selfobject transference" and "self psychology."

I am in complete agreement with Basch's contention that current findings in the behavioral and biological sciences refute the validity of Freud's theory of instinctual drive and support instead a view of human nature and human development compatible with the selfobject concept. Even more important, I would suggest, is Basch's assertion that instinct and drive do not even fall within the proper conceptual domain of psychoanalytic theory, a claim which calls to mind George Klein's (1976) discussions of the distinction between the metapsychology and the clinical theory of psychoanalysis. Metapsychology and clinical theory, Klein held, derive from two completely different universes of discourse. Metapsychology, which rests upon the theory of instinctual drive, deals with the material substrate of subjective experience, and is thus couched in the natural science framework of impersonal mechanisms, discharge apparatuses, and drive energies, all of which are presumed to "exist" as entities or events in the realm of objective reality. In contrast, clinical theory, which derives from the psychoanalytic situation and guides psychoanalytic practice, deals with intentionality and the personal meaning of subjective experiences, seen from the perspective of the individual's unique life history. Klein wished to disentangle metapsychological and clinical concepts, and to retain only the clinical ones as the legitimate content of psychoanalytic theory—a goal consistent with Kohut's (1959) view that psychoanalysis as an empirical science is defined and delimited by its observational method of introspection and empathy.

I have argued elsewhere (1983) that self psychology in its mature form—what Kohut (1977) calls psychology of the self in the broad sense—is essentially a clinical psychoanalytic theory in Klein's sense, and that this is one of its principal virtues. As

Basch has described, the central theoretical constructs of self psychology were derived directly from the psychoanalytic situation–specifically, from sustained empathic-introspective immersions in patients' subjective worlds as reflected in the microcosm of the transference (Ornstein, 1978). To paraphrase Basch, in the beginning was the psychoanalytic experience. Correspondingly, self psychology's central constructs pertain to the realm of the experience-near, and therefore embody a personalistic, rather than a mechanistic perspective.

These two features of clinical theory—experience-nearness and derivation from the clinical situation—are nowhere better exemplified than in the concept of a selfobject. This concept of an object that is experienced as incompletely separated from the self and that serves to maintain the sense of self (Kohut, 1971, 1977) finally lifts the shadow that fell upon Freud's (1914) theory of object choice when he tried to formulate the personal narcissistic *meaning* of attachments in terms of the impersonal workings of an energy-discharge apparatus. More importantly, the concept of a selfobject radically alters our understanding of the meaning of patients' experiences in the analytic situation. Our listening perspective is refined and broadened to encompass a patient's use of the analytic bond as an essential aspect of his own self-experience (Schwaber, 1979), and our interpretive focus is shifted from what the patient might wish to ward off to what he needs to restore and maintain (Stolorow and Lachmann, 1980)—to the idealizing and mirroring ties, thwarted during his formative years, on which he now comes to rely for his sense of self-cohesion, self-continuity, and self-esteem.

Returning to Basch's concern about the scientific standing of psychoanalytic constructs, since the selfobject concept is derivative of and uniquely appropriate to meanings which can be apprehended in the psychoanalytic situation through empathy and introspection, it promises to make psychoanalytic theory more scientific—that is, more closely grounded in psychoanalytic data. Such rootedness in psychoanalytic data contrasts sharply with those traditional metapsychological constructs that are relics of 19th-century physiology and that, as Basch points out, are essentially unrelated to the psychoanalytic situation.

If I have agreed with Basch's assessment of the relative scientific merits of Freud's instinct theory and Kohut's selfobject concept, I can endorse just as wholeheartedly his emphasis on the centrality of affect (rather than instinct) in human motivation and in the psychoanalytic situation, and on the need for a more adequate psychoanalytic theory of affect and affective development. An aspect of affect theory that has been of particular interest to me is the artificial separation of affect from cognition that has characterized not only psychoanalytic theory, but Western psychology in general. I have argued elsewhere (Lachmann and Stolorow, 1980; Stolorow and Atwood, 1983) that psychoanalytic developmental psychology should be concerned with the ontogenesis of unitary configurations of experience of self and other in which affect and cognition are indivisible. As Basch suggests, the empathic responses of selfobjects play a crucial role in such development by helping the child articulate, differentiate, modulate, and interpret the meaning of his affective experiences. This progressive articulation of the child's affective life, in turn, facilitates the evolution and structuralization of his nuclear sense of self.

Let me turn now to Basch's objection to the term "selfobject transference" on the grounds that there are no other psychoanalytic transferences besides the selfobject ones and that to imply otherwise is to perpetuate a false dichotomy between one kind of transference and another. In partial disagreement with Basch's position, I favor retaining the term "selfobject transference," but not to refer to a *type* of transference, but rather to a *dimension* of transference—indeed, as Basch suggests, a dimension of all transference. This viewpoint has the advantage of remaining open to the possibility that at times other dimensions of experience and of human motivation may emerge as the most salient ones in structuring the transference—for example, conflicts over loving, hating, desiring, and competing with others. What I am proposing here is a variation on Kohut's concept of complementarity between self psychology and classical conflict theory, except that for me conflict refers always and only to a subjective state completely divested of the metapsychological doctrine of instinctual drive and energy discharge.

The figure-ground distinction drawn from perceptual psychology has, for me, been particularly helpful in conceptualizing this issue in my analytic work with patients. The selfobject dimension occupies the position of figure in the transference relationship and in the analysis to the extent that restoring or maintaining the organization of self-experience is the paramount psychological purpose motivating the patient's specific tie to the analyst. Even when the selfobject dimension is not figure, however, it is never absent from the transference. So long as it is undisturbed, it operates silently in the background, providing a facilitating medium that enables the patient to dare to confront and work through the frightening and painful emotional dilemmas that trouble him. In this respect, every mutative therapeutic moment—even when based on interpretation of intrapsychic conflict—contains some element of selfobject transference cure.

One reason that I favor retaining the term "selfobject transference" as referring to a dimension of the analytic relationship is that it designates an enormously important area for further psychoanalytic research—namely, the investigation in the psychoanalytic situation of the nearly endless varieties of selfobject experience that derive from all phases of the human life cycle. Basch has shown that the concept of selfobject transference, originally formulated in the context of treating narcissistic personality disorders, has been extended to include the revivals of the specific selfobject needs of the oedipal period encountered in the analysis of neurotic structures. My own particular interest has been in acquiring a deeper understanding of the extremely archaic selfobject transference relationships formed by more disturbed patients—those manifesting so-called borderline and psychotic psychopathology (Brandchaft and Stolorow, 1984). In this context, the selfobject concept has permitted me to gain an experience-near comprehension of certain theoretical ideas which before had seemed elusive and opaque, such as Winnicott's (1965) notion of the holding environment and Bion's (1977) metaphor of the container and the contained—terms which I now believe refer to reliance on ties to archaic selfobjects to maintain the basic structural integrity and stability of the sense of self and to prevent its structural dissolution. Revivals of the early specific need for selfobjects to aid in the articulation and containment of affective experience are particularly characteristic of patients with severe developmental arrests.

The most archaic selfobject transference relationships tend to be very intense, labile, highly vulnerable to disruption, and extremely taxing of the therapist's empathy and tolerance. Furthermore, when these ties are obstructed or ruptured by empathic failures or separations, the patient's reactions may be quite catastrophic, since what becomes threatened is the central capacity for self-regulation. However, when the archaic selfobject transferences are correctly understood, accepted, and protected from prolonged traumatic disruption, the more florid psychopathology tends to recede or disappear, and the former borderline or even psychotic patient may become analyzable without parameters (Brandchaft and Stolorow, 1984; see Chapter 6). By contrast, so-called "negative therapeutic reactions" and entrenchment of the psychopathology are produced not by the patient's inherent instinctual viciousness and destructive envy, as some would claim (Kernberg, 1975), but rather by intersubjective situations in which the patient's selfobject transference needs are consistently misunderstood and thereby rejected (Stolorow and Lachmann, 1980).

Finally, let me consider Basch's objection to the appellation "self psychology." Although I agree that all psychoanalytic psychology explicitly or implicitly deals with self-experience, and that the term "self psychology" has been misused by its opponents to falsely isolate it from the Freudian tradition, nevertheless I favor retention of the term because I feel that, rather than arrogating psychoanalysis to the status of a total psychology, it focuses attention on the specific, radical alteration in theoretical outlook whereby Kohut located the experience of self and its development at the very center of psychoanalytic inquiry. This fundamental change in outlook, involving a conceptual shift from the motivational primacy of instinctual drive to the motivational primacy of self-experience, enables us to picture our patients not as mental apparatuses processing drive energies and dealing with instinctual tension, but as *persons* striving through ties to selfobjects to develop, restore, maintain, and consolidate their nuclear sense of self.

I would like to close my discussion by affirming one point concerning which I think Basch and I are in complete harmony—namely, the singular importance of the selfobject concept in extending the limits of our theoretical understanding, of our capacity for empathic comprehension, and of our therapeutic effectiveness, to hitherto inaccessible regions of human subjectivity.

REFERENCES

Bion, W. (1977). *Seven Servants.* New York: Aronson.

Brandchaft, B., & Stolorow, R. (1984). The borderline concept: Pathological character or iatrogenic myth? In *Empathy*, ed. J. Lichtenberg. Hillsdale, N.J.: The Analytic Press (Vol. 2).

Freud, S. (1914). On narcissism: An introduction. *S. E.*, 14.

Kernberg, O. (1975). *Borderline Conditions and Pathological Narcissism.* New York: Aronson.

Klein, G. (1976). *Psychoanalytic Theory: An Exploration of Essentials.* New York: International Universities Press.

Kohut, H. (1959). Introspection, empathy, and psychoanalysis. In *The Search for the Self*, ed. P. Ornstein. New York: International Universities Press, 1978.

_____ (1971). *The Analysis of the Self.* New York: International Universities Press.

_____ (1977). *The Restoration of the Self.* New York: International Universities Press.

Lachmann, F. & Stolorow, R. (1980). The developmental significance of affective states. *The Annual of Psychoanalysis*, 8:215–229.

Ornstein, P. (1978). Introduction to *The Search for the Self*, by H. Kohut. New York: International Universities Press.

Schwaber, E. (1979). On the "self" within the matrix of analytic theory. *Int. J. Psycho-Anal.*, 60:467–479.

Stolorow, R. (1984). Self psychology—A structural psychology. In *Reflections on Self Psychology*, eds. J. Lichtenberg & S. Kaplan. Hillsdale, N.J.: The Analytic Press.

_____ & Atwood, G. (1983). Psychoanalytic phenomenology: Progress toward a theory of personality. In *The Future of Psychoanalysis*, ed. A. Goldberg. New York: International Universities Press.

_____ & Lachmann, F. (1980). *Psychoanalysis of Developmental Arrests: Theory and Treatment*. New York: International Universities Press.

Winnicott, D. (1965). *The Maturational Processes and the Facilitating Environment*. New York: International Universities Press.

4 Notes toward a Psychology of the Feminine Self

Joan A. Lang, M.D.

FOR AT LEAST AS LONG as society ascribes decisive importance to an individual's gender and makes gender the basis for significant social demands, expectations, life-option limitations, and sanctions, then awareness of one's gender will occupy a central place in one's sense of self.

That statement may seem obvious to most readers; to many, it may actually sound odd. For gender has always been, in every society or culture about which we know anything, a crucial differentiator of persons. In fact, Mahler (Mahler, Pine, and Bergmann, 1975) considers "gender-defined self-identity" to be one of two fundamental levels of the sense of identity (p. 224). Thus, even to imagine a society where gender might be of minor significance can be difficult. This difficulty increases to the degree one believes that socially defined gender differences are inevitable outgrowths of biological givens—that anatomy and biochemistry determine social destiny.

Yet, interestingly, in the psychology of the self no specific elaboration has yet been made of the significance of gender identity in the nuclear self, nor of the specific processes by which this aspect of the self is consolidated within the matrix of selfobject relationships, nor of the differences of process or outcome which may occur in male and female self development. (For one recent exception, see Lachmann, 1982.)

There are many possible reasons for this omission, the simplest being that no one has gotten around to it yet. Or it may be that the theory's deemphasis of drives and instincts is partly responsible. There does seem to be an underlying assumption, detectable in Kohut's (1978) writings, that "obvious biological truths" (p. 228) provide a sufficient explanation for the "natural" unfolding of sex and gender differences and psychosexuality. Thus, like drives, these contents of the self may be secondary and not especially interesting theoretical concerns of a psychology of the self. The thesis would presumably be that a properly empathic selfobject milieu will facilitate the unfolding of nature's blueprints, and boys will become masculine and girls feminine without anyone needing to pay specific attention to the matter—beyond, of course, the healthy mirroring of parental joy in these developments, and the healthy acceptance of sex-role-related idealizations, along with others.

In some ways, this is not a bad perspective, because it avoids building into developmental theory the assumption that certain stereotypically defined end results—rather than processes—define healthy psychosexual development.

To put it differently, I would *prefer* that our theory (especially clinical theory, which tends to prescribe interventions and behaviors) take the position that parents should interfere as little as possible with their children's development, rather than that parents are "supposed" actively to ensure their children's masculinity or femininity.

Such a preference is, however, political and practical. Judged for theoretical soundness, a thesis such as the one sketched above depends upon the validity of one or another extremely vulnerable assumptions about gender differences: (1) that such differences are really biologically determined, or (2) that, although socially defined, gender roles are so compatible with children's inner agendas that parental and cultural transmission of these roles (in self-psychological terms, the dispensing of selfobject functions in ways determined by gender stereotypes) will not constitute distorting empathic failures.

The first of these assumptions—the fundamentally biological basis for gender differences—has been undermined by so many challenges that I will here cite only the decisive work of Stoller and others on gender identity. They have clearly demonstrated that gender identity is firmly established by eighteen months to three years of age in conformity with parental beliefs about their child's sex, regardless of the chromosomal reality (Stoller, 1968; Money and Ehrhardt, 1972).

This finding does not, of course, mean that there are no biological predispositions, nor that conscious and unconscious perceptions of anatomical and psysiological realities cannot be invested with psychological significance; I assume that they are. But it does mean that any theory of gender identity cannot rest solely on an assumption of biological determinism, but must include an account of the way in which sociocultural role definitions become translated into psychic structure. (The question of how the role definitions themselves become elaborated within a culture can also be investigated by psychoanalytically informed approaches, of course, and the concept of reciprocal interactions wherein psychic needs shape cultural institutions, which in turn shape psychological development, is an important one. I will return to some considerations of such psychosocial interactions later.)

As for the assumption that the parental responses involved in transmitting socially defined gender roles do not represent distortions of selfobject empathic responsiveness, I hope it is obvious that careful research and clinical exploration are required to demonstrate this; until then, such an assumption is wholly unsupported.

It is of interest then to ask what applying the conceptual tools of the psychology of the self might reveal about the development of those aspects of the self which specifically involve one's sexual or gender self-experiences. We might, for example, investigate such questions as:

—Are there consistent gender-based developmental vicissitudes in the process of consolidating a nuclear self?

—Are there gender-specific differences in the kinds or qualities of selfobject relationships experienced by children?

—Do men and women serve different selfobject functions because of their gender differences?

—How do any such gender-specific differences affect the final constitution of the nuclear self—its constituent poles, its structures, its psychic life?

This paper represents an initial attempt to answer one aspect of such questions, specifically: What can we learn by using the concepts of self psychology to investigate the processes of consolidation of the feminine self, as we observe these processes to occur within our field of observation, which is the socioculturally and psychobiologically patterned subjective world within which our women patients negotiated their selfobject needs and consolidated their nuclear selves?

I have limited my subject to feminine self-structure because my personal experiences and clinical data have most interested me in and best prepared me to address this area. The related questions of the detailed developmental psychology of the self in males (and in Lesbian, gay, or androgynous psyches) are no less relevant, but must be attempted by others.

The question has also been so formulated as to indicate its precise nature: An inquiry into how and why certain things happen, using specific methodology to observe, analyze, and make inferences about the socially and historically specific set of interpersonal relationships within which we have structured the rearing of our children. Implied in this specification is the crucially important, sometimes forgotten nature of the answers we may generate: They will be accounts of what happens—not of what inevitably has to happen under all circumstances, and not prescriptions as to what should happen.

I have also been mainly concerned with one aspect of feminine self development that has been a persistent clinical puzzle: namely, women's self-devaluation, and collusion in their own subordination to male domination.

KOHUT'S WRITINGS

I was not fully aware until I reviewed Kohut's works with specific attention to the questions of gender identity and feminine self-structuralization of the extent to which he did not deal directly with these issues. In elaborating his formulation of the oedipal situation, for example, he abstracts and neuters the description by using such phrases as

> The empathic *heterogenital parent* will grasp the fact of having become the target of *the child's* libidinal desires. . . . The *homogenital parent, too* . . . [1977, p. 231; emphasis added].

There are thus no references to differing vicissitudes of male and female development. Although he does at times refer to such differences—for example, with a brief indication that "a nuclear self . . . will . . . henceforth be more definitely a male or female self" (1977, p. 240), this abstraction is characteristic of Kohut's theoretical formulations (though not of his more informal illustrations and examples). Consistent with his goal of establishing the principles of a psychology of the self as a structure distinct from its drives, and of providing a descriptive outline of the processes by which this self is formed, Kohut, I believe, deliberately sought to abstract his schema, leaving the fleshing out of the "how and when questions" to others.

One exception to this generalization is Kohut's (1975) paper "A Note on Female Sexuality." Replying to criticisms of some remarks he had made (at an earlier symposium) concerning the position of women in society, Kohut questions "whether the difference between my views regarding the area of female sexuality and the [classical psychoanalytic] views of my critics is really as great as they seem to think" (p. 783), given his agreement that penis envy "has an incidence of one hundred percent" (p. 786). He questions, however, the psychogenetic significance of this "injury" in female personality formations and psychic disturbances (p. 786), in particular rejecting the view that the wish for a baby derives from the wish for a penis. The thrust of this paper is to summarize his view that "infantile sexuality . . . is not biological bedrock but psychological surface. Behind it lies the child's experience of . . . the selfobjects" (p. 789). In the course of his discussion, however, he puts forth some specific points which are relevant here:

(1) He indicates that sex- and gender-related experiences concerning "the sight of the male genital" (p. 783), the "non-

possession of a penis" (p. 785), "the little girl's experience of her genitality," and the like will "among other factors . . . leave a distinctive imprint on the personality of women" (p. 783) by tending to "reinforce (and lend a specific content to)" universally occurring human propensities (such as envy or grandiosity).

(2) Among the "other factors," he clearly indicates that "the convergence of biological and cultural factors" (p. 786) and the support and direction of "the cultural milieu" (p. 787) are relevant forces which "channelize" and give "concretely defined content to the woman's self-expressive needs" (p. 786).

In summary, I think it is fair to characterize Kohut's implied theoretical stance in the following way: The nuclear self and its needs (for mirroring, for a target for its healthy idealizations, for empathic understanding and responsiveness, for self-expression) can be understood in the abstract as androgynous; that is, the "supraordinate" urges and motivational forces are in principle the same for both men and women, as are the processes of self-structure formation (Lachmann, 1982). But the concrete contents of the self that is formed, and the specific channels settled upon for satisfaction of the self-expressive needs, will be defined by both biological givens and the specifics of the cultural milieu, which will differ significantly in the experiences of boys and girls. The detailed working out of the complexities of the developmental processes and their differing vicissitudes in males and females, and of the respective contributions of biology, selfobjects, and cultural milieu, is left to later workers.

A CLINICAL ILLUSTRATION AND A PERSONAL ODYSSEY

The main basis for any elaboration of the significance of gender identity by the developmental psychology of the self must be, as in Kohut's own work, the raw material of clinical experience (not excluding our own self-experience). And, indeed, it was my work with women patients which led me to some of the puzzles and beginning insights to which the psychology of the

self, when I first read Kohut's work, brought so much illumina-
tion. Some of the puzzles were like those presented by a patient
I saw in psychoanalytic psychotherapy some years ago.

> Dr. X. was a respected and successful surgeon, intelligent,
> healthy, attractive, productive, yet "inexplicably" depressed. She
> and her busy lawyer husband both took it for granted that,
> although both worked full-time (her practice was actually both
> more arduous and more remunerative), she should assume total
> responsibility for managing their home and children. My in-
> terpretations of her deep unconscious resentment of this ar-
> rangement were rejected by her for a long time, and she was
> impatient with my interpretations of her unconscious devalua-
> tion of herself as a woman. But one morning she came to my
> office pale and shaken. She had worked all night in the operat-
> ing room trying to save a baby, but the child had died, and it fell
> to her to tell the parents. As she walked out, collecting herself
> for this painful task, she found herself thinking, "Thank God it
> wan't a son!"

My work with this woman revolved for a long time around
interpretations of oedipal conflict, penis envy, and sibling rivalry
to explain her depreciated self-image, devaluation of herself as a
woman, unconscious contempt for women, narcissistic vulnerability, absolute dependence on her husband and automatic
deference to him or any man, concealed anger and envy toward
men, and underlying feelings of depression and depletion.
Modest gains were made, but despite her apparent agreement
with my interpretations, the regular production of additional
memories and associations which seemed to confirm them, we
both recognized a sense of dissatisfaction and impasse in the
work.

Let me summarize the theoretical confusion I was experiencing with this woman and many who presented similarly. (I shall
return to her case in the following section.) On the one hand,
the traditional psychoanalytic formulations which seemed to
identify intrapsychic dynamics as responsible for their symptoms did not do much to help them. Thus, I—who had never
placed much stock in the women's liberation movement (I had,
I thought, no problem attributable to sexist oppression; there-

fore, it did not exist)—came gradually to raise my own consciousness. I began to read the feminist literature. Other, more personal data sources—my own psychoanalysis, personal relationships, mothering my daughters—all converged. I began to question old assumptions, recognize and challenge cultural mythologies. It became increasingly clear to me that our theories of intrapsychic conflict and psychological structure simply did not adequately take into account the truly damaging consequences of oppressive sociocultural realities such as sexism. Yet, for all the power of feminist and other sources of sociocultural analysis, these theories, too, were ultimately unsatisfactory. An "enlightened" woman does not necessarily change; even the removal of "external" barriers—legal, economic, educational—left the psyches of my women patients little touched; they were still afraid, angry, and depressed, and they still colluded in their own devaluation. Furthermore, at the intellectual level, I was uneasy with the assumption that "culture" was purely a male creation, or that the intrapsychic needs of both men and women had not shaped our institutions and mythologies.

To condense the story of my odyssey of the last several years and to get to the point of this paper, I have come to believe, and will attempt to advance arguments here to demonstrate, that the psychology of the self, particularly Kohut's brilliant conception of selfobject relationships, provides the missing link between the biological determinism and intrapsychic focus of classical psychoanalysis on the one hand, and the insistence of the cultural school on direct environmental determinism on the other. The selfobject relationship is the crucial mediator between external and psychic reality. The motivational primacy of the self and its need to secure selfobject relationships, the role of mirroring and idealizing selfobject functions in the consolidation of the nuclear self, the concept of transmuting internalization, the selective processes of inculsion and exclusion of mental contents into "self" or "non-self" (Kohut, 1977, p. 183), the traumatic derailing of self development that results from repeated empathic failures, and the lifelong primacy of the need to maintain self-cohesion, these concepts offer enormous power and flexibility in investigating the way in which the psyche reflects the internalization and structuralization of self-experiences that are in significant ways culturally and gender-specifically determined.

IMPLICATIONS OF SELF-PSYCHOLOGICAL THEORY FOR THE FORMATION OF THE FEMININE SELF: AN INITIAL OUTLINE

The implications for the formation of the feminine self that can be discerned in the developmental psychology of the self as we currently understand it arise from two of its aspects:

(1) While "mirroring" and "accepting idealization" are self-object *functions*, which can be described in the abstract as long as we are talking about a theoretical model of human development, in practice a self must develop via selfobject relationships with real people. Thus, it will be materially influenced by the specifics of which qualities are mirrored (and which are not) and which attributes are presented as appropriate for idealization (and which are not). Kohut refers to the "imprints" which will remain from specific attributes of selfobjects (1971, pp. 43, 108).

(2) The impact on the developing self of consistently unempathic selfobject responses is far more grave than merely the production of conflict or ignorance: There is a deficit in psychic structure, the exclusion from the consolidating self of some of its original potentials as being "not me," and the distortion and derailing of the whole course of development.

Kohut's concept of transmuting internalizations has relevance for the first of these considerations. According to this formulation, the specifics of various experiences with a real selfobject are more or less "homogenized out" under favorable conditions by being taken in as functions (of soothing, admiring, and so on)—shorn of their personalized aspects—which can be performed by the self for itself (Kohut, 1971, pp. 49–50). This notion requires an assumption that the child can separate the "signal" from the "noise," and that it is the functional aspects of how others respond which the child will preserve, discarding as unessential the specific contents of the interactions. But can we consider that the real world provides the "favorable conditions" which Kohut considers to be requisite for the operation of transmuting internalization, as far as self-experiences and functions related to gender are concerned? Consider the following conditions:

(1) The baby's growing capacities are mirrored or not depending upon how those capacities fit predetermined and arbitrary rules and categories which the selfobject consciously or unconsciously considers gender-appropriate, rather than in ways that are freely responsive to the child's actual capabilities or inner agendas.

(2) The empathic failures caused by imposing gender-stereotyped external agendas on the child's own are not limited to idiosyncratic responses dictated by one parental personality, but—being culturally prescribed—will be more or less consistently presented by both parents and most selfobjects the child encounters. Thus the traumatic self-constrictions must be experienced by the child as "signal," rather than as incidental trappings. Furthermore, the failures will occur in all poles of the nuclear self, so that opportunities to compensate for failures in one pole by finding appropriate responsiveness in another will also be constricted.

(3) Many of the attributes presented to the child as (a) worthy of admiration, and (b) possible eventually to attain are similarly more or less rigidly classified by gender.

I suggest that as long as such conditions hold, Kohut's formulations lead us to predict gross interference with the processes of transmuting internalization and consolidation of the gendered self. I further suggest that Kohut's conceptualization of the psychology of the self can then be used to develop a more complete and careful understanding of the role played by psychosocial factors in the formation of the individual (male or female) psyche in a world so constituted. The directly distorting influences of conscious and unconscious gender-based constrictions of the empathic responsiveness of the mirroring and idealizing selfobjects can be specified, and the consequences in terms of the consolidation of the core self, particularly in terms of unresponded to and disavowed parts of the nuclear self and its inner agenda, can be mapped.

To return to my patient, Dr. X., for example: When I stopped trying to anchor her experiences in the constructs of oedipal conflict theory and listened instead to her repeated—at first and for a long time frustratingly vague but insistent— efforts to convey to me what she actually felt, two new themes emerged. The first: A strong but previously disavowed and well-camouflaged "inner voice" of sound good judgment, integrity, and perceptiveness which had always tried to provide her with commentary and guidance in life situations, but which she had learned rigorously to discredit. The second: Her means of self-discrediting, and the reason for it, lay in a powerful and automatic judgment triggered (we came to know) by certain kinds of temptations—most notably, to be aggressive or self-assertive, particularly to men or older women. This judgment was a loud "That's NOT ME!," and represented an absolute, unchallengeable signal to desist and submit.

Space does not permit me to detail here the further mapping of her specific selfobject relationships and their vicissitudes, traumas, and her defenses and compensations in the face of them. Suffice it to say that the stalemated therapy took on new direction and vigor—and, more importantly, so did she.

Since then, I have come to recognize that this imperative "That's NOT ME!" is of central importance in the conflicts of many of my patients. It is my view that a "deficient" self *does* experience severe conflicts, which are not organized around instinctual drives per se, but around the threat to the sense of self-cohesion which is posed to an insufficiently consolidated self by any violation of the established and selfobject-sanctioned boundaries of the incomplete self-structure, with its necessary enmeshment with archaic selfobjects. The primary fear is not of castration or loss of love (though these, too, are experienced), but of disintegration or total devaluation of the self. The primary motivational drive is not to discharge instincts, but the need to maintain the "structural cohesiveness, temporal stability, and positive affective coloring" (Stolorow and Lachmann, 1980) of the self.

This is true in principle (and process) for both men and women, but the specifics vary in gender-consistent ways. We are only beginning to spell these out. In a great number of my women patients the "NOT ME!" is characteristically triggered, as in Dr. X, by the expression of aggression or self-assertion. The observation that many women characteristically sacrifice self-interest to avoid open aggression or competition with others (especially men) is certainly not new, but I am proposing that self psychology offers a more powerful explanation for the dynamics than do such older formulations as those of innate masochism, passivity, or dependency.

In a preliminary and tentative way, the equation reads thusly for many girls: (1) To own a "good" self requires that you be "feminine"; (2) to be "feminine" requires that you should *not* be "aggressive" (because aggression is defined as masculine, and aggressive women as unfeminine, castrating, and therefore both bad and unlovable); (3) therefore, if you are aggressive, you are endangering your self, repudiating some idealized selfobjects, and risking the loss of other mirroring selfobject relationships!

Another example: At one point in her psychotherapy, a middle-aged married woman, a successful academic, decided to buy a car. It would be the first car she had ever chosen and owned for herself. We worked through in turn her fears that it was "NOT ME" to become knowledgeable about cars, to choose one for herself, to bargain directly and effectively for it. Finally—to her own amazement (and with her husband's casually ungrudging support, which also amazed her—and which is not in all cases so readily available), she bought herself a sports car, left the showroom triumphantly—and promptly threw up!

I would once have viewed and interpreted all of this material as revolving around penis envy, sibling rivalry, and castration anxiety, and, indeed, elements of these were present and at times interpreted. But I believe that the far more effective therapeutic focus centered upon the construction described above. As this patient learned to recognize, trace the roots of, and challenge the "NOT ME" injunctions of her archaic selfobject relationships, she restored the feelings of pride and pleasure in healthy self-assertiveness. And, as commonly happens, her barely masked fury and envy—symptoms not of primary excessive aggression or penis envy but of her disavowed self's rage at the surrender to being what she felt she had to be to please others and secure from them the urgently needed, self-maintaining selfobject functions—resolved also.

Turning now to what Kohut has called "psychotropic social factors" (1977, p. 270), the findings of self psychology can also be seen to have important implications for the psychosocial realities implicit in our culture's parenting arrangements. In theory, there is no obvious reason why men and women cannot fulfill both mirroring and idealizing functions equally for boys and girls (or, at least, in ways which are not strictly determined by gender alone). In practice, our gender-based childcare arrangements make this highly unlikely. Kohut himself does not envision such equifunctionality of parents. Consider the following quotations:

> It is also more than likely that the earlier constituents of the self are usually predominantly derived from the relation with the maternal self-object (the mother's mirroring acceptance confirms nuclear grandiosity; her holding and carrying allows merger-experiences with the self-object's idealized omnipotence), whereas the constituents acquired later may relate to parental figures of either sex [1977, p. 179].

> The developmental move frequently proceeds—especially in the boy—from the mother as self-object (predominantly with the function of mirroring the child) to the father as a self-object (predominantly with the function of being idealized by the child). Not infrequently, however—especially in the girl—the child's successively mobilized developmental needs for different self-objects en route to the laying down of the nuclear self are directed toward the same parent. And, finally, exceptional circumstances in the environment may occasionally force a child to turn to his parents in the reverse order (from a mirroring father to an idealized mother) [1977, p. 185].

> Briefly, we can say that if the mother had failed to establish a firmly cohesive nuclear self in the child, the father may yet succeed in doing so [1971, p. 185].

What is happening, I believe, is that Kohut's observations concern two different developmental sequences which he does not clearly distinguish. There is the developmental progress from more archaic to more differentiated forms of selfobject relationships implied in his references to earlier and later constituents of the self and to "successively mobilized developmental needs." But there is also, given the sociocultural patterns of our familial and childrearing arrangements, a developmental move which most children make away from an originally intense and exclusive dyadic relationship with the mother to the father as a selfobject and then to the wider world. Indeed, in some theories of child development one of the father's principal functions is held to be that of essentially seducing the child away from symbiosis with the mother (Abelin, 1971; Mahler, Pine, and Bergmann, 1975; Stoller and Herdt, 1982). It is this sequence which Kohut apparently has in mind when he refers to the likelihood that "the earlier constituents of the self are usually predominantly derived from the relation with the maternal self-object . . . whereas the constituents acquired later may relate to parental figures of either sex."

What tends to happen is that the characteristics of the earlier or later stages of maturational development are not distinguished from the circumstances of the earlier or later stages of the socioculturally patterned sequence of relationships. This might not matter if the two sequences were inevitably parallel to one another, but in fact they are not—as Kohut recognizes when he refers to variations. In fact, it is extremely important to recognize that a maturational sequence is "programmed" to unfold sequentially, so our best course as parents or therapists would ideally be one of facilitation rather than interference. But the same is not true for sociocultural patterns: We *create* these, and a great deal can depend on just how we choose to organize them.

Kohut alludes to this possibility of socially determined variations affecting developmental outcomes:

> In patriarchally organized groups, for example, the parental attitudes toward the oedipal boy foster, as a result of his oedipal experience, the development of a mental apparatus that is characterized by a firm superego and a set of strong masculine ideals . . . parental attitudes in groups in which gender differentiation has lessened, may produce, in consequence of different

responses to the oedipal child, girls whose superego firmness and ideals correspond more to that normally found in boys of the patriarchal group [1977, p. 232].

We must, then, inquire about the significance—to an individual child's self-structuralizations, and to our common psychic and social life as men and women in society—of child-rearing arrangements which assign virtually all children of both sexes to the exclusive care of women during the time when their most archaic selfobject needs exist, and the core processes of laying down the nuclear self are beginning, introducing male selfobjects into an important role only at a later stage of development. If, furthermore, Kohut's allusions to a predominant function for women of mirroring, for men of being idealized, have general validity, this polarization would almost have to have significant consequences which we do not know much about but should begin to map.

So far, these "how and when" questions have not been precisely addressed by self psychologists, nor has a chronological timetable for the consolidation of the nuclear self or its constituent parts been mapped. But, interestingly enough, the suggestions I have just sketched can be read as converging with the work of feminist and sociocultural historians (Dinnerstein, 1976; Miller, 1976; Chodorow, 1978; Thompson, 1981; Capra, 1982) who attach enormous importance to the institution of mothering for many features of our individual psychology, male/female arrangements, and cultural and planetary agendas. I will not endeavor to summarize their works here, since this would take us far afield. But, for our purposes, let me outline briefly how the sequence of relationships that evolve in our Western family milieu might look from the vantage point of what we do know about the psychology of the self:

(1) In the typical Western family, the mother (or some female substitute) is almost exclusively responsible for child rearing, and thus it is she who is "omnipresent" for the infant (some think "fused" with it), she who presumably does (or fails to do) most of the mirroring of the child's archaic grandiosity, and she who is omnipotently idealized by the child (as in the earlier cited quote from Kohut).

(2) Correspondingly, the mother must inevitably at times be experienced as the original primary frustrater of the child's selfobject needs—in particular, the destroyer of the child's archaic grandiosity.

(3) Later, when the father becomes more prominent in the child's sphere of selfobject relationships, it is he who turns out to be the possessor of most of what society defines as really admirable and powerful.

(4) A young girl thus learns that certain masculine-assigned potentials of her self are to be disavowed and excluded, made "not me," that it is those very traits that society most values, and that those feminine-assigned potentials left to her are generally devalued by society. (A similar self-constricting process of course occurs in a boy who learns that his feminine-assigned attributes must be disavowed. But he can console himself to some degree with the inflated phallic narcissism he is encouraged to experience.)

(5) Children of both sexes must presumably then undergo a rather drastic revision of their former omnipotent idealization of the mother. I am suggesting here a hypothesis that only clinical experience will be able to test: namely, that the child here sustains the kind of traumatic disillusionment which Kohut (1971) has described as preventing transmuting internalization:

Transmuting internalization is prevented, however, if, for example, the disappointment in the perfection of the object concerns the total object, e.g., when the child suddenly recognizes that the omnipotent object is powerless [p. 50].

I am further suggesting that such a massive disillusionment in the mother (as opposed to "micro" disappointments in selfobjects of both sexes) must have extremely important consequences for the subsequent attitudes which will be held by both men and women about their own gender identity and about masculinity and femininity in general. And I am suggesting that, at this point in development, when the child moves cognitively and developmentally into a revision of former archaic selfobject needs and perceptions, there is a decisive difference in the development of girls and boys. That is: When the archaic idealizations of the mother are disrupted, she is still usable as a mirroring selfobject by both sexes, but no longer as a valid idealized selfobject. The boy is more likely to succeed in rescuing the idealizing pole of his self by turning to his father as a selfobject serving these functions, because social reality supports this move. The little boy is *supposed* to want and expect to grow up to be a man "just like Daddy." But what of the little girl? While the father may accept her idealizations of him, it is likely to be with a very different message: "Yes, look up to me and admire my powerfulness—and I, in return, will enjoy your 'femininity' (e.g., your flirtatiousness). But you can't and shouldn't ever expect to be like me." Reality does not usually support a little girl's efforts to identify with or emulate "masculine" ideals, values, or goals.

The situation thus created is not without its advantages for girls, nor its disadvantages for boys, as feminist and some psychoanalytic theorists have pointed out (Bettelheim, 1954; Greenson, 1968; Stoller, 1968; Dinnerstein, 1976; Miller, 1976; Chodorow, 1978; Stoller and Herdt, 1982). Notably, the boy may react to his disillusionment with mother by basing his sense of having a masculine self on being rigorously "not feminine," thus losing many valuable parts of his potential self. The girl, on the other hand, may be able to retain an undisturbed and secure sense of having a feminine self, but the development of that pole of her nuclear self which is organized around ideals and values may be severely derailed, even arrested, or at least disavowed, as in the case of Dr. X. This probably accounts for the longstanding psychoanalytic conceptualization of the feminine superego as being somehow "weaker" or differently formed (but see Gilligan, 1982). Furthermore, the arrested development in the young girl may impair her separation and individuation processes, so that she retains her mother as a selfobject needed in predominantly archaic ways, needs which may then be repeated in subsequent relationships, such as that with her husband or lover.

As a final point, consider that it is these same non-self-realized girls (vulnerable, according to Kohut's theory of psychopathology, to at least subclinical depression, low self-esteem, hypochondria, panic, etc.) who will later be expected to function as the primary archaic selfobjects for their own infants (male and female).

It seems to me highly probable that, under such conditions, the empathic milieu that Kohut describes as essential for the healthy development of a child's self will be strained, distorted, and badly impaired, particularly—though certainly not exclusively—for little girls. It would also seem that an obvious and important implication for change, following directly from Kohut's formulations about the development of the self, would coincide with some of the recommendations made by writers who arrived at their conclusion from a different (feminist) direction: that infants should be parented (provided with consistently available, empathic selfobjects) by both men and women, and that the emerging selves of boys and girls should be freely responded to without the constraints imposed by artificial and distorting cultural myths defining masculinity and femininity.

REFERENCES

Abelin, E. L. (1971). The role of the father in the separation-individuation process. In *Separation-Individuation*, eds. J. B. McDevitt & C. F. Settlage. New York: International Universities Press.

Bettelheim, B. (1954). *Symbolic Wounds*. Glencoe, Ill.: Free Press.

Capra, F. (1982). *The Turning Point: Science, Society, and the Rising Culture*. New York: Simon & Schuster.

Chodorow, N. (1978). *The Reproduction of Mothering: Psychoanalysis and the Sociology of Gender*. Berkeley: University of California Press.

Dinnerstein, D. (1976). *The Mermaid and the Minotaur*. New York: Harper & Row.

Gilligan, C. (1982). *In a Different Voice: Psychological Theory and Women's Development*. Cambridge, Mass.: Harvard University Press.

Greenson, R. (1968). Disidentifying from mother: Its special importance for the boy. *Int. J. Psycho-Anal.*, 49:370–374.

Kohut, H. (1971). *The Analysis of the Self*. New York: International Universities Press.

――― (1975). A note on female sexuality. In *The Search for the Self*, ed. P. Ornstein. New York: International Universities Press, 1978.

_____ (1977). *The Restoration of the Self*. New York: International Universities Press.

_____ (1978). *The Search for the Self*, ed. P. Ornstein. New York: International Universities Press.

Lachmann, F. (1982). Narcissistic development. In *Early Female Development: Current Psychoanalytic Views*, ed. D. Mendell. New York: Spectrum.

Mahler, M., Pine, F., & Bergman, A. (1975). *The Psychological Birth of the Human Infant*. New York: Basic Books.

Miller, J. B. (1976). *Toward a New Psychology of Women*. Boston: Becon Press.

Money, J., & Ehrhardt, A. A. (1972). *Man and Woman, Boy and Girl*. Baltimore: The Johns Hopkins University Press.

Stoller, R. (1968). *Sex and Gender*, Vol. I. New York: Science House.

_____ & Herdt, G. H. (1982). The development of masculinity: A cross-cultural contribution. *J. Amer. Psychoanal. Assn.*, 30:29–58.

Stolorow, R., & Lachmann, F. (1980). *Psychoanalysis of Developmental Arrests*. New York: International Universities Press.

Thompson, W. I. (1981). *The Time Falling Bodies Take to Light: Mythology, Sexuality and the Origins of Culture*. New York: St. Martin's Press.

5 Shame and the Psychology of the Self

Andrew P. Morrison, M.D.

IN THIS PAPER I shall argue that shame is an affect central to the pathological core of narcissism. If guilt be the emotion of Freud's conflicted Guilty Man, shame, I would suggest, is the affect central to Kohut's Tragic Man. In the course of my argument I shall consider the construct of the "ideal self," and its relationship to the "idealized parental imago" and to shame, and draw on language and conceptualizations from Kohut's writings to indicate that shame is an affect important to his understanding of self deficits.

In a recent publication (Morrison, 1983), I reviewed some previous writings on shame and its relationship to guilt, the ego ideal, and the ideal self. With several other authors (Lynd, 1958; Lewis, 1971; Thrane, 1979; Wurmser, 1981) I assumed that shame is an affect of equal importance, theoretically and phenomenologically, to guilt. I included within the designation "shame" those related phenomena of humiliation, mortification, remorse, apathy, embarrassment, and lowered self-esteem. While there is good reason to attempt to differentiate these phenomena from shame and from one another, I believe that,

Portions of this paper appeared in preliminary form in "Shame, Ideal Self, and Narcissism," *Contemporary Psychoanalysis*, 19:295–318, 1983.

for the purposes of this examination, they are closely enough related emotions to be subsumed under "shame" as a signifying affect. Reflecting the focus of this volume, I shall only briefly summarize earlier contributions on shame, before turning directly to shame's relationship to self psychology and the work of Kohut.

Freud discussed shame from the perspective of genital exposure and exhibitionism (1930), and related it to the female's sense of castration and genital inferiority (1933). He also implied that the young boy experiences shame in the context of oedipal defeat and the resolution of the Oedipus complex (see Hazard, 1969). In an implicit extension of Freud's thinking, Piers (Piers and Singer, 1953) suggested that shame results from a tension between the ego and ego ideal (that ill-defined construct of the superego), and specifically from failure of the ego to attain a goal of the ego ideal, leading to the threat of abandonment and rejection. Piers described a guilt-shame cycle of impulse inhibition resulting from guilt, leading to passivity and shame, with reactive impulse expression and renewed guilt. Finally, Piers suggested that shame is a reflection of body functions and comparison of self to others, with resultant feelings of inferiority and an inclination toward compensatory hiding (i.e., of the defective body part).

Contemporaneous with Kohut's formulation of the self's evolution, Lewis (1971) emphasized the role of the self in the phenomenology of shame, focusing on the "experiential registration of the person's activities as his own . . ." (p. 30). For Lewis, shame is about the *whole* self, and its failure to live up to an ideal. Defenses against shame include hiding or running away, with hostility against the self experienced passively as depression. Whereas shame reflects deficiency and incapacity, guilt is experienced for transgression (an action or a thought), and thus feels more active and voluntary. Lynd (1958), referring to identity formation, related shame and doubt to self-esteem, again implying an awareness of the whole self.

To these authors, then, shame variously reflects feelings about a defect and inadequacy of the self, a lowering of self-esteem, a falling short of the goals of the ego ideal, a flaw in identity representation. We can detect some movement toward a greater appreciation of the experience of the whole self in the phenomenology of shame. But because of the relatively late attention paid by psychoanalytic theory to the self as distinct from intrapsychic structures, and to deficit and developmental arrest as distinct from intrapsychic (intersystemic) conflict; because guilt has consequently been considered a more worthy, deeper, and more structurally embedded emotion than shame; and finally because of the tendency of patients to conceal shameful self-perceptions in psychotherapy (since the danger is abandonment or rejection by a "perceiving other" [Levin, 1967]) shame has maintained a relatively low profile in psychoanalytic writing. While Freud's elucidation of the ego ideal and its relationship to narcissism (1914) offered an opportunity for the psychoanalytic study of shame, with the shift of his attention to aggression and libidinal wishes, and the consequent retaliatory response of the superego (castration anxiety and oedipal resolution), guilt—the dominant emotion of intrapsychic conflict—became the major leitmotif in this area of psychoanalytic investigation.

The construct of the "ideal self" is of relatively recent origin (Reich, 1954, 1960; Schafer, 1960; Hartmann and Lowenstein, 1962; Jacobson, 1964; Schecter, 1979), and an appreciation of its relationship to the superego and ego ideal can be most useful, in my view, in understanding shame. Defined as a representation of the goal of perfection in the subjective experience of the self, it can be contrasted with the ego ideal, a metapsychological construct derived from the superego, representing an internalized, objective set of goals, values, and esteemed object representations toward which the ego strives. The ideal self can thus be seen to be more subjective and experience-near, less specific and cognitive, than the ego ideal—the representation of the individual's personal and subjectively experienced aspirations with regard to the self, rather than aspirations which, however much internalized, are experienced by the individual as objectively determined byproducts of encounters with highly cathected objects.[1] Failure of the self to approximate the repre-

---

[1]For valuable discussions of the ideal self, and its relationship to the ego ideal, see Sandler, Holder, and Meers, 1963; Schafer, 1967; Schecter, 1974.

sentation of the ideal self leads to that sense of self defect and shortcoming central to the experience of shame. In the face of such failure, modification of the aspirations implicit in the ideal self's quest for perfection leads to enhanced *self-acceptance,* an experience different from *forgiveness* of the self for transgressions that have resulted in guilt.[2]

SHAME IN KOHUT'S EARLY WRITINGS

Kohut's self psychology is particularly helpful in understanding shame, since it offers a perspective on the self's structural defects and shortcomings, particularly "self depletion." Self depletion reflects insufficiency of the selfobject's response to the need for affirmation, merger, and idealization, leading to that "guiltless depression" resulting from lowered self-esteem. Kohut (1966) recognized early the relationship of shame to the lack of affirmation of the narcissistic self's exhibitionistic demands. Still working within the framework of structure-drive metapsychology, he discussed shame in relationship to the ego ideal. He saw the ego ideal as "related to drive control," while the narcissistic self is the source of ambition, the wish "to be looked at and admired" (1966, pp. 435–436). Later he stated: "Shame, on the other hand, arises when the ego is unable to provide a proper discharge for the exhibitionistic demands of the narcissistic self" (p. 441). The shame-prone individual is ambitious and success-driven, responding to all *failures* (in the pursuit of moral perfection or external success) with shame. Thus, shame results when the ego is overwhelmed by the grandiosity of the narcissistic self. The ego ideal functions to protect the self from narcissistic

---

[2]Compare the perspective of psychoanalytic metapsychology, in which the "loving superego" (see Schafer, 1960) seeks to *accept* rather than to forgive the self when it falls short of superego ideals, so that psychoanalysis can help to strengthen the loving superego by modifying and making more flexible the goals and standards of the ego ideal. The role of self-acceptance in the palliation of shame will be explored from the perspective of Kohut's contributions in subsequent sections. So too will the relationship of the ideal self to the "idealized parental imago," one anchoring selfobject of Kohut's bipolar self.

vulnerability and shame by "controlling" the expression of exhibitionistic "drives."

In 1971, Kohut explicitly rejected the thesis of Piers and others that shame is "a reaction of an ego that has failed to fulfill the (perhaps unrealistic) demands and expectations of a strong ego ideal" (1971, p. 181). Rather, he stated again, the shame of narcissistic patients "is due to a flooding of the ego with unneutralized exhibitionism and not to a relative ego weakness vis-á-vis an overly strong system of ideals" (p. 181); i.e., such patients are driven by grandiose ambitions. Progress in the analysis of shame-prone individuals is achieved through a shift in narcissistic investments from the grandiose self to the idealized parental imago and ultimately to the superego through its progressive idealization (p. 175). This shift occurs in the context of the analyst's admiring acceptance and confirmation of the patient's grandiose self. Thus, archaic grandiosity and "shame-provoking exhibitionism" become transformed into self-esteem and pleasure in success.

Kohut's concept of the bipolar self, anchored on the one side by the grandiose self and on the other by the idealized parental imago, posits a tension arc between ambitions and ideals, and the notion, as I see it, of a second chance at development of a fully cohesive self through empathic acceptance of the wish to merge with and idealize an omnipotent, tension-regulating selfobject. The first opportunity for development of self-cohesion arises early, usually with the mother, and requires adequate empathic mirroring in response to the exhibitionistic grandiose self; the second chance comes later, usually with the father, and requires empathic acceptance of the child's "voyeuristic" idealization and wish for merger. Kohut (1971, p. 107) argues against viewing the grandiose self as more primitive than the idealized parental imago, suggesting that the tendency to do so reflects a prejudice that assigns object love supremacy over narcissism. Rather, grandiose self and idealized parental imago represent parallel forms of narcissistic development. Throughout *The Analysis of the Self*, however, Kohut *does* imply that the idealizing transference—which reflects a movement outward in an object-seeking direction, just as "voyeuristic" idealization suggests a similar movement outward—constitutes a developmental step beyond investments in the grandiose self. For instance: "The therapeutic mobilization of the grandiose self may thus arise either directly (*primary mirror transference*), or as a temporary *retreat* [italics mine] from an idealizing transference (*reactive remobilization of the grandiose self*)" (p. 133). Or again: ". . . an initial period of idealization, followed by a secondary mirror transference, repeated a sequence of events in his childhood (the brief attempt at idealization which was followed by a *return* to the hypercathexis of the grandiose self" (p. 140; italics mine).

Despite Kohut's disclaimers, then, he does suggest a developmental sequence of narcissism from (1) investment in the grandiose self, to (2) a movement outward in an object-seeking direction toward investment in the idealized parental imago, to (3) firming of the idealized parental imago, and its internalization (with the formation of psychic structure) through idealization of the superego, and the resultant establishment of ideals. I believe that this developmental sequence is important for our understanding of shame in the context of self psychology. Certainly, grandiosity/exhibitionism and idealization/voyeurism coexist in patients with primary self pathology. But I suggest that the developmental thrust outlined above represents a real maturational sequence which allows us to move beyond an explanation of shame solely on the basis of overwhelming grandiosity, as Kohut would have it, and which, further, suggests an object-seeking (affiliative) direction in the development of the self which potentially links narcissistic development with the quest for object ties. These points will be elaborated below, in my discussion of *The Restoration of the Self* (1977).

THE RESTORATION OF THE SELF

By 1977, Kohut had relinquished the drive-conflict elements of Freud's metapsychology in his elaboration of self deficits, positing at best a parallel development of conflictual/structural elements and the self, with the self assuming a supraordinate position with regard to intrapsychic structure. The major danger to the vulnerable self was "disintegration" (loss of cohesion), with the relevant signal of impending loss of cohesion being "disintegration anxiety." Kohut included within disintegration anxiety fears of "fragmentation, serious enfeeblement, or uncontrollable rage" (1977, p. 138). Or again: "The core of disintegration anxiety is the anticipation of the breakup of the self . . ." (p. 104).

Thus, Kohut did not differentiate fragmentation from enfeeblement/depletion as elements in the disintegration of the self. On the basis of the developmental schema proposed above, however, I would suggest that fragmentation is the more archaic manifestation of self disintegration, reflecting primitive, prestructural failure in the mirroring/affirming selfobject function with regard to the self's grandiosity and exhibitionism. Enfeeblement/depletion, in contrast, would tend to reflect failure of the idealized selfobject's function in responding to the self's idealizing/merger needs with regard to its quest for an omnipotent, tension-regulating selfobject. If this assumption is accepted, depletion/enfeeblement anxiety would then reflect the threatened loss of the earliest sought-after object, leading to feelings of emptiness and archaic depression.

Kohut describes fragmentation vividly: "the dread of the loss of his self—the fragmentation of and the estrangement from his body and mind in space, the breakup of the sense of his continuity in time" (1977, p. 105). Tolpin (1978) acknowledges the distinction between fragmentation and depletion anxiety (and depression): "Thus the term [disintegration anxiety] refers not only to the fear of fragmentation of the self, it also refers to the fear of impending loss of its vitality and to the fear of psychological depletion" (p. 175). Fragmentation is a primitive state reflecting the danger of regression to psychosis; depletion relates, I would suggest, to a more cohesive self state, with greater capacity for structuralization and selfobject idealization, and thus with vulnerability to the loss of the sought-after object and internalized ideals,[3] with empty depression the usual result.

---

[3]This distinction cannot be rigidly maintained, since fragmentation and depletion concerns usually coexist in states of disintegration anxiety. But the developmental direction of these two conditions can be clinically observed and substantiated, as I hope to demonstrate in a future paper.

Two clinical vignettes will help exemplify the difference between incipient fragmentation and feelings of depletion as distinct manifestations of self disintegration:

Mrs. B., a woman in her mid-thirties, had been working in therapy on her low self-esteem, anxieties about being alone, and disorganizing attraction to a female coworker (a self-esteem-regulating relationship with merger and twinship elements). During my absence for a week, she was in a serious skiing accident in which she could have been badly hurt. On my return, she at first explored whether she had been trying to punish herself for some unknown wish or action, an explanation that lacked immediacy or conviction. I then wondered whether her self-aggrandizing wishes had gotten out of control in my absence, and whether she had risked a ski jump which, with some reflection, she would have recognized as being beyond her capabilities. This connected. She thereafter worked effectively on her grandiosity and her need for my presence to help keep it in bounds, and her concern that she could so readily lose touch with her realistic limitations.

Mr. R., a passive, depressed, narcissistic man who had been in treatment for many years, had been progressing in his exploration of his idealization of me. He had spent much time earlier in treatment working through his grandiose expectations that professional success would come easily to him, and his feelings of shame at not having attained his desired status at work. More recently, he had shared concerns that he must hide his imperfections out of fear of my abandoning him. In one hour, I commented on his large outstanding therapy bill. He became angry and sullen, and thought of leaving the hour prematurely. I wondered whether he felt angry and ashamed at owing me money. He confirmed this, saying that I should indeed be paid for my work with him, and he felt disturbed at not being able readily to come forth with the balance. Further work indicated his dependent idealization of me, and his fear (and shame) at not living up to his own ideal of self-sufficiency.

Mrs. B.'s accident reflected, I believe, the breakthrough of her archaic grandiosity without my affirming presence to stabilize her reality sense. She used me as a mirroring selfobject, without much appreciation of my independent human qualities. She was overwhelmed at realizing the degree of her own disavowed grandiosity, and the life-threatening, fragmenting nature of its manifestations. Mr. R., on the other hand, had progressed in facing and dealing with his archaic grandiosity, and was acknowledging my (somewhat) separate existence in his use of me as an empathic, idealized, omnipotent selfobject. As such, he feared losing me in that role if I came to share his own contempt for himself, and thereby came to reject him. My acceptance of his financial plight as an issue which we could consider together helped him to review his life situation, regain his fragile self-esteem, and overcome his depressive feelings.

How do self deficits develop with regard to exhibitionistic and idealizing selfobject needs? According to Kohut (1977, pp. 3–4), defects are manifested both in the early development of the psychological structure of the self and in secondary structures related to the primary defect—"defensive" and "compensatory" structures. A defensive structure functions to cover over the self's primary defect, whereas the compensatory structure strives to make up for the defect. Thus, the compensatory structure attempts to counterbalance a weakness in one pole of the self (usually in the area of exhibitionism and ambitions) by increasing self-esteem through the pursuit of ideals. Pseudovitality in a narcissistic patient may be defensive against (i.e., may attempt to hide) "low self-esteem and depression—a deep sense of uncared-for worthlessness and rejection, an incessant hunger for response, a yearning for reassurance" (1977, p. 5).[4]

Kohut relates the primary structural defect in the nuclear self to the genetic failure of the mother as a selfobject in mirroring the child's healthy, age-appropriate exhibitionism. Defects in the self's *compensatory* structures, on the other hand, frequently reflect failure of the father as a selfobject in responding to the child's idealizations (1977, p. 7). Consistent

---

[4]This description by Kohut of a narcissistic personality disorder fits well, I suggest, with the psychodynamics of manic-depressive illness. I believe that shame and narcissistic vulnerability are central problems for the manic-depressive, which manic flight attempts to conceal in fantasied merger with the ideal self.

with the developmental sequence I have proposed, we see the first pole in self formation (ambitions and the nuclear self) becoming established early, the second pole (ideals and compensatory structures) relatively later in development. This view of compensatory structures articulates, in turn, with my view of self depletion as a developmentally later experience of the loss of self-cohesion. Depletion, I would suggest, reflects not the primary defect of a fragmented self, but, most prominently, failures in compensatory structures of a self in the process of attaining tenuous cohesion, seeking to make up for its enfeeblement through merger with an idealized selfobject. In his discussion of the case of Mr. M., Kohut supports my view of the relationship between the "genetically later" failure of compensatory structures and "the father's selfobject function as an idealized image" (1977, p. 7). The absence of ideals and goals as a result of failure of compensatory structures is a primary source of self depletion.

The process of psychoanalytic treatment involves, then, either repair of the self's nuclear defect through repeated "transmuting internalizations" (in the analytic context, through transference to the *mostly* empathic analyst as a responsive selfobject) or modification of compensatory structures by establishing more flexible and realistic ambitions, goals, and ideals. As I shall elaborate below, modification of grandiose ambitions and/or the ideal of perfection may eventuate through identification with the *accepting,* empathic selfobject/analyst, with important consequences for the palliation of shame.

According to Kohut, self pathology reflects inadequacies in the structure of the parent's self which have caused the child to be deprived of empathic mirroring responses or empathic acceptance of his idealization needs. Based on the developmental model presented earlier, I would suggest that fragmentation indicates defects of the nuclear self proceeding from insufficient mirroring and affirmation of age-appropriate grandiose needs. Self depletion, in contrast, would tend to reflect problems with compensatory structures proceeding from deficiencies in the responsiveness of the idealized selfobject to voyeuristic (object-oriented) needs. Reparation through psychoanalysis occurs when the analyst provides a context of empathic mirroring and/or allows for optimal idealization. Adequate nuclear self structure can be built anew, or adequate compensatory structure increased, through exploration and interpretation of the (perceived) empathic microfailures of the analyst, allowing for the transmuting internalization and structure-building necessary to strengthen the patient's self.

SHAME IN *THE RESTORATION OF THE SELF*

In discussing the "guiltless despair . . . of those who in late middle age discover that the basic patterns of their self as laid down in their nuclear ambitions and ideals have not been realized" (p. 238), Kohut (1977) speaks of a time

> of utter hopelessness for some, of utter lethargy, of that depression without guilt and self-directed aggression, which overtakes those who feel that they have failed and cannot remedy the failure in the time and with the energies still at their disposal. The suicides of this period are not the expression of a punitive superego, but a remedial act—the wish to wipe out the *unbearable sense of mortification and nameless shame* imposed by the ultimate *recognition of a failure* of all-encompassing magnitude [1977, p. 241; italics mine].

Kohut's reference here to "nameless shame" is one of the few references to shame in *The Restoration of the Self*. But throughout the book there are references to feelings that I believe are closely related to shame: "mortification" (p. 137, p. 224), "disturbed self-acceptance" (p. 94), and "dejection" (p. 97, p. 224). These occur repeatedly in discussions of the self's "defeat" in the realization of its goals. To provide only one example:

> [theories of drives and defenses fail to do justice to] the experiences that relate to the crucially important task of building and maintaining a cohesive nuclear self (with the correlated joy of achieving this goal and the correlated *nameless mortification . . .* of not achieving it) and, secondarily, to the experiences that relate to the crucially important striving of the nuclear self, once it is laid down, to express its basic patterns (with the corre-

lated triumph and *dejection* at having succeeded or failed in this
end) [p. 224; italics mine].

I believe that the feelings correlated with this "defeat" can all
conveniently be conceptualized in terms of shame—the shame,
mortification, dejection of the self at having failed to achieve its
ambitions and ideals. The patient suffers from "disturbed self-
acceptance" because he is *ashamed* at not having realized the
"basic patterns" of the self. No other single word adequately
captures the sense of the self's evaluation of itself and its performance. Only "guilt" has the same self-referential quality, but
clearly guilt is very different from the subjectively experienced
defeat of the self in the pursuit of its goals. For this reason, I
would suggest, it is the language of shame which permeates
Kohut's thinking, and which requires us to conceive of shame as
involving more than overwhelming grandiosity.

Is the experience of shame possible for the patient with fragmentation anxiety (as I would argue, the more primitive narcissistic personality disorder) as well as the patient with depletion anxiety (the less severe narcissistic personality disorder)? I
would suggest that a certain level of attainment of self-cohesion
is necessary in order to experience shame, whether it be in
response to overwhelming grandiosity or failure to attain ideals. Kohut (1977) states:

> I suggest that we first subdivide the disturbances of the self into
> two groups of vastly different significance; the *primary* and the
> *secondary* (or reactive) disturbances. The latter constitute the
> acute and chronic reactions of a consolidated, firmly established
> self to the vicissitudes of the experiences of life, whether in
> childhood, adolescence, maturity, or senescence. The entire
> gamut of emotions reflecting the states of the self in victory and
> defeat belongs here, including the self's secondary reactions
> (rage, despondency, hope) to the restrictions imposed on it by
> the symptoms and inhibitions of the psychoneuroses and of the
> primary disorders of the self [p. 191].

I believe that shame deserves a prominent place in the list of
the self's secondary reactions, and that, as Kohut's language
suggests ("acute and chronic reactions of a consolidated, firmly

established self"), the experience of shame requires a certain degree of self-cohesion, be it to register inadequate responsiveness of a selfobject, failure in attainment of a goal, disappointment with regard to ideals or even with regard to bodily functions. A self that is fragmenting does not have the energy or luxury to register shame, but rather is overwhelmed with panic and boundary diffusion.

As a "secondary reaction" of the self, I would argue that shame is a prominent response to the failure of a compensatory self structure. One characteristic example of compensatory structure offered by Kohut is the enhancement of self-esteem through the pursuit of ideals. Thus, when Kohut maintains that shame reflects only the breakthrough of unneutralized grandiosity, and not failure to meet the goals and expectations of the ego ideal (or ideal self, as I prefer to view it), I believe his view to be too limited, and that shame can be experienced as well with respect to failure in relationship to the idealized parental imago. I suspect that Kohut rejects the connection between shame and the ego ideal because he (quite correctly) views shame as a manifestation of narcissism and its vissisitudes, and the ego ideal as a metapsychological construct reflecting an internalization of the libidinized object. But the relationship with the idealized parental imago is an aspect of *narcissistic development* according to Kohut's theory, so that shame over failure in the compensatory pursuit of ideals, for example, or over *any* failure with regard to the idealized selfobject, is as real as the shame of unneutralized grandiosity, and no less a product of narcissistic development. Indeed, to the extent that idealization implies greater differentiation from the selfobject than does grandiosity and the need for mirroring, and to the extent that the formation of the idealized parental imago represents an advance in narcissistic development beyond the stage of the grandiose self, as I have argued above, rupture in the bond to the idealized selfobject should result in a greater sense of self defeat and personal responsibility—a greater sense of shame— than rupture of the bond with the mirroring selfobject. Reflecting the developmental sequence from grandiosity to idealization, shame experienced in relation to the idealized parental imago will tend to be less archaic and more differentiated than that experienced as a result of overwhelming unneutralized grandiosity.

Failure in attaining an ideal or goal is, then, a major precipitant of shame, with the concomitant threat of rejection or abandonment by the "significant object." Of course, the threat of abandonment may also reflect an earlier experience of failed mirroring responsiveness by the parental selfobject to the self's healthy exhibitionistic strivings. Such an experience may then lead, as I have argued above, to a compensatory pursuit of ideals, aimed at reversing the perceived disinterest and apathy of the parental selfobject. It is in this way that defensive strivings may be transformed into compensatory structure in healthier narcissistic patients. But recurrent failures of empathic responsiveness of the idealized selfobject to the quest for merger will, in turn, lead to a sense of emptiness, depletion, and despair.

What is the relationship between the idealized parental imago and the ideal self? In 1971, Kohut identified the idealized parental imago as a way station in the evolution of the self from grandiosity to the internalization of the idealizing function with the formation of psychic structure through idealization of the superego. By 1977, he had dispensed with metapsychological structure altogether in explaining the development of the self. I would suggest, however, that some representation of the idealizing function must be maintained in the narcissistic transformations which accompany the development of self-cohesion. As idealizing selfobject functions are relinquished during establishment of a firmly cohesive self, I believe that these functions *are* internalized, but not in the form of an idealized superego. Rather, they become attached to the already structuralized, firm self and its vigorous, esteemed, and valued qualities. This constellation of optimal, experience-near qualities and ideals forms the ideal self—the representation of the goal of perfection in the subjective experience of the self. The ideal self is thus an endpoint in the development of the self—from grandiosity, to idealization of the selfobject, to final internalization of the "self as it aspires to be": cohesive, independent, vigorous, and representative of values and ideals.

Earlier I indicated my view that depletion anxiety is the product of less severe self pathology than fragmentation anxiety, the result of a failure of the "more or less" cohesive self, and that the shame of depletion can thus be a "secondary reaction" to failure of a compensatory structure to attain an ideal, including the ideal of gaining for the striving self the admiration/mirroring of a responsive selfobject. This should not be taken to mean that shame cannot also be a secondary reaction purely—without mediation by compensatory structure—to failure in the self's quest for the mirroring responsiveness of the selfobject, as in the case of overwhelming grandiosity. Rather, I mean only that such grandiosity cannot be the *too* overwhelming grandiosity of fragmentation states, since, as I have argued, the experience of shame requires a certain degree of self-cohesion. But whether shame reflects the subjective experience of frustrated grandiose ambitions, failed attempts to compensate for frustrated ambitions, or failed attempts to satisfy ideals, it is the hallmark of the defeated self in the state of depletion, the self that has fallen short of its goals.

If shame reflects self depletion, what is the relationship between shame and depression? I have already considered Kohut's view of the "guiltless despair" that results from the self's failure to realize its ambitions and ideals. This "guiltless despair" is characteristic of self depletion in the depression of middle life over failure to attain the goals of the nuclear self. In a discussion of depression very closely related to Kohut's views, Bibring (1953) implies that depression results from the failure to attain ambitions and ideals. While he does not explicitly discuss shame, Bibring comes close to my conceptualization when he states: ". . . the depression sets in whenever the fear of being inferior or defective seems to come true, whenever and in whatever way the person comes to feel that all effort was in vain, that he is definitely doomed to be a 'failure'" (p. 25). Or again: "In depression, the ego is shocked into passivity not because there is a conflict regarding the goals, but because of its incapacity to live up to the undisputed narcissistic aspirations" (p. 30).

Thus, the views of both Kohut and Bibring suggest that there is a close relationship between shame and depression, and that, for some patients, particularly those suffering from narcissistic personality disorders, the relationship of depression to failure in attaining ambitions and ideals may be most compelling. But we also know that all individuals, including the relatively healthy (those with a firmly cohesive nuclear self), suffer at times from the affect of shame (especially, as Lewis [1971] has described, those who are relatively field dependent). I suggest that shame in healthy people can also be understood in terms of microfailures in meeting the aspirations of the (relatively cohesive and differentiated) ideal self. Put another way, the ideal self is a construct relevant to self-cohesion (or neurotic character structure) as well as to more primitive archaic self states. At issue here is the *intensity* and *magnitude* of failure in affirmation of ambitions and development of attainable ideals. When viewed from the perspective of the self in the "broader" sense, we can understand that failures in attaining aspirations of the ideal self need not necessarily reflect severe psychopathology.

PSYCHOANALYTIC TREATMENT OF SHAME

While shame is frequently accompanied by depression, too often it is only the depression which is treated in therapy. This lack of therapeutic attention to shame may also occur in the analysis of manifestations of narcissistic rage. In essence, narcissistic individuals cannot achieve even a modicum of self-acceptance, and cannot believe that anyone else could possibly accept them in view of their emptiness and failure to achieve their own self-appointed, grandiose life tasks. This *lack of acceptance* by self and other is, I suggest, a central narcissistic dilemma, related to the deeply felt shame of the narcissistic patient, and should be a target in treatment of the narcissistic personality.

Protracted "empathic immersion" in the feeling state of any patient (but particularly the narcissistic patient) will unveil deep and painful shame feelings. These are often difficult to detect for the many defenses directed at covering over shame experiences, and the grandiosity, defects, failures, and emptiness which engender them. But their discovery, examination, and working through by the patient, and the ultimate realization that the analyst and patient alike can accept them, represent a major curative factor in each and every successful analysis. In achieving this goal, the analyst should be helped and guided by his recognition, through vicarious introspection, of his own failures to achieve goals, to realize ambitions and ideals, of his own grandiosity and defects. In short, the analyst must be willing to face and acknowledge his own shame, and the pain which accompanies it.

Many have argued that the tenets of self psychology can be integrated within the theoretical framework of classical psychoanalytic theory. But with regard to the affective experience of shame, it would seem that structural theory could never completely explain its importance, particularly in the narcissistic patient's psychopathology. Unlike guilt, which can be understood in terms of the conflicting vectors of traditional metapsychology, shame can best be appreciated as a reflection not of conflicting drives, but of passive failure, defect, or depletion. Whereas guilt motivates the patient to confess, shame motivates him to conceal—for this reason, shame has been less richly evaluated in the psychoanalytic literature and less frequently dealt with in psychoanalytic therapy. For guilt, the antidote is *forgiveness;* shame tends to seek the healing response of *acceptance*—acceptance of the self despite its weaknesses, defects, and failures. The selfobject/analyst must strive to facilitate self acceptance through his own protracted empathic immersion in the patient's psychological depths. Modification of grandiose ambitions and/or the ideal of perfection may then eventuate through identification with the accepting, empathic analyst.

SHAME AND RAGE

Kohut seems to view shame and rage in a complementary way, the former as a response to the self overwhelmed by unmirrored grandiosity (1971), the latter as a reaction to the self's lack of absolute control over an archaic environment (1972). Whereas some theorists of self psychology consider rage to be the affect central to Kohut's Tragic Man—the individual with major deficits of the self—I would suggest, rather, that *shame* is the principal affect of Tragic Man—particularly of the depleted self, suffering as it does, in Kohut's terms, the empty, guiltless depression resulting from unmirrored ambitions and unrealized ideals.

What, then, is the relationship of rage to shame? I believe that shame (and the related phenomenon of humiliation) is an affect—a signal that the individual feels exposed and vulnerable—which serves as a primary stimulus to rage. Shame, whether in the face of unmirrored grandiosity or failure to meet the fantasied expectations of the idealized parental imago, frequently acts as an internal trigger to the more socially discordant and observable expressions of rage and aggression. This relationship has been noted in so-called "shame cultures" by anthropologists (e.g., Singer, in Piers and Singer, 1953), and in the psychology of antisocial personalities (e.g., Gilligan, 1976). Because the narcissistic rage which results from shame is frequently more dramatic and clearly delineated than shame, which is characteristically hidden in treatment, as in life, inadequate therapeutic attention is sometimes paid to the underlying experience of shame in the analysis of manifestations of narcissistic rage.

SUMMARY

In this paper I have reviewed and attempted to integrate some previous metapsychological and phenomenological discussions of shame. I have related shame to the self, and have elaborated on the concept of the ideal self and its position in relation to the ego ideal and the idealized parental imago. I have then considered shame (and related phenomena) from the perspective of self psychology, arguing that Kohut's framework is particularly useful in our attempt to understand shame's role in the patient's affective experience. For narcissistic patients, in particular, shame is a central affect, one which underlies much of their character pathology. Their quest for self-acceptance and acceptance by others represents a focal narcissistic problem. Shame, moreover, plays a central role in the psychology of narcissistic patients suffering from a failure to achieve ideals, as well as narcissistic patients suffering from overwhelming grandiosity.

REFERENCES

Bibring, E. (1953). The mechanism of depression. In *Affective Disorders*, ed. P. Greenacre. New York: International Universities Press.

Freud, S. (1930). Civilization and its discontents. *S.E.*, 21.

_____ (1933). New introductory lectures on psycho-analysis. *S.E.*, 22.

Gilligan, J. (1976). Beyond morality: Psychoanalytic reflections on shame, guilt, and love. In *Moral Development and Behavior*, ed. T. Lickona. New York: Holt, Rinehart, & Winston.

Hartmann, H. & Loewenstein, R. (1962). Notes on the superego. *The Psychoanalytic Study of the Child*, 17:42–81.

Hazard, P. (1969). Freud's teaching on shame. *Naval Theologique et Philosophique*, 25:234–267.

Jacobson, E. (1964). *The Self and the Object World*. New York: International Universities Press.

Kohut, H. (1966). Forms and transformations of narcissism. In *The Search for the Self*, ed. P. Ornstein. New York: International Universities Press, 1978.

_____ (1971). *The Analysis of the Self*. New York: International Universities Press.

_____ (1972). Thoughts on narcissism and narcissistic rage. *The Psychoanalytic Study of the Child*, 27:360–399.

_____ (1977). *The Restoration of the Self*. New York: International Universities Press.

Levin, S. (1967). Some metapsychological considerations on the differentiation between shame and guilt. *Int. J. Psycho-Anal.*, 48:267–276.

Lewis, H. B. (1971). *Shame and Guilt in Neurosis*. New York: International Universities Press.

Lynd, H. M. (1958). *On Shame and the Search for Identity*. New York: Harcourt, Brace and World.

Morrison, A. P. (1983). Shame, the ideal self, and narcissism. *Contemp. Psychoanal.*, 19:295–318.

Piers, G. & Singer, M. (1953). *Shame and Guilt*. New York: Norton.

Reich, A. (1954). Early identifications as archaic elements in the superego. *J. Amer. Psychoanal. Assn.*, 2:218–238.

_____ (1960). Pathologic forms of self-esteem regulation. *The Psychoanalytic Study of the Child*, 15:215–232.

Sandler, J., Holder, A., & Meers, D. (1963). The ego ideal and the ideal self. *The Psychoanalytic Study of the Child,* 18:139–158.

Schafer, R. (1960). The loving and beloved superego in Freud's structural theory. *The Psychoanalytic Study of the Child,* 15: 163–188.

_____ (1967). Ideals, the ego ideal, and the ideal self. In *Motives and Thought: Psychoanalytic Essays in Honor of David Rapaport,* ed. R. Holt. *Psychological Issues,* Monograph 5. New York: International Universities Press.

Schecter, D. (1974). The ideal self and other. *Contemp. Psychoanal.,* 10:103–115.

_____ (1979). The loving and persecuting superego. *Contemp. Psychoanal.,* 15:361–379.

Thrane, G. (1979). Shame and the construction of the self. *The Annual of Psychoanalysis,* 7:321–341.

Tolpin, M. (1978). Self-objects and oedipal objects: A crucial developmental distinction. *The Psychoanalytic Study of the Child,* 33: 167–184.

Wurmser, L. (1981). *The Mask of Shame.* Baltimore: Johns Hopkins University Press.

III SELF AND SELFOBJECT: NEW DIMENSIONS IN PSYCHOANALYTIC PRACTICE

6 A Current Perspective on Difficult Patients

Bernard Brandchaft, M.D., and Robert D. Stolorow, Ph.D.

THE SINGLE FEATURE most characteristic of so-called "borderline" patients is that therapists find them particularly difficult to treat. So it is well to recall that the history of psychoanalysis began with "difficult" patients. Even earlier Freud had recognized that the difficulty presented by "difficult" patients did not rest with the patients alone but with how they were understood and consequently how they were treated. As a young neurologist, Freud became dissatisfied with the understanding of aphasia propounded by his teachers, Meynert and others. The essence of his disagreement lay in his belief that various aphasias could not be explained, as they were then being explained, by minute localizing schemes of discrete subcortical lesions. Rather, Freud held, all varieties of aphasia were to be explained by varying degrees of functional derangement radiating from a centrally damaged area (Jones, 1953, pp. 214–215). From the outset he recognized that it was imperative to discover new methods for investigating his subject—nervous tissue—and he was exultant when following a hint by Flechsig he used a gold chloride stain and found that the picture which emerged was entirely different, "wonderfully clear and precise" (Jones, 1953 p. 205).

Freud's discovery was an early example of the general principle that "mode of observation defines the contents and limits of the observed field and thereby also determines the theories of an empirical science" (Kohut, 1959, p. 212). It is just as imperative in our day as it was in Freud's that we continually reexamine our theories and their observational base if our science is to expand. This is especially so with regard to attempts to understand "borderline" disorders whose difficulties seem to mark the boundary of current psychoanalytic knowledge.

The first syndrome that elicited Freud's psychological interest was hysteria, the quintessential stigma of the late-19th-century difficult patient. At the time, hysterical women were the target of contempt and indignation on the part of physicians, the best of whom regarded the illness as a matter of simulation (manipulation) or "imagination." In the past, thinking it a peculiar disorder of the womb, they had treated it by extirpation of the clitoris or by valerian, for some believed the smell would cure the wandering womb by "putting it in its place." Bertha Pappenheim (Anna O.), the first of Freud's difficult patients, was to sweep clean a great deal of the scientific dogma of that day, in addition to her own disordered mind, and we need look no further than her relationship with Breuer for evidence that the difficulty with difficult patients never arose solely from within the patient but "must be viewed as a difficulty in the more inclusive patient-therapist system" (Stolorow, Brandchaft, and Atwood, 1983).

From its beginnings to the present, psychoanalysis has had to deal with patients who failed to conform to or benefit from existing paradigms arrived at by existing methods of investigation. And the development of psychoanalysis has always been nourished by its failures with such difficult patients. It is they who challenge our complacency with what is known and who force us to extend the boundaries of our understanding. The scientists of Charcot's day almost uniformly regarded hysterics as impossibly difficult. But despite their nearly universal agreement, theirs was still a subjective view. It was an alteration of that view that brought about the scientific revolution known as psychoanalysis. Human interactions take place in a field of reciprocal regulations, and there can be little doubt that when hysterical patients were viewed and responded to as highly abnormal and extremely troublesome, this in itself affected how they experienced themselves, and thereby tended to exacerbate and intensify their symptoms, as it does with today's borderline patients. Freud was able to alter his perspective, as he had previously done with the new stain of nervous tissue, and adopt a new mode of observation, from *within* the hysterical patient's subjective frame of reference. His shift in stance constituted a monumental scientific achievement.

Very early, narcissism emerged as a difficult problem for Freud and his followers. Abraham (1919) noted a chronic resistance in certain of his patients to observation of the fundamental rule, although this was by no means the only rule to which they failed to conform. In these patients he detected an "unusual degree of defiance" (p. 305). They reported only ego-syntonic matters, and were "continually on their guard against suffering and humiliations" (p. 305). They were preoccupied with signs of personal interest and wanted to be treated with affection; they reacted intensely to slights and injuries to their self-esteem. These were not the kinds of "nervous disabilities" which analysis at the time had set out to cure, and Abraham noted that his own predetermined treatment plans receded into the background to the extent that "narcissistic interests predominate[d]" (p. 306). He concluded that the most fundamental explanation for what he was observing was that his patients wished to thwart him and to grudge him "the role of the father" (p. 306).

Abraham's paper, in its time, represented a noteworthy advance. But it is of interest to us primarily for the way it reflects discordant views of the purpose of psychoanalysis on the part of disjunct subjectivities, those of patient and analyst, and a conflict arising not solely from within the patient, but also from the system formed by patient and analyst together. Kohut (1959) was later to define the narcissistic purpose as arising not from any primary need to thwart the therapist, but from an injured and poorly structured psyche "struggling to maintain contact with an archaic object" (p. 218) in order thereby to maintain its basic self-regulatory functions. Abraham in his own day was applying the newly discovered insights about drives and defenses as primary organizers of psychic functioning. From that perspective he concluded that the neediness and clinging of his patients demonstrated their fixation at the oral level of psychosexual development. Since he believed that normal development proceeded from autoerotism through a narcissistic phase to genitality and object love—"mature object relations"—he concluded that his patients' narcissistic preoccupations represented a defense against love for and appreciation of the analyst. When his patients insisted on their narcissistic preoccupations and reacted with anger to his interpretations of their presumed defensive maneuvers, he believed that they did so solely from innate, unconscious destructive forces within themselves. Unconscious oedipal rivalry or preoedipal sadism was the basic cause of pathological development and of the difficulties encountered in treatment—an example, we believe, of mistaking effect for cause.

The term "borderline" first appeared in a paper by Stern (1938). Stern reported that a large group of patients did not fit into the existing diagnostic categories of neurosis or psychosis. The clinical picture included narcissism, "psychic bleeding," hypersensitivity, rigidity of personality, negative therapeutic reactions, constitutionally rooted feelings of inferiority, and deep organic anxiety. The symptomatology can be recognized today as that of severe self disorders (Kohut and Wolf, 1978). And indeed Stern noted that in the borderline group, narcissism formed the basis of the entire clinical picture. He wrote that the disorder seemed to be rooted in very early childhood relations which had adversely affected the patients' narcissistic development, anticipating Kohut's conclusion that for such patients "the analyst is not the screen for the projection of internal structures but the direct continuation of an early reality that was too distant, too rejecting, or too unreliable to be transformed into solid psychic structures" (1959, pp. 218–219). In at least seventy-five percent of the histories, the primary caretakers were decidedly neurotic or psychotic, and "inflicted injuries on their children by virtue of a deficiency of spontaneous maternal affection" (Stern, 1938, p. 469). As food deficiencies result in nutritional defects, so these patients, never having acquired "a sense of security by being loved" (p. 469), were malnourished, as it were, in their narcissistic development.

Despite these findings, the questions raised by borderline patients continued to revolve mainly around whether they could be treated by psychoanalysis. The more important question—"treated for what"—receded into the background. Concessions in the form of parameters were made, with the hope that, after an initial period of attention by the analyst to the specific needs of the patient, the patient would then be able to be analyzed "properly," that is, with the focus on the unconscious intrapsychic structural or drive-related conflicts and defenses that psychoanalysts had come to believe *had* to be lurking beneath every treatable disorder. So thoroughly has psychoanalysis become imbued with this article of faith that even today psychoanalysts insist that if these drive-related conflicts are not engaged in the transference in a primary way, it is because of the tenacity of the resistance with which the analyst has likely been colluding (Stein, 1981).

Kernberg (1975) has attempted to delineate a discrete pathological syndrome, the borderline personality organization, and to distinguish it from the narcissistic personality structure. He maintains that the following are primary characteristics of the borderline disorders: (1) "non-specific ego weaknesses" (lack of anxiety tolerance, impulse control, and sublimating channels); (2) shifts toward primary process thinking; (3) pathognomonic primitive defenses, especially "the intensification and pathological fixation of splitting processes" (p. 28) which segregate "good" and "bad" self- and object representations. "The major defect in development," Kernberg writes, "lies . . . in the incapacity to synthesize . . . the aggressively determined and libidinally determined self and object images" (p. 28). In direct line with Abraham's findings of a half-century earlier, Kernberg concludes that the primary pathogenic factor is excessive aggression.

Patients with borderline organization, Kernberg claims, externalize all-bad, aggressive self- and object images, and consequently experience objects as dangerous and retaliatory. They then feel as though they must defend themselves against the fantasied harm. Significantly, the evidence for this set of far-reaching propositions comes from instances in which narcissistic and borderline patients experienced their *analysts* as dangerous and retaliatory, when the analysts did not so perceive themselves.

Kernberg describes the narcissistic personality disorder as a variant of the underlying borderline disorder, in his view the major diagnostic category. He reserves the term narcissistic for patients whose main problem is a disturbance in self-regard— who show an unusual degree of self-reference and an inordinate need to be loved and admired by others. Pathognomonic for this group, according to Kernberg, is an integrated though highly pathological grandiose self reflecting a condensation of real-self, ideal-self, and ideal-object images. He does not regard these features as symptoms of a weakness in the structural foundations underlying the subjective sense of self and its affective valence, with a consequent urgent need for constant and extreme buttressing. Rather, he claims, these narcissistic configurations are used to defend against "real" dependency and the aggression it is presumed to mobilize.

In a recent paper (Brandchaft and Stolorow, 1984) we discussed the borderline concept in some detail. We took issue with the view "that borderline refers to a discrete, stable, pathological character structure rooted in specific, pathognomonic instinctual conflicts and primitive defenses." We noted that all such patients seemed to show underlying structural vulnerability and weaknesses and propensities for, or rigid defenses against, fragmentation and dysfunction. These disorders of the structural cohesion and temporal stability of the sense of self (Stolorow and Lachmann, 1980) we regarded as pathognomonic of severe primary self disorders.

In that paper we formulated and cited evidence for the following thesis: "The psychological essence of what we call borderline is not that it is a pathological condition located *solely* in the patient. Rather, it refers to phenomena arising in an intersubjective field—a field consisting of a precarious, vulnerable self and a failing, archaic selfobject" (Brandchaft and Stolorow, 1984).

We recognize that borderline symptomatology exists outside the therapeutic situation and precedes it, and that it can arise in any situation in which any selfobject is experienced as failing in functions needed to sustain a brittle and vulnerable self. We do not overlook or minimize the contribution of the patient's archaic states, needs, and fragmentation-prone self, but stress that in the therapeutic situation the patient's manifest psychopathology (and its subsequent course) is always *codetermined* by *both* the patient's self disorder *and* the therapist's ability to understand it. While we do not claim that borderline *symptomatology* is iatrogenic, we do believe that the *concept* of a borderline personality structure rooted in pathognomonic conflicts and fixed defenses is symptomatic of the difficulty therapists and analysts have in comprehending the archaic intersubjective contexts in which borderline pathology arises.

Thus have contemporary views crystallized, after a prolonged period of germination, in very different notions of narcissistic and borderline patients. How are these differences to be explained?

THE STANCE OF THE OBSERVER

The most essential difference between these contrasting views, and that upon which all other differences rest, is the perspective used to gather and organize the data from which inferences are drawn and by which the various theoretical conclusions are supported. Kohut's (1959) paper "Introspection, Empathy and Psychoanalysis" set the stage for a reconsideration of the basic methods by which we gather the data that enable us to know what we know about mental life. Where he originally saw "resistances" as arising from internal pressures and endopsychic sources, with his role being that of a neutral observer outside the psychological field, he was able to see, through a profound and crucial shift in focus to his patient's subjective experience of himself and his interpretations, that his own specific contributions were intrinsic to the very nature of his patient's reactions. Patients' experiences could be more fully understood only in the context of their perceptions of the analyst, and the subjective validity of those perceptions (Schwaber, 1979).

We have subsequently attempted to spell out the difference between psychoanalysis seen as a science of the intrapsychic, focused on events presumed to occur within an isolated "mental apparatus," the classical analytic stance, and psychoanalysis viewed as a science of the intersubjective focused on the interplay between the differently organized subjective worlds of the observer and the observed (Stolorow, Brandchaft, and Atwood, 1983). We are fully in accord with Kohut in stressing the importance of an observational stance which places primary emphasis on understanding the impact of the analyst from within the patient's subjective frame of reference.

This stance is methodologically necessary, we believe, in order to investigate and understand in depth those "difficult" archaic states which involve a loss of self-regulatory function (and its recovery), fragmentation symptomatology, erotization, autoerotization, and narcissistic rage. The loss of self-regulatory functions has been subsumed under the heading of "ego weakness," and consistent with the traditional analytic stance has generally been attributed to the effect upon the ego of repression (Fenichel), primitive ego defenses such as splitting and projection, and pathologically intensified pregenital sadistic impulses (M. Klein, Rosenfeld, Kernberg). These assumptions were derived from the almost unchallenged doctrine that the patient's psychic reality is secondary to and determined by unconscious defensive measures and primary instinctually determined configurations.

When we view the therapeutic interchange from the vantage point of the patient's subjective perception of the analyst as a fundamental determinent of his ensuing experience, that view yields markedly different data and distinctly different explanatory hypotheses. A similar reorientation in observational stance is now occurring within the field of infant observation, whereby the entire developmental process is increasingly coming to be understood as "the property of an interacting infant-environment system of mutual regulation" (Sander, 1975, p. 7). We have elsewhere cited evidence for concluding that psychological development and pathogenesis are best conceptualized in terms of the specific intersubjective contexts that facilitate or obstruct the child's negotiation of critical developmental tasks and that shape the course of the entire developmental process throughout its successive phases (Stolorow and Brandchaft, 1984). Sander has emphasized the different outcome that results from this observational shift, in that the questions asked, the route of discovery, and the understandings available are all different.

It has been claimed (e.g., Kernberg, 1982) that such a stance leads to a "psychology of the conscious." On the contrary, a strict focus on subjective experience not only leads to the discovery of unconscious meanings and purposes, it makes possible as well an unveiling of the forms and patterns that conscious experience repetitively and unconsciously assumes. Access is thereby gained to the underlying structures and organizing principles that unconsciously govern psychological life.

CLINICAL ILLUSTRATION

The following is excerpted from the analysis of a patient with a brittle self and borderline symptomatology. It illustrates the extent to which such symptomatology is embedded in an intersubjective context.

Mr. J., a business executive, entered analysis with a history that betrayed a thoroughly chaotic life. In neither his personal nor professional life could he maintain control. His home life was marked by frequent bouts of violent rage against his wife, toward whom he would hurl the most extreme insults. At work he was unable to maintain discipline over himself or his employees. His intense need for approval led to his being taken advantage of repeatedly, after which he would lapse into long periods of self-reproach for his "weakness," interspersed with outbursts of resentment. He was predisposed to take offense at the slightest rejection or failure to appreciate or respond to his needs, and would suffer severe disruptive states marked by rage, withdrawal, or urgent compensatory measures to recover his self-esteem or redress his grievances. He reported episodes of delinquency in adolescence.

Mr. J. was unable to attend to details, was regularly late to appointments, and generally mismanaged his business relationships. In search of relief from the chaotic conditions around him, and from his sense of inner disorganization and recurrent feelings of deadness and meaninglessness, he was driven to enter sexual relationships with a number of women. These were often marked by drug use, which he said made him feel more alive. He was also tormented by recurrent, severe episodes of hypochondriasis, for which he could find relief only by searching out the highest authority in the field of whatever bodily disorder with which he thought himself afflicted.

With the development of an idealizing transference to the analyst, his hypochondriacal symptoms subsided. On weekends, however, he continued to engage in driven sexuality, and was unable to control his profligate eating and spending habits.

One Monday, during a phase in the analysis in which his relationship with his father had begun to occupy the focus, he appeared for his session on time, unusual for any day and hitherto unknown on Mondays. He seemed more animated than usual and bore a sheaf of papers which he began to read, after first saying, "I've been working on this all weekend." The papers chronicled an introspective journey into his early relationship with his father, concerning which a number of memories had emerged that fit together to form a pattern of relatedness of which he had previously been unaware. It was beautifully put together and contained a series of highly important, even brilliant insights. The analyst found himself enthralled by the story that unfolded and, eager to make the most of the opportunity, used the patient's report to tie together a series of elements in the patient's symptomatology and behavior which had previously been puzzling and frustrating but now seemed absolutely clear. The patient accepted the explanations and the hour continued. But where originally he had been enthusiastic and bouyant, now he began to sound increasingly dull, repetitive, and uninspired. The analyst noted the change and inquired as to whether the patient was aware of it and whether he could account for it. Thereupon Mr. J. exploded: "You are just like my father—that is exactly what I was writing about. He could never just be pleased with how I was or what I did; he kept showing me and telling me how much better, smarter, and ahead of me he was, how much better a son he had been to his mother than I, what great things he could have accomplished if only he had had the glorious opportunities he was providing me with!"

The patient missed the next session, came late for the following one, and reported that he had just spent a night filled with sexual excitement. He had also turned to various drugs in an attempt to counteract feelings of deadness and inner chaos, which feelings had caused him to absent himself from work. Subsequently the analyst was to discover that Mr. J.'s adolescent delinquency had been rooted in childhood experiences closely similar to what had just occurred in the transference.

The analyst of course had failed to notice and reflect the patient's pride in the momentous step he felt he had taken in organizing himself in a creative act, modelled after the analyst's ideal of attention to the inner world and presented to the analyst in the hope of evoking his enthusiastic recognition and affirmation. A significant shift in the selfobject transference toward reliance on the analyst's mirror function for self-integration had gone unanswered, resulting in Mr. J.'s fragmented state, rage, and primitive sexualized self-restorative efforts.

Mr. J.'s symptomatology, when he began treatment, fit into the "borderline" category that has been described. Included in the array, in addition to his severe hypochondriacal anxieties, were nonspecific "ego-weaknesses," lack of impulse control, and a scarcity of sublimatory channels. He was disposed to magical and primary process thinking, particularly to ideas of reference. For example, he viewed himself as the cause of any misfortune which members of his family might incur. He also believed in omens and in expiatory acts to influence a God whom he experienced as tyrannical and sometimes implacable. His behavior towards objects, including the analyst in the transference, could be easily conceptualized as evidence of the "pathognomonic" primitive defenses of splitting and projective identification. His rage when he was thwarted or felt humiliated could not be controlled, sometimes leading to physical attacks, and when in this state, he showed no indication of any awareness of positive aspects of the relationship.

The borderline symptomatology, which had gradually subsided within a responsive analytic milieu, now reappeared when this new but unsteady intersubjective field disintegrated and a traumatic repetition of elements of an original childhood pathogenic field temporarily replaced it.

Such failures, from the perspective of the subjective experience of a patient attempting to revive a developmental process, are common and absolutely inevitable. The unfolding of the particular selfobject need (for unlimited recognition), when understood within its developmental context and worked through, would eventually enable Mr. J. to acquire a sustaining confidence in himself and in his ability to understand himself and his object world. It would reduce his dependence upon idealized women, sexualized crude exhibitionism, and drugs— his "fixes"—to sustain and recover a positive sense of himself. First, however, it was necessary to focus upon his traumatic disappointment in the analyst and its sequelae, his rage and the other events that had followed. Reactions to disappointments or injuries that repeat chronic traumatic developmental interferences constitute, in our view, the essence of what is often described as the negative transference. The expressions of violent anger and other assertions of self will usually be associated with a background of specific meanings and experiences for the patient. Accordingly, the analyst first took up the patient's expectations of the impact of his anger and subsequent absence on the analyst's feelings about himself and toward Mr. J. This inquiry yielded important memories of his early relations with his parents, in which acts of self-demarcation and self-assertion produced hurt and withdrawal from his mother and physical retaliation and threats from his father.

Mr. J.'s expression of hurt and his criticism of the analyst had left him terrified of the analyst's anger and retaliation, providing compelling evidence, in our view, of his urgent need for a more comforting and responsive archaic selfobject. In sexualized form it repeated regressive retreats of his early childhood in which he sought solace from damaging and humiliating encounters with his father by turning to his mother. In his childhood, this had necessitated a commitment on his part to concentrate his efforts on what would please or delight and not upset her. In his sexualized replaying of this sequence, he repeated the compulsion to please at the same time as he preserved the memory of the comforting qualities of his mother in his sexual partner.

The analysis and working through of these reactions clarified the origins of Mr. J.'s chronic rage, his disposition to what some analysts might perceive as an excess of aggression. When the channels for the normal expression of assertiveness and anger at injuries to a child's vulnerable pride and self-esteem are foreclosed, the child has no way of directly repairing the damage and integrating the experience within the context of the total relationship. He retains his vulnerability in the form of a brittleness. He capitulates and preserves the idealization of his objects at the expense of his own development, and he develops various compensatory activities to cover over the wounds and the defect. So it was with Mr. J. His mother could never acknowledge that any action of hers might be damaging to him. She insisted, for example, that he be immaculately dressed, inspecting him minutely each day before he left for school. She paid no attention to his complaints that this resulted in his being teased mercilessly by his schoolmates and made him feel awkward and out of step. His father could never say that he was sorry for anything that he did or said to his son, instead always blaming Mr. J. for being "too sensitive" and lacking in "balls."

In the analytic situation just recounted, the analyst's interpretation of Mr. J.'s anxieties following his outburst—in terms of his fear of retaliation by a failing archaic selfobject—had the effect of reducing the severity of his defensive distancing. It was then possible for the analyst to communicate his understanding of Mr. J.'s hurt and anger as reactions to the analyst's faulty responsiveness to his prideful display of the psychological tapestry he had so painstakingly woven. Together analyst and patient were then able to expand the exploration of the many meanings of this experience and the encapsulated and encoded memories it contained and revived. The disruption subsided, the symptomatology disappeared, and the analysis proceeded in greater depth.

We do not doubt, from our previous experiences in such instances (Brandchaft, 1983; Brandchaft and Stolorow, 1984), the consequences that would have followed had the analyst interpreted the situation just described according to concepts which are more familiar. Interpretations might point to a fear of depending upon the analyst or purport to describe a display arising from outmoded, omnipotent, and grandiose needs and an underlying desire to defeat and humble the analyst. In our opinion, these would have been inappropriate and counterproductive. The same might be said about interpreting Mr. J.'s angry response as demonstrating the operation of primitive defenses such as splitting and projection, or as indicative of his inability to synthesize good and bad internal object representations or lack of appreciation of the analyst's well-intended efforts and interpretive help. Such interpretations, which are often more exculpatory of the analyst than explanatory of and for the patient, both exacerbate the symptomatology and isolate it from its intersubjective context. It is in response to such views of the patient that the characteristics which have come to be associated with the borderline personality organization often become entrenched.

OBJECT RELATIONS

Current perspectives on borderline and narcissistic disorders embody widely divergent views on the nature of the object relations that are engaged. These divergencies reflect the contrasting "stains" of each observer, drawn from the analyst's subjective view of transferences that occupy the focus of attention in analytic investigation and provide its observational data. The analyst's conclusions themselves become part of the interacting patient-therapist system and affect subsequent transference configurations. We are in agreement with Rosenfeld's (1964) statement that "as the transference is the main vehicle for any analytic investigation, it seems essential for the understanding of narcissism that the behaviour of the narcissist in the analytic situation should be minutely observed" (p. 169). We would add that the intersubjective field within which such behavior takes place should now be equally minutely studied.

Analysts generally regard the nature of object relations as crucial in borderline patients. Frequently emphasized is the incapacity to synthesize good and bad introjections and identifications. All-good and all-bad internal object representations together with all-good and all-bad parts of the self are maintained and repetitively reinforced by splitting, these observers hold, in order to avert painful feelings of dependence upon less than ideal objects. Other factors stressed are a preference for the pleasure principle so as to avoid the pain, humiliation, and rage that the recognition of reality entails, "unneutralized" primitive destructiveness, and unbearable guilt in the mourning process that comes about when the patient is forced to acknowledge that the loved analyst and the hated analyst are one and the same. Most observers maintain that these archaic all-good and all-bad internal object representations or parts of the self—in the form, for example, of a primitive and malignant superego—are constantly projected onto the analyst in the transference, and that this leads to the negative transference and negative therapeutic reactions.

Such concepts, in one or another form, frame and underlie the approach of most analysts treating borderline and narcissistic patients. An absolute precondition for success in treatments which adhere to these concepts is that the patient agree that his own perceptions of the analyst are essentially invalid or of secondary importance. Failure on the part of the patient to do so and thus validate the analyst's perception of himself and of the patient is treated as a "resistance." If the patient persists in expressing his own experience of the analyst, a judgment is generally made that the patient's "reality testing" is impaired, and that the "therapeutic alliance" necessary for the treatment does not exist. The patient is considered to be further over the "borderline" and to warrant a poor prognosis. Other forms of treatment may then be recommended.

Mahler and those who follow her developmental schema believe that this presumed defensive splitting is responsible for the failure to develop object constancy and that this in turn accounts for the severe anxiety over separation and aloneness. The splitting, Mahler also believes, is maintained because of an excess of unneutralized aggression and serves to avert, delay, or prevent the resolution of painful differentiating and mourning processes (Mahler, Pine, and Bergmann, 1975). In this connection, our observations indicate that when the structural foundations supporting the patient's sense of self crumble, his object representations also may disintegrate. The analyst's consistent focus on the intersubjective contexts underlying these archaic states of disruption and their anxieties serves to reinstate an aborted developmental process and reestablishes the sense of an intact self in an enduring selfobject relationship. When these archaic states of disruption recur over a long period of time, the patient becomes extremely sensitive to signs of the analyst's disappointment and feelings of failure. This revives specific, early intersubjective disjunctions in which the patient was needed, and failed, as a selfobject for the parents to buttress their own feelings of competence and avert the collapse of their own sense of self.

Our understanding of human development, of psychoanalytic transferences, and of the profoundly intersubjective nature of the psychoanalytic situation have all been immeasurably deepened by Kohut's (1971, 1977) concept of selfobjects and selfobject transferences. The selfobject theory of development is a contemporary theory of object relations. It concerns the most archaic relationships to objects experienced as part of the self, merged with the self, or in the service of the self. These selfobject relationships are necessary in order to maintain the stability and cohesion of the self while the child gradually acquires, bit by bit, the psychological structure it needs to maintain its own self-regulatory capability. The course of selfobject relations reflects the continuity and harmony of the developmental process through its various hierarchically organized stages. In the "omnipotence" which has been described as characteristic of the pathology of archaic object relations (M. Klein, Rosenfeld, Kernberg) we can recognize the persistence of the confident expectation that these selfobject needs will be met (Winnicott, 1965; Mahler, Pine, and Bergmann, 1975). Where archaic selfobject needs persist, the differentiation, integration, and consolidation of self structures and the developmental line of selfobject relationships have been interrupted. Thus archaic, poorly differentiated and integrated selfobjects continue to be needed, expected, and used as substitutes for missing psychological structure. When the selfobject unit is intact, the patient experiences himself as "well" and the world as "all right." When the unit is disrupted by physical or psychological absence or prolonged, unrecognized disjunction, symptoms of narcissistic and borderline disorders derived from precariously consolidated and brittle self structures appear. Such symptoms include fragmentation and depletion phenomena, addiction-like craving for praise or for union with idealized selfobjects (sometimes sexualized), as well as rigid defensive postures, schizoid or paranoid, erected to protect the underlying vulnerability. The predominant anxiety accompanying separations is the terror of disintegration, and the harm that such patients fear in analysis is not, in our view, "fantasied harm," but actual. Psychosis, psychological and physical self-mutilation, and suicide are only extremes of a host of actual dangers to a patient whose vulnerable self structures are exposed.

It was Melanie Klein who first attempted the study of transferences in children. Considering the child's subjective experiences of its objects from the background of her own theoretical assumptions, she concluded that her child patients' experiences of her as a (self)object—that is, their persistent claims and needs for her to maintain their endangered or precariously organized selves—were derivations of defensive, instinctually determined "fantasies." Therein she failed to consider the child's experience of its incompletely differentiated objects as a phase-appropriate, *primary* psychological phenomenon. She thereby laid the groundwork for succeeding generations of analysts of differing theoretical orientation to continue to regard archaic subjectivity as a second-order phenomenon, evidence of splitting into all-good and all-bad, and defensive against the reality principle and against a presumptive primary destructiveness and mourning.

The analysis of selfobject transferences indicates that narcissistic and borderline patients defend against or seek to reestablish an arrested, archaic bond with the analyst. If the defenses employed to protect a fragile self are recognized and explained, a selfobject rransference will emerge and coalesce around the analyst. The terms "mirror transference" and "idealizing transference" refer to the most intense aspects of the patient's reawakened archaic longings, not to the behavior of the analyst, however much any particular analyst ignores this principle. Countertransference reactions cut through all conceptual frameworks. What is essential in the analysis of selfobject transferences is the provision of a milieu in which the patient's subjective experience, including especially his experience of the analyst, can be sensed, noted, and articulated freely, with the analyst committed to understanding that experience from within the perspective of the patient's subjective world. The archaic needs of the patient are then recognizable as at one time having been those of a normal small child, however intensified and distorted they became in their passage through the particular life experience being scrutinized and reconstructed.

The analysis of selfobject transferences involves those areas of self-development and self-experience, and consequently of selfobject relations, in which development was derailed or arrested. Through the transference those derailments and arrests and their unconscious determinants can emerge and be demonstrated and understood. When they are understood, an authentic pattern of development may be resumed, together with a process of gradual differentiation of self from object, which so many analysts hold is being "denied" for defensive reasons. *The analysis of those innumerable and inevitable experiences of frustration and disappointment in which the patient perceives the analyst as failing in respect to a particular archaic wish or need is an indispensible part of the treatment.* The understanding in depth of the conscious and unconscious meanings of such empathic failures restores the disrupted tie and thereby permits the analysis and development to proceed. *Such a technique provides an analytic alternative to nonanalytic procedures in which either the patient must renounce his deepest personal "narcissistic" wishes, or the analyst disregards his own boundaries and supplies "parameters."* Respect for another's subjective experience, we emphasize, need not imply compliance or enslavement of the analyst.

When the patient feels that the analyst understands, respects, and is concerned with his archaic longings, rooted in a vulnerable and arrested self, the resumption of an interrupted developmental process becomes possible. Then concern and consideration for and gratitude to the analyst can develop naturally and spontaneously, as they seem to do in normal children whose needs, perceptions, vulnerabilities, and assertions have been understood, respected, and responded to by their parents. Feeling valued, they do not exhibit devaluation. If, however, these transferences are engaged, and the patient fails to elicit the analyst's consistent interest in his unique self-experience, the analyst may come to regard the patient's continued attempts to evoke the needed interest as manipulative and the patient's self-experience or its constituents as outmoded, defensive, or expressive of a primary hostility toward or envy of the analyst. The process of self delineation then will predictably come to a halt, and all the complications and reactions which have been described in the literature can appear. These include negative therapeutic reactions, interminable analyses, transference psychoses, intractable "resistances," "borderline symptomatology"—all of the characteristics of "difficult" patients. Perhaps even worse are the "cures" that come about when the patient is compelled by his need for the analyst to substitute the analyst's subjective view of his reality for his own.

SYNTHESIS OF "GOOD" AND "BAD" PARTS OF SELF AND OBJECT

The experience of objects or the self as "all-good" and "all-bad" has been widely regarded as prima facie evidence of defensive splitting and projective identification. The supporting data are derived from transferences in which the analyst is at times the target of intense anger or disparagement, and at other times experienced as ideal, loving, and loved. In either case it is believed that the experience is defensive against the countervalent affective configuration. These data are then seen to confirm certain background assumptions regarding the patient's early object relations.

When these interactions are viewed from the perspective of the patient's subjective frame of reference an entirely different ordering of the data emerges. Then it can be seen that idealiza-

tions in narcissistic and borderline patients do not most commonly arise as a defense against hostility or disparagement, as
"red herrings" designed to throw the analyst off his guard.
They arise as a direct continuation of the aborted idealizations
of childhood, as a resumption of a tie to an early object which
was ruptured by loss or traumatic disappointment. They revive
an early developmental phase when only a figure perceived as
flawless and godlike can protect against the dangers to existence for which the infant has no other source of protection.
The emergence of such an idealization requires no commitment on the part of the analyst to fulfill the patient's archaic
expectations, only that the inevitable disappointments be explored non-defensively from the perspective of their current
and genetic, conscious and unconscious, subjectively construed
contexts.

The violent negative reactions similarly viewed from within
the perspective of the patient's subjective experience of the
analyst will be seen to indicate specific structural weaknesses
and vulnerabilities, rooted in specific developmental interferences. When their expression is freely permitted, we have
found, they owe their intensity to the fact that they contain
encoded and encapsulated memories of traumatically damaging experiences. This was the case, as was seen, with Mr. J.

We regularly find that divergences from the focus on the
patient's subjective reality and shifts to an assumption that that
reality is secondary to more deeply lying pathological defenses
or drive derivatives come about when the patient's experience
of the analyst cannot be comfortably assimilated into the structure of the analyst's subjective world. What is therefore required of the analyst is the ability to "decenter" from the structures of his own subjectivity in order to be able to understand
those of his patient. When we have been able to do this success-
fully, we have found that the patient's experience of us becomes readily intelligible in the context of specific, discrete elements within the preceding interchange. These elements may
have been unnoticed or considered unimportant by us, but can
be shown to have enormous significance to the patient. We
stress that such disjunctions of experience cannot and should
not be reduced by considering them distorting mechanisms on

the part of either participant. Instead they must be considered as inevitable consequences of the interaction between differently organized subjectivities. This altered stance on the part of the analyst makes possible the articulation and exploration of their meanings for the patient, and when this is accomplished, a consolidation can occur at a higher level of organization, together with a lessening of vulnerability, a modulation of affect, and a strengthening of the underlying structure.

AGGRESSION

We cannot conclude this presentation without touching on the differing view of aggression that accompanies a stance from within the subjective experience of the patient and a focus on the more inclusive patient-therapist system as a field of interacting subjectivities. We emphatically disagree with the claim that "excessive pregenital aggression" is the etiological bedrock of borderline and narcissistic pathology. Such excessive aggression is the inevitable, unwitting consequence of a therapeutic approach which insists that certain arrested archaic needs and the archaic states of mind associated with them are in their essence pathological defenses against dependency on or hostility toward the analyst. It is the inevitable consequence of the persistent superimposition of the analyst's subjective reality on that of the patient. When this occurs in the treatment, the patient, attempting to revive a previously aborted or derailed developmental step, comes to experience such interpretations, whatever the intent of the interpreter, as severe breaches of trust and as traumatic narcissistic wounds.

A vulnerable patient revives his most personal, nuclear, and vital needs in the relationship to the analyst. When these are misunderstood and misconstrued, and once again the patient is required to see his experiences from another's viewpoint when he so desperately longs for someone to see them from his own, it is not surprising that intense rage, destructiveness, and distrust may follow. It is the therapist's consistent inability to comprehend the developmental meaning of the patient's archaic states and of the archaic bond that the patient needs to establish with him that secondarily produces the pervasive rage that can make such patients seem so difficult. We are convinced this is a difficulty which arises not entirely from pathological endo-psychic sources within the patient. That this difficulty occurs so frequently emphasizes for us the necessity for psychoanalysts to follow the courageous lead of the young Freud, and to try for themselves a new way of comprehending the data—as a function of the more inclusive patient-therapist system. For them, as for Freud, more things on heaven and earth will then appear than men have as yet dared to dream.

REFERENCES

Abraham, K. (1919). A particular form of neurotic resistance to the psychoanalytic method. In *The Selected Papers of Karl Abraham*. London: Hogarth Press, 1927.

Brandchaft, B. (1983). The negativism of the negative therapeutic reaction and the psychology of the self. 327–359. In *The Future of Psychoanalysis*, ed. A. Goldberg. New York: International Universities Press.

_____ & Stolorow, R. (1984). The borderline concept: Pathological character or iatrogenic myth? In *Empathy II*, eds. J. Lichtenberg, M. Bornstein & D. Silver. Hillsdale, N.J.: The Analytic Press. 333–357.

Jones, E. (1953). *The Life and Work of Sigmund Freud*, Vol. I. New York: Basic Books.

Kernberg, O. (1975). *Borderline Conditions and Pathological Narcissism*. New York: Aronson.

_____ (1982). Review of *Advances in Self Psychology*, edited by A. Goldberg. *Amer. J. Psychoanal.*, 139:374–375.

Kohut, H. (1959). Introspection, empathy and psychoanalysis. In *The Search for the Self.*, ed. P. Ornstein. New York: International Universities Press, 1978.

_____ (1971). *The Analysis of the Self*. New York: International Universities Press.

_____ (1977). *The Restoration of the Self*. New York: International Universities Press.

_____ & Wolf, E. (1978). The disorders of the self and their treatment: An outline. *Int. J. Psycho-Anal.*, 59:413–425.

Mahler, M., Pine, F., & Bergmann, A. (1975). *The Psychological Birth of the Human Infant*. New York: Basic Books.

Rosenfeld, H. (1964). On the psychopathology of narcissism: A clinical approach. In *Psychotic States: A Psychoanalytical Approach*. London: Hogarth Press.

Sander, L. (1975). Infant and caretaking environment—Investigation and conceptualization of adaptive behaviour in a system of increasing complexity. In *Explorations in Child Psychiatry*, ed. E. J. Anthony. New York: Plenum.

Schwaber, E. (1979). On the "self" within the matrix of analytic theory. *Int. J. Psycho-Anal.*, 60:467–479.

Stein, M. (1981). The unobjectionable part of the transference. *J. Amer. Psychoanal. Assn.*, 29:869–893.

Stern, A. (1938). Psychoanalytic investigation of and therapy in the borderline group of neuroses. *Psychoanal. Quart.*, 7:467–489.

Stolorow, R. & Brandchaft, B. (1984). Intersubjectivity: II. Development and pathogenesis. In *Structures of Subjectivity: Explorations in Psychoanalytic Phenomenology*, eds. G. Atwood & R. Stolorow. Hillsdale, N.J.: The Analytic Press. 65–83.

_____, Brandchaft, B. & Atwood, G. (1983). Intersubjectivity in psychoanalytic treatment: With special reference to archaic states. *Bull. Menn. Clin.*, 47:117–128.

_____ & Lachmann, F. (1980). *Psychoanalysis of Developmental Arrests*. New York: International Universities Press.

Winnicott, D. (1965). *The Maturational Processes and the Facilitating Environment*. New York: International Universities Press.

7

Issues in the Treatment of the Borderline Patient

Gerald Adler, M.D.

BORDERLINE PERSONALITY DISORDER as a diagnostic category continues to be a subject of much debate. Does it allow us to conceptualize the issues of a particular group of narcissistically vulnerable patients, and apply these conceptualizations in useful ways in psychoanalytic treatment? Or is it nothing more than a "wastebasket" term, a manifestation of our muddled thinking, perhaps an iatrogenic myth based upon our failure to understand some severely vulnerable patients?

Because many clinicians interested in self psychology have been psychoanalysts concerned primarily with the treatment of neurotic and narcissistic personality disorders, the self psychology literature addressing the understanding of borderline and psychotic patients is just developing. Recent contributions by P. Tolpin (1980) and Brandchaft and Stolorow (1984), as well as those by Buie and myself (Adler and Buie, 1979; Adler, 1981; Buie and Adler, 1982), examine Kohut's views of these severe forms of self pathology, raise issues concerning the treatability of borderline patients, and sometimes question the validity of borderline as a separate diagnostic category.

In this paper I shall present data based upon my clinical and supervisory experiences to suggest that borderline personality disorder, both as a concept and as a diagnostic category, helps to clarify our theoretical understanding; it is therefore useful in the treatment of a certain group of primitive, narcissistically vulnerable patients. The diagnosis, once established, helps to alert us to specific patient vulnerabilities related to issues of serious self pathology, as well as to difficulties in the patient-therapist relationship that are characteristic of this group of patients. The borderline diagnosis can also highlight the contributions of self psychology to the conceptualization and treatment of these severely vulnerable patients. In the course of discussing these issues, I shall describe the specific defects of the borderline patient, the relationship between borderline and narcissistic personality disorders, the changes in the vulnerability of the self in borderline patients during the course of successful treatment, and the countertransference difficulties experienced by the therapist treating these patients.

DIAGNOSTIC CONSIDERATIONS

DSM-III includes for the first time the diagnostic categories borderline personality disorder and narcissistic personality disorder, and provides operational definitions of each. The DSM-III description of borderline personality disorder is consistent with recent clinical research studies (Gunderson and Singer, 1975; Gunderson and Kolb, 1978; Perry and Klerman, 1980) that stress the impulsivity of borderline patients, their intense and unstable relationships, their difficulties with anger, their affect and identity instability, and their propensity to hurt themselves physically. Also described in DSM-III are the "chronic feelings of emptiness and boredom" experienced by these patients and their "intolerance of being alone; e.g., [their] frantic efforts to avoid being alone, [as well as being] depressed when alone."

When we compare this description of the borderline personality disorder with that of the narcissistic personality disorder in DSM-III, we note certain important differences and similarities. In contrast to the DSM-III emphasis on the grandiosity, grandiose fantasies, aloofness, vulnerability to criticism, or indifference toward others of the narcissistic personality disorder, the borderline personality disorder is characterized by intense neediness, lability of affect, and perhaps most important of all, by problems with being alone. Significantly, however, patients in both categories need a response from the other person. Although the patient with narcissistic personality disorder is more capable of maintaining an aloof indifference, patients with both disorders overidealize, devalue, and manipulate. DSM-III may thus be recognizing aspects of two relatively distinct disorders with overlapping areas, perhaps as part of a pragmatic attempt to categorize clinical material about primitive patients. Consistent with my previous work (1981), I believe that a borderline-narcissistic personality disorder continuum can be postulated, with a distinct diagnostic category at each end of the continuum.

THE BORDERLINE PATIENT IN TREATMENT

A patient who fits the DSM-III description of borderline personality disorder may at first be mistaken for a patient with narcissistic personality disorder. At the beginning of treatment, he may form relatively stable selfobject transferences of the mirror and/or idealizing variety which transiently fragment when he experiences empathic failures in the treatment. Gradually, however, or sometimes in a more sudden and dramatic way, an increasing feeling of dissatisfaction, emptiness, and anger begins to emerge, often associated with weekends and/or other separations from the therapist or analyst. An aspect of this dissatisfaction is anger that builds with increasing intensity, and responds only momentarily to the empathic statements of the therapist who tries to understand the reasons for it and the context in which it arises from the patient's perspective. For some of these patients, the anger is accompanied by increasing panic which the patient relates to an intolerable feeling of aloneness. This experience of aloneness can be terrifying. The patient often has difficulty remembering the therapist or analyst between sessions, may only be able to summon malevolent, angry images of him, or may feel he has somehow destroyed or harmed the therapist. A few patients in very intense moments can even experience terror as a result of not being able to recognize the therapist even while in his presence. These experiences of aloneness, sometimes accompanied by panic, are unique to borderline patients, and are manifestations of specific defects which differentiate them from those patients with narcissistic personality disorders who are solidly at the other end of the continuum. Often in relating their histories, borderline patients describe similar experiences of aloneness as part of their disappointment and anger in their relationships with the important people in their lives.

Another characteristic of borderline patients which may help to distinguish them from patients with narcissistic personality disorder is the apparent primitive, archaic, punitive nature of their superegos. Consequently, self-destructive and suicidal concerns are much more of a preoccupation and danger for them than for those with narcissistic personality disorder. Many borderline patients repeatedly devalue themselves, viewing themselves, both consciously and unconsciously, as overwhelmingly bad and deserving punishment. Not infrequently, these self images have a painful, unremitting quality that does not allow for positive feelings or results. Some of these patients exemplify very well the superego aspects of the negative therapeutic reaction (Freud, 1923). The superegos of these patients also resemble descriptions of punitive, critical superego aspects which have not been neutralized by loving components related to ideals and values (Jacobson, 1964; Kernberg, 1975). Kohut (1971, 1977) makes little mention of such archaic superego elements in his discussions concerning the treatment of narcissistic personality disorders. It could be that primitive superego formation in some groups of narcissistically vulnerable patients not only predisposes them to borderline personality disorder, but also tends to maintain the disorder once it exists. In addition, as Basch (personal communication) has pointed out, what appear to be manifestations of a primitive superego could be the patient's defenses against overwhelming fear of fragmentation. In such formulations, the superego exists as a structure only after the resolution of the Oedipus complex, and cannot be described in its prestages.

The emergence of what I believe are indeed primitive superego components in many of these patients occurs most clearly at the time of the borderline patient's mounting rage in the transference. Concurrent with the rage, or experienced in place of it, may be the primitive borderline's intense, self-punishing conviction that he is bad and does not deserve to live. When coupled with his vulnerability to aloneness experiences at such times, a potentially lethal situation may develop in which panic, annihilatory rage, and suicidal preoccupations rapidly emerge.

Both borderline and narcissistic personality disorder patients share a vulnerable self-cohesiveness and a need for selfobjects in order to feel complete. They both form mirror and idealizing selfobject transferences, although the borderline's self-cohesiveness and capacity to maintain these selfobject transferences is much more tenuous and more likely to disintegrate. The result can be severe fragmentation experiences when the inevitable disappointments and anger at the therapist and therapy emerge, often secondary to the patient's experience of empathic failures.

When the borderline patient has allowed himself to become involved in his treatment and has experienced the soothing and comfort of the selfobject as part of the selfobject transferences, he is more vulnerable to the experiences of aloneness and panic which occur when his anger appears. At the same time, however, his involvement causes him to fear the loss of his separateness. In contrast, patients with narcissistic personality disorder can more comfortably maintain varying degrees of merger as part of their selfobject transferences without significant concerns about loss of separateness. Borderline patients intensely fear this loss, which can be conceptualized as a loss of distinct self and object representations. Whereas psychotics actually experience this fusion of self and object representations (Jacobson, 1964; Kernberg, 1975), borderlines largely *fear* its occurrence, and when they do experience it, experience it only transiently. But it remains a fear, akin to Burnham, Gladstone, and Gibson's (1969) need-fear dilemma of schizophrenics. This fear, then, is another factor that prevents borderline patients from being able to maintain safe, stable selfobject transferences, and heightens the disruption which follows experiences of disappointment and anger in treatment. They long for the warmth, holding, and soothing that selfobject transferences provide, but fear the threat of loss of separateness that accompanies these experiences.

The relationship between borderline and narcissistic personality disorders becomes clearer when long-term treatment of borderline patients is studied (Adler, 1981). That is, borderline patients, once they resolve the issue of aloneness, become more and more like patients with narcissistic personality disorder. They form increasingly stable selfobject transferences which are more resilient to disruption in the face of disappointments in the therapist and the therapy. Although they may regress to states of aloneness in the middle phases of treatment when their anger becomes too intense, these experiences are shorter-lived; they reestablish stable selfobject transferences more readily as they progress along the continuum from borderline to narcissistic personality. When borderline patients finally form stable selfobject transferences, they are more likely to idealize the holding aspects of their therapist than are patients with narcissistic personality disorder who have never been borderline (Buie and Adler, 1982).

ALONENESS AND BORDERLINE PATHOLOGY

In order to clarify further the distinctions between borderline and narcissistic personality disorders, the nature of the aloneness experiences of borderline patients requires amplification. Observation of these aloneness states and the panic that accompanies them reveals the difficulty these patients have in maintaining positive memories of important people, both past and present. Specifically, the holding and soothing qualities of important others are emphasized in the fantasies of these patients when selfobject transferences exist, but disappear during experiences of aloneness. Buie and I (Adler and Buie, 1979; Buie and Adler, 1982) have viewed these sustaining affective memories as evidence of introjects—felt presences of important others that are available intrapsychically to perform holding and soothing functions when the individual is under stress. Borderline patients have an inability to utilize such intrapsychic resources to tolerate separation anxiety. In the face of disappointment, separation, or loss, their increasing anger heralds a regression in which they transiently lose the capacity to maintain these introjects. Separation anxiety gives way to annihilation anxiety. With the loss of holding introjects, they feel their very psychic and physical survival to be at stake. In contrast, patients with narcissistic personality disorder have progressed developmentally beyond these issues and are concerned with the complex questions of self-worth and completeness.

Although peripheral to the task of this paper, it is of interest to note briefly that the borderline patient's experience of aloneness has much in common with certain observations in the child development literature. Piaget (1937) describes the development of object constancy in children and their capacity at 18 months of age to know that an object has permanence, that is, independent existence. Fraiberg (1969) defines this milestone as evocative memory capacity, in contrast to recognition memory capacity, which is present at five to eight months of age. With recognition memory capacity the infant recognizes the object but cannot evoke its memory when it is not present. Winnicott's (1965) description of transitional objects relates to Piaget's and Fraiberg's contributions. Transitional objects help the child evoke the memory of an idealized holding mother before the child is able to remember her reliably when she is not there. As M. Tolpin (1971) has written, the transitional object is not mourned when it is given up because the memories and images it evokes have become internalized through transmuting internalization at the time when the child is capable of object constancy. The consistency of these latter observations with those of Piaget and Fraiberg is remarkable, for transitional objects are first important to infants when they are approximately six months of age, the time when recognition memory capacity develops. They are given up as an object of intense need at about 18 to 24 months of age, coincident with the formation of solid evocative memory.

The aloneness issues characteristic of borderline patients, which result from their inability to maintain stable holding introjects, can be viewed as a developmentally prior aspect of the primary defect of the self that Kohut (1977) has described with respect to narcissistic personality disorders. The concept of "stunted development of the grandiose-exhibitionistic aspect of the self" (p. 7), which Kohut placed at the core of narcissistic personality disorders, must be expanded when borderline patients are included in our study of narcissistically vulnerable patients. For the primary defect of the self in borderline patients arises from an earlier developmental stage, and is characterized by their inability to maintain stable holding introjects. Until the issues of aloneness, survival, and annihilation of the self are resolved, these patients remain borderline and are not developmentally prepared to work on issues of incompleteness and self-worth. Their tenuous evocative memory capacity threatens a terrifying experience involving the annihilation of the self when they become angry in response to disappointment in important dyadic relationships, thereby precluding relatively stable selfobject transferences at those times.

Borderline patients in psychotherapy or analysis will, by definition, regress to some variant of the aloneness problems which are at the core of their disorder, either transiently or in a more profound way. In order for them to make use of the selfobject in the stable manner of the patient with a narcissistic personality disorder, they must first come to terms with their own and the selfobject's psychic and physical survival. They must ultimately learn that their anger does not destroy, nor lead to abandonment by the selfobject. Such patients cannot reliably utilize a selfobject as a merged or fused part of themselves until they are certain that the selfobject is dependable both as a selfobject and as a separate entity, and is nondestructible and nonmalignant. To feel that certainty, they must establish within themselves an increasing capacity to maintain a holding introject of the selfobject therapist.

The necessary experience in treatment is one in which the patient's anger, often of momentarily overwhelming intensity, is acknowledged, respected, and understood. Whenever possible this anger can be related to the patient's life story of disappointing, enraging selfobjects as they are reexperienced in the transference. The result is the gradual building up of holding introjects increasingly resilient to regressive loss in the face of the patient's anger. Ultimately, evocative memory capacity for the therapist as a holding, sustaining, soothing figure is established. For some patients, this process can occur in months, for others, only in several years. In time, however, the patient may show increasing evidence of a capacity to tolerate separations and empathic failures without disintegrative, annihilatory rage. As a result, for many patients, self-destructive behaviors and suicidal fantasies gradually diminish. The building of these new capacities occurs in small increments and can be conceptualized as part of the process of transmuting internalization.

COUNTERTRANSFERENCE

The borderline patient poses special countertransference problems for the therapist, particularly the therapist who values his empathic and introspective capacities. In the transference the patient often relives the hopelessness and helplessness of his childhood (Adler, 1972), including preverbal experiences with repeatedly disappointing and enraging selfobjects. These experiences sometimes include traumatic separations from the selfobject at particularly vulnerable times. In his therapy, the patient often seeks to recreate these earlier feelings in terms of the therapist's lack of perfection as a holding selfobject. He may devalue the therapist, be unable to utilize his clarifying statements, or withdraw into an angry, hopeless silence. Regardless of the therapist's clinical experience, he cannot help but feel something akin to the patient's anger, despair, and hopelessness.

There are two major frameworks to use in order to understand these countertransference experiences: self psychology and object relations. Although they are not mutually exclusive, they utilize very different schema. The self psychology perspective emphasizes the therapist's experience of failure as a selfobject or rejection as an adequate selfobject, leading to characteristic countertransference feelings. The object relations viewpoint describes countertransference responses as the mobilization of primitive object relations in the therapist, secondary to their emergence in the patient.

Countertransference and Self Psychology

Among the many contributions of self psychology is its recognition that selfobject needs exist in all people to varying degrees throughout their lives. Relatively mature therapists and analysts require some validation from their patients that they are competent, effective clinicians. They receive this validation from experiences of understanding their patients and being useful to them, from the realization that the functions they perform for their patients ultimately lead to their patients' growth. As long as the patient uses his therapist and responds to him sufficiently to confirm his competence, the therapist will maintain a solid, comfortable feeling about himself as someone of worth and value. But when the therapist has one or more borderline patients who feel helpless and hopeless, and devalue, reject, or deny his attempts to help, consistent with the nature of their emerging transference, the therapist may then find himself feeling very much as the patient does.

The therapist's hopelessness, helplessness, despair, and anger can be viewed as a response to his experience of feeling that he has failed as a selfobject. That is, he does not appear to be performing the selfobject functions that the patient says he wants from him. Usually unrecognized by both patient and therapist are the silent (and therefore often preconscious or unconscious) idealizing selfobject transferences (Adler, 1980) which provide the holding and stability to permit unresolved issues of the past to emerge. Disappointment, helplessness, hopelessness, despair, and anger from the past are thus reactivated and relived in the transference. They elicit countertransference responses in the therapist to the extent that they involve him as the failing selfobject recreated from the patient's past failing selfobjects. Since neither the patient nor therapist is in touch with the positive idealizing selfobject bond that allows these feelings to emerge, both experience pain in the transference-countertransference. The patient feels helpless and hopeless in the transference; the therapist, because he cannot soothe, satisfy, adequately understand, or help the patient from both his and the patient's perspective, experiences the situation as his own failure. When chronically repeated, this experience ultimately relates to the therapist's failure to receive the validation of his professional competence that he requires. A paradox of this transference-countertransference situation is that, in the *successful* transference reliving, the therapist experiences his failure as a selfobject only after he has first succeeded as a (silently idealized) selfobject; and the patient, in experiencing the therapist as the failing selfobject, fails the therapist by not performing the selfobject validating function that the therapist intermittently needs. (This should not be taken to mean that it is the patient's *task* to perform this validating function, only that when at such times the patient does not validate the therapist's sense of competence sufficiently, the described countertransference experiences are usually inevitable.)

Countertransference and Object Relations Theory

Kernberg (1975) describes countertransference in terms of internalized primitive object relations which first emerge in the patient as the borderline transferences develop; they then elicit parallel primitive object relations in the therapist. For example, in projective identification, the patient (symbolically) projects a part of himself onto his therapist who then has the experience of that projected part being mobilized within himself. The patient also attempts to control the therapist as a way of managing the projected part of himself. The therapist experiences the patient's projections in an "empathic" way because primitive internalized object relations similar to the patient's are available in him to be mobilized.

Although both frameworks describe the same countertransference feelings in work with borderline patients, their emphases are different. Self psychology stresses the patient's transference experience with the failing or rejecting selfobject. Its countertransference formulation emphasizes the therapist's sense of lack of validation when he feels that he cannot soothe or hold. The object relations framework focuses on the primitive object relations mobilized not only in the patient but in the therapist as well. While Kohut (1971) does describe the primitive, grandiose, and exhibitionistic aspects of the *therapist* that can be activated as part of his countertransference, and while these can be related to the reactivation of memories of failing selfobjects in the therapist's childhood, the clinical writings of self psychology also point to the therapist's experience of feeling that he has failed as a soothing and understanding selfobject.

When the therapist can view his countertransference experience as his empathic response to the feelings of his patient, he has a clue to the nature of the patient's current and past experiences. But it is not easy to maintain a balance between immersion in the patient's feelings and the requisite distance from them necessary to function most effectively as therapist and selfobject. The task is particularly difficult to the extent that the therapist's intense countertransference experiences often include a transient or more prolonged conviction that he indeed does not understand, or that he lacks an adequate empathic capacity with, this specific patient. He may, as described, question what he previously felt were solidly established aspects of his own self and his therapeutic skills.

The therapist's countertransference vulnerability may lead to his withdrawal from the patient, or to a transient experience of his own emptiness and fragmentation, or may express itself in rageful wishes to rid himself of the patient. The rage may include sadistic confrontations in which the therapist may formulate a need for realistic limit setting or redefinition of the therapeutic tasks (Adler, 1970; Adler and Buie, 1972).

At the same time, the therapist must evaluate the validity of the patient's view of him as a failing selfobject. Are the patient's feelings of hopelessness, rage, and rejection of the therapist the reliving in the transference of early selfobject failures? And are they being experienced in response to the expectable failures of a good to excellent selfobject therapist? Or has the therapist indeed failed the patient because of his significant empathic limitations or countertransference difficulties with the specific patient? The fact that the therapist can raise these questions puts him in a good position to examine the various possibilities as he continues his work with his patient. Sometimes consultations with a trusted and respected colleague are necessary to sort out these complex issues and gain some perspective.

Some borderline patients can get into serious difficulties with poor therapists, and some patients who are diagnostically between borderline and narcissistic personality disorder on the continuum can appear more borderline and reveal more of their aloneness difficulties with inadequate therapists. (I do not mean that these patients do not still have borderline vulnerabilities by definition.) The aloneness issues can be less painful and potentially less lethal when the patient is in treatment with a therapist who functions most optimally as a selfobject. But the primary issue for the early stages of treatment with these borderline patients is their vulnerability to the loss of holding introjects when their disappointment and rage emerge in treatment. The optimally capable empathic therapist still has to help his patient with this issue. To the degree that the therapist's failure as a selfobject is a transference manifestation, it is more likely to be resolved ultimately through the process of transmuting internalization.

Although the anger and panic that accompany the loss of evocative memory may repeatedly be manifest during the treatment of the borderline patient, it is not sought or provoked by the therapist. It is inevitable even with the best therapist working with the more vulnerable borderline patients. The experience that leads to transmuting internalization is not primarily based on the fact that the patient experiences his rage and panic in relation to the therapist. Rather, the therapist, by remaining with the patient over time, always attempting to understand and not retaliate or reassure superficially, provides the holding, containing, soothing, and comforting selfobject function that was missing at crucial times in the patient's childhood. At the same time, the patient requires help in understanding the fear of fusion that accompanies his longing for the holding selfobject as it appears in the transference.

Borderline patients teach us something more about the holding and soothing qualities of selfobject transferences. They illustrate the ways in which the selfobject transferences can become established in patients with a primary defect of the self involving difficulties in maintaining holding introjects. Some of these patients need to hear their therapist's voice during brief phone calls to remember he exists when the intense transference experiences, already described, occur. He may also need transitional object evidences of the therapist, such as a postcard when the therapist is on vacation. Other patients may require hospitalization when there is a more prolonged loss of evocative memory capacity, often accompanied by increasing suicidal thoughts. Decisions in these matters, which are best made in discussions with the patient, provide further evidence to the patient that he is understood and responded to by a holding selfobject therapist. When the patient is out of control and suicidal, the therapist's decision to hospitalize the patient against the patient's stated desires may still be empathically correct, and may thus become part of the therapist's selfobject functions. At such times, limit setting, an expression often used pejoratively, helps reestablish the holding selfobject transference. Thus, such patients also teach us about the selfobject functions performed by groups, hospitals, and hospital milieus until the needed capacities ultimately become a permanent part of the patient through the process of transmuting internalization.

I shall describe several vignettes from the long-term treatment of a borderline patient (Adler, 1981) to illustrate some of the themes discussed.

Ms. A. sought treatment in her thirties because of difficulties in completing her graduate degree. Initially, she was most concerned with her longstanding problems in studying. These problems dated back to her early years in school when she fought with her mother because she felt her mother was not providing adequate homework help. She had always turned for help to teachers whom she idealized, and had always needed their appreciation and praise to do well. Although her grades were excellent, she felt driven, inadequate, and incomplete except for the brief respites when she felt she had pleased a mentor.

In addition to her feeling that her mother was chronically depressed and only intermittently available, and that her father was preoccupied with his successful business career, Ms. A. cited a serious automobile accident her parents had had when she was two years old. During the three-month period that followed the accident, Ms. A. and her three older siblings had stayed with their emotionally cold grandmother. One of her earliest memories consisted of an image of herself in a playpen in a gray, cold room; she had no images of other people, recalling only shadowy, distant voices.

Ms. A. felt that the rest of her childhood had been unremarkable, and did not feel that she had experienced significant unhappiness until she went to school. There, in addition to idealizing some of her teachers, she envied her friends for having warmer, more available parents, especially when their mothers were kind to her. Her first conscious feelings of aloneness occurred in high school, when she felt bleak and black as she thought of the future and the emptiness of her life. She became aware of the depth of her neediness in college when her first relationship with a man elicited intense yearnings and feelings of emptiness when she was not with him. After that relationship ended, she retreated to her academic career and her fantasies of pleasing admired professors, whom she felt would increasingly expect more and more from her.

The early months of her twice-weekly psychotherapy were uneventful. The patient established what seemed to be mirror and idealizing selfobject transferences as she told her complicated story. She had little difficulty with the therapist's four-week vacation when it occurred after two months of therapy. Gradually, however, over the next six months, Ms. A. became increasingly unhappy. In addition to reporting that she could not please her professors, she felt more empty and panicky between sessions, and felt particularly alone before weekends; she felt abandoned, which she likened to being dropped. Her sessions were increased to three and then four times a week, but this only temporarily alleviated such feelings.

Gradually Ms. A. began to describe her conviction that she was a terrible person who deserved to die. These feelings intensified to a point that she would pound her head and thighs and scratch at her face during sessions. Painfully, she acknowledged that she was furious with her therapist, a totally unacceptable feeling for her. She did not deserve to live because of her badness and feelings of hatred that the therapist had abandoned her when he could not see her all the time. The more frequent sessions and brief daily phone calls helped contain these feelings—until the therapist went away for a week. At this time, she required a three-week hospitalization because she could not tolerate her anger, emptiness, and panic; in addition, she could not be certain she would not act on her wishes to die. After discharge she was able to resume her outpatient psychotherapy.

These angry, self-punishing sessions continued for almost three years, although gradually diminishing in intensity after a year. Ms. A. formulated the experience as one in which "the abandoned child had her due." As her anger abated, the mirror and idealizing transferences became more stable and dependable, although there were numerous, increasingly brief regressions to the aloneness feelings. After the therapist's summer vacation at the end of her third year of therapy, she reported for the first time that she had missed him, a very different experience from the previous panic she had felt. Concomitant with this, she described warm, positive memories of her mother instead of entirely critical ones laced with guilt and self-hatred.

The countertransference feelings of her therapist were varied and complex. His initial sense of comfort with the patient ended when her suicidal preoccupations and rage emerged. Not only was he concerned about the patient's safety between sessions, but he felt intermittently frightened and helpless in the face of her self-punishing activities during the therapy hour. The persistence of her self-punishment and rages over the three-year period often left him with the conviction that he did not understand his patient, and was stuck in a hopelessly stalemated treatment. At times he felt murderously angry at her, especially during her chronic angry outbursts. Only reluctantly could he acknowledge to himself how guilty he felt for his hatred, hatred which included the occasional thought that he would be relieved if his patient killed herself. His offer of extra phone calls concerned him. Would the patient call more and more frequently in a crescendo of neediness? His clarification in response to her similar concerns helped both of them; he explained to her that if occasional calls were insufficient, something additional, such as hospitalization, was available. In fact, one of the patient's brief hospitalizations was the result of such a sequence of neediness.

Once stable mirror and idealizing selfobject transferences were established, countertransference difficulties were similar to those described by Kohut (1971). The therapist's intermittent boredom was balanced by his genuine liking for the patient. His feelings of being validated in his work with the patient occasionally disappeared as short-lived regressions to the aloneness issues reoccurred.

Patients such as Ms. A. illustrate the complex issues involved in the treatment of borderline patients and in their progression to the narcissistic personality disorder level of development. A formulation of borderline personality disorder which emphasizes the concepts of aloneness and vulnerability to the loss of holding introjects provides the therapist with the framework to understand and work with the issues of severe fragmentation at the core of the disorder. Viewing these patients along a continuum from borderline to narcissistic personality disorder allows us to use the concepts of self psychology in a way that illuminates the patient's growth. The increasing capacity to maintain relatively stable selfobject transferences in the face of disappointment and rage heralds the patient's solid growth toward the narcissistic personality disorder end of the continuum. This framework also helps us formulate the countertransference problems at either end of the continuum.

REFERENCES

Adler, G. (1970). Valuing and devaluing in the psychotherapeutic process. *Arch. Gen. Psychiat.*, 22:454–461.

_____ (1972). Helplessness in the helpers. *Brit. J. Med. Psychol.*, 45:315–326.

_____ (1980). Transference, real relationship, and alliance. *Int. J. Psycho-Anal.*, 61:547–558.

_____ (1981). The borderline-narcissistic personality disorder continuum. *Amer. J. Psychiat.*, 138:46–50.

_____ & Buie, D. H. (1972). The misuses of confrontation with borderline patients. *Int. J. Psychoanal. Psychother.*, 1:109–120.

_____ & _____ (1979). Aloneness and borderline psychopathology: The possible relevance of child development issues. *Int. J. Psycho-Anal.*, 60:83–96.

Brandchaft, B., & Stolorow, R. D. (1984). The borderline concept: Pathological character or iatrogenic myth? In *Empathy II*, eds. J. Lichtenberg, M. Bornstein & D. Silver. Hillsdale, N.J.: The Analytic Press.

Buie, D. H., & Adler, G. (1982). Definitive treatment of the borderline patient. *Int. J. Psychoanal. Psychother.*, 9:51–87.

Burnham, D. G., Gladstone, A. I., & Gibson, R. W. (1969). *Schizophrenia and the Need-Fear Dilemma*. New York: International Universities Press.

Fraiberg, S. (1969). Libidinal object constancy and mental representation. *The Psychoanalytic Study of the Child*, 24:9–47.

Freud, S. (1923). The ego and the id. *S.E.*, 19.

Gunderson, J. G., & Kolb, J. E. (1978). Discriminating features of borderline patients. *Amer. J. Psychiat.* 135:792–796.

_____ & Singer, M. T. (1975). Describing borderline patients: An overview. *Amer. J. Psychiat.* 132:1–10.

Jacobson, E. (1964). *The Self and the Object World*. New York: International Universities Press.

Kernberg, O. (1975). *Borderline Conditions and Pathological Narcissism*. New York: Aronson.

Kohut, H. (1971). *The Analysis of the Self*. New York: International Universities Press.

_____ (1977). *The Restoration of the Self*. New York: International Universities Press.

Perry, J. C., & Klerman, G. (1980). Clinical features of the borderline personality. *Amer. J. Psychiat.* 137:165–173.

Piaget, J. (1937). *The Construction of Reality in the Child*. New York: Basic Books, 1954.

Tolpin, M. (1971). On the beginnings of a cohesive self: An application of the concept of transmuting internalization to the study of transitional objects and anxiety. *The Psychoanalytic Study of the Child*, 26:316–352.

Tolpin, P. (1980). The borderline personality: Its make-up and analyzability. In *Advances in Self Psychology*, ed. A. Goldberg. New York: International Universities Press.

Winnicott, D. W. (1965). *The Maturational Processes and the Facilitating Environment*. New York: International Universities Press.

Difficult Patients

Discussion of "A Current Perspective on Difficult Patients," by Bernard Brandchaft and Robert D. Stolorow, and "Issues in the Treatment of the Borderline Patient," by Gerald Adler

Paul H. Tolpin, M. D.

THESE PAPERS DEAL WITH the borderline or difficult patient from different perspectives and with somewhat different purposes in mind. Dr. Adler's is more descriptive, more focused on phenomenology, and, using self psychological concepts, more concerned with the clarification of theoretical and clinical issues in the *treatment* of the borderline patient. Drs. Brandchaft and Stolorow *use* the issue of the difficult patient as a taking-off point to demonstrate how a systematic use of precepts derived from the psychology of the self, including the stance of the therapist in relation to the patient, significantly alters one's understanding of the clinical material. I shall begin with Adler's paper, though some of my comments overlap and extend to the other presentation as well.

I shall attempt to answer Adler's opening question regarding the value and meaning of the borderline concept by providing my own definition of the disorder. Broadly stated, borderline disorder refers to a conglomerate group of patients who are severely ill and, often, very difficult to treat. While a particular group of them are treatable by analysis, special sensitivity and ability is required on the part of the analyst. Borderline patients are highly vulnerable, rigidly or poorly defended individuals whose compensatory and identificatory systems are relatively inadequate to stabilize their insufficiently cohesive core selves.

Adler's description of such patients as "narcissistically vulnerable" is thus similar to mine, but his subsequent discussion indicates that we differ in some respects. For I believe that the consistent use of the framework of self psychology, particularly the concept of a self-selfobject system, allows greater access to the understanding of these patients' extreme vulnerabilities and to their primary disturbance than do any of the variations of a drive-defense model of the mind. And I would include in that model formulations in terms of oedipal and preoedipal pathology and the pathology of internalized object relations. I have no problem with drive-defense terminology as such, but I believe that the implications of the theoretical position it implies tend to lead one's thinking along a narrower path than is suited to the task. What is specifically lacking in drive-defense concepts is a consideration of the ramifications of the meaning of a self-selfobject unit.

Regarding the issue of the continuum vs. the separate entity status of borderline and narcissistic personality disorders, it seems to me that this is, up to a point at least, an issue only of degree. Within limits one can have it either way, depending on what clinical problems one wants to highlight. As I see it, the problem is the often difficult one of determining how much of a solid core self underlies the manifest symptom disturbance. If primary selfobject needs are still present and can be mobilized in the transference, treatment to some extent is possible. How far one can go with this depends on many interlocking factors including, especially, the rigidity of defenses against reexposure to early traumatic states. The more empty or disorganized or collapsed the core self and the more rigid the defenses, the closer the borderline disorder is to the psychoses. Sometimes this is a stable instability that can't really be altered. Borderline disorder should then be considered an entity separate from narcissistic personality disorder. Sometimes there is a more living core and a less rigid defense system, so that in treatment the patient can begin to make selfobject connections again. There are gradations of these in terms of accessibility to in-depth experiences. In other words, there are various types of borderline disturbances. And clearly the ability of the therapist to make contact with still-searching selfobject needs and with the core of the personality is crucial. Brandchaft and Stolorow hold a similar point of view.

Two other ideas discussed by Adler are the fear of loss of separateness and the experience of aloneness. Despite a clear sense of recognition of, and partial agreement with what he says, my emphasis would be different. That is, it seems to me that Adler highlights a secondary phenomenon rather than the core problem. I agree with him when he indicates that the need for separateness is a defensive necessity arising out of fear of the overwhelming neediness for archaic merger and idealizing experiences, a neediness which reflects past experiences of injurious frustrations that have left the cohesiveness of the self at serious risk. But I would emphasize *that* aspect of the danger rather than the issue of the distinctiveness of self and object boundaries, which has always seemed like an artificial construct to me, one that I could not sense in my clinical experience. I would prefer to underscore the massiveness of the danger experience which the loss of connection with the selfobject brings once it has become reinvested with primary childhood intensities. The idea of loss of boundaries needs refinement if one accepts the concept of a selfobject, which implies after all that one can use the perceived functions of another person or object as if they were one's own without confusing one's physical self with the other's physical self. And while I agree that fear of the danger of reawakening primary selfobject experiences is enormous in some borderline patients, such as the schizoid and paranoid types, in my experience it is also present more subtly but just as pervasively in other kinds of disturbances of the self. Finally, there is a group of borderline or near borderline patients for whom distancing defenses are relatively inoperative. In fact the opposite is the case. This group of selfobject-hungry patients *actively seek* various types of intimacy with others, but are still unable to feel satisfied because their archaic merger and idealizing needs are not or cannot be met, or are readily frustrated. The urge in these types is to attempt to remedy a deficit in the self by intense connections rather than by distancing. Still, the essential deficit and lack of cohesiveness of the nuclear self may be quite similar in both types, so that we may be looking at two sides of the same coin.

I am in overall agreement with Adler regarding the importance of the experience of aloneness in some borderline patients, but for me the word aloneness is too weak and not sufficiently experientially evocative to describe the kind of fragmen-
tation-annihilation-depletion-panic experiences which the borderline patient is subject to and which underly his aloneness. I
think it is useful to keep such disorganizing affective states in
mind in attempting to connect empathically with these patients,
in attempting to understand what motivates them to feel the
utter depths beyond aloneness, or to search desperately for
their particular addictive relief, or to hide behind armor-plate
defenses against emotional involvement.

Adler discusses the superego of the borderline patient, specifically, "the apparent primitive, archaic, punitive nature" of
the superego, which, he says, "may help to distinguish them
from patients with narcissistic personality disorder." He suggests that, as a result of such an archaic superego, self-destructive and suicidal concerns are more prominent and are a greater danger than in narcissistic personality disorders. On the one
hand, I find his description of the phenomenology of the self-
punitive, self-destructive borderline patient quite consistent
with *some*—certainly not all—cases I have had experience with,
but I am uneasy with his further, more theoretical discussion of
the problem. I believe this uneasiness stems from our being
guided in this instance by two different orientations about what
goes on in the unconscious of patients with self disorders—
whether they are borderline disturbances or not. The concept
of a massively punitive pre- or post-oedipal superego as such
that reacts to or replaces rage reactions does not play a significant role in my clinical understanding of how the minds of
these patients work. What I look for in patients who devalue
themselves or, more often, have little, or a very shaky, sense of
their positive value, who sometimes see themselves as useless,
worthless, no good, bad, and who are self-destructive, are specific experiences with selfobjects in their pasts that have led to
such feelings of inadequacy, shaky self-esteem, self-loathing.
And, further, how these negative experiences at a sensorimotor
level and with selfobjects have shaped or, better, have distorted
that individual's nuclear self, and how that self functions to

maintain its cohesiveness when its present-day selfobjects repeat the injuries of the past and leave the patient without the life-support systems he requires to survive. In other words, it is not the terminology I object to; it is rather the limitations that the terminology seems to me to set on broader empathic experiences by the analyst of the patient. Nevertheless, I agree that self psychology has not yet addressed issues related to the concept of the superego and that more work remains to be done in this area. Perhaps what self psychology emphasizes in terms of fragmentation of the nuclear self and of massive depletions of self-esteem is approached by structural psychology in terms of the superego. As I have said, there is more work to be done here.

On the related matter of aggression, certainly for some borderline patients the issue of aggression in its various forms and transformations is of crucial importance. This is true of the paranoid personality who feels that the world is a vengeful, hateful, dangerous place and who retreats from it or, in a burst of rage, acts out against his persecutors. Alternately, there is the aggression of the vulnerable, injured self that takes the form of chronic narcissistic rage against people or institutions. And there is the aggression that is turned against the self in self-destructive acts. The disposition of the rage does not depend on the formation of the pre- or post-oedipal superego but on other factors which I suggest are related not only to endowment but to the specifics of the self-selfobject unit in development. I believe that the shift to a self-psychological point of view leads us to focus attention on the question of what the deficiencies are in the organization of the nuclear self which lead to those intense vulnerabilities and associated acute and chronic rage reactions. This shift requires us to examine the vicissitudes of the development of the self in fine detail, and it keeps us from turning to proliferated, noisily prominent, and fixated end products of fragmentation experiences which are mistaken for manifestations of the primary disease and taken as an explanation for the borderline-aggression issue.

In the last section of his paper, Adler discusses countertransference issues and it is here, particularly, that his sensitive clinical and self-reflective judgment shines through in a beautiful description of the interacting variables of the therapist's reaction to the patient's reactions to treatment, and the therapist's reactions to those reactions, ranging from doubts about his own competency to an examination of inevitable empathic failures to an examination of the patient's particular sensitivities. Adler and I come together here with practically no disagreement. I can only commend him for his valuable description of the everyday labors of therapist and patient. In the final analysis, that is where our theories are tested, our difficulties revealed, and our effectiveness measured.

Brandchaft and Stolorow argue that how the analyst understands and responds to his patient will have a profound effect on the patient and *his* response to the analyst and his feelings about himself. The therapist's particular theoretical set will lead to a particular view of the patient and will govern his attitude and responses to the patient. A set that fosters the analyst's role as microscopist and/or is too limited or tangential will lead to distortions rather than to clarifications of the patient's primary disorder. Subtle to grotesque iatrogenic pathologies will be created and superimposed on the patient's original disturbance and will then be identified as the primary pathology. The patient's actual underlying primary pathology will not be revealed because it does not exist in the analyst's mind and because the therapeutic atmosphere is uncongenial to its development. That therapeutic atmosphere is shaped by a group of theories which Brandchaft and Stolorow discuss.

They say we have gone wrong in terms of oedipal and preoedipal formulations and particularly in terms of object relations theories of the synthesis of "good" and "bad" parts of the self and object and of the primacy of the role of aggression. The authors forcefully demonstrate how these particular concepts, stretched in specific directions, are artificial creations— once one accepts the centrality of the self-selfobject concept in healthy and pathological development.

I would like to present here a brief clinical vignette to illustrate how such a self-selfobject point of view coupled with empathic resonance to the patient's transference can effectively open up a world of experience for the patient and the analyst which could not be adequately explored within the framework of classical analytic theory and technique or some of its variants.

The patient was a successful, married businessman in his early forties who came to treatment because of a low-grade chronic depression, fatigue, and feelings of inadequacy. He felt that his life had become drab and pointless. He felt that any venture he undertook was worthless despite the fact that he had had reasonable successes in most areas of his life. After about a year of treatment he began to feel better at times, though he could not explain why. He said he liked the analyst because the analyst seemed to like him and it felt good to be listened to by an older man who seemed to understand him. After a three-day weekend interruption, the patient returned to treatment on Monday saying that he felt terrible. His old familiar depressive feelings had returned. He had not been able to get interested in anything over the weekend. His wife, he said, was demanding, his children noisy brats. He only felt "okay" when he distracted himself by watching television. He went on complaining in an increasingly agitated and almost tearful way about his fate, saying finally that he just felt hopeless. He was waving his hand in the air at that moment, pointing his index finger for emphasis. The analyst said: "You know I have the feeling I'd like to take your finger in my hand and just hold it." The patient was shocked, by surprise and pleasure, and his mood immediately began to change. He felt washed over by a mixture of rapidly intensifying emotions of pleasure and deep sadness. He began to cry.

What does this all mean? Within the framework of self psychology the analyst conveyed to the patient what they had both known and worked on before—but never with such vividness or focused immediacy. The patient and analyst both understood, again as they had before, that the patient's recurrent childhood sense of having been deserted by a self-absorbed mother had been remobilized by the analyst's absence over the weekend. Their vital connection had been lost. The patient was back into his well-known, often experienced childhood state of miserable loneliness and psychological emptiness. In a graphic word picture the analyst had said in effect: "I understand how you feel. I know what you wanted in the past and what you want to experience with me now—a reaching out to you to restore the lost emotional tie, the connection that makes you feel alive and worthwhile."

There is no need to continue with this. I should only point out my assumption here that a primary selfobject need for connection with the vitalizing selfobject, along with secondary rage at its absence, had been mobilized over the weekend. The possibly symbolic sexual meaning of the analyst's remark to the patient and the patient's soothed reaction was not an issue in this instance—though if it had come up it would have been understood as the sexualized expression of the need for the connection to the missing selfobject. The issue of rage at the loss would have been dealt with similarly. I could go on to discuss other possibilities. But I mean only to illustrate the essence of what Brandchaft and Stolorow have presented in their paper, that is, how an empathic analytic stance within a self-selfobject theoretical system may operate, and how one may understand and respond empathically to the patient's primary disease, recognizing the effects of intersubjectivity, as they have called the subtle interplay of patient and therapist. Not to have these possibilities open to one because of a theoretical set that places relatively isolated drives and defenses against those drives in the center of psychoanalytic theory is to foreclose the possibility of understanding a whole area of human experience and relationships that *must* be taken into account and given its proper place at the center of our analytic understanding if we are to reach the difficult patient where he lives.

I should like to close with a new reading of the familiar cautionary tale of the blind men and the elephant. Each man, the reader will recall, described the elephant in terms of the part of its body he felt. Each man developed his theory of elephantness from limited empirical data. The fault of their reasoning was clear: They should have pooled their data. But the assumption of the story is that the beast was an elephant. Actually it was not—it was a different beast altogether. The blind men were attaching elephant significance to another animal. That animal is called the self. In the course of their investigations the blind men ought to keep that in mind.

9 Disruptions in the Psychoanalytic Treatment of Disorders of the Self

Ernest S. Wolf, M.D.

ONE OF THE MOST noticeable effects of the influence of Kohut's conceptualizations on the clinical practice of psychoanalysis is the changed ambience in the psychoanalytic consulting room. No longer are analyst and analysand locked in adversary clench, and a loose and lively dialogue has replaced laconic checkmate. I suspect I am not alone in making this observation. This does not mean that peace and harmony reign over our couches. Perhaps nothing illustrates better that "negative transference" and hostility have not been suppressed than an examination of the disruptions of the selfobject transference relationship that are the subject of this paper. These disruptions occur in all successful psychoanalytic treatments, self-psychologically oriented or not. But in order to avoid misunderstandings and to highlight how familiar psychoanalytic data can be viewed through the lens of a theory which has been modified by the findings of self psychology I must first outline those basic principles that frame the theories of the psychology of the self.

I shall state these principles as briefly as possible here:

(1) Psychoanalysis is the objective study of man's subjectivity.

(2) Introspection is the method of access to one's own subjective experience; empathy—vicarious introspection—gives access to the subjective experience of others.

(3) The center of attention in self psychology is the self in an environmental matrix that functions to shape and maintain the structure of the self. Selfobjects are objects who function to sustain the self.

(4) The healthy development of the self depends on the maturation of a given set of potentials that are activated and sustained by an appropriately functioning selfobject environment.

(5) Faulty self-selfobject relations, particularly during a phase of vulnerability of developing nascent structures, lead to developmental arrests, to chronically weak or damaged self structures, and, consequently, to defensively distorted self-selfobject relations in the present. During the course of psychoanalysis these distorted self-selfobject relations are manifested as selfobject transferences, i.e., as expectations and demands on an analyst experienced by the patient primarily as a carrier, as it were, of the selfobject function.

Orientation to the centrality of the self and its selfobject relations has resulted in a reexamination of the aims and methods of psychoanalytic treatment. In 1978 Kohut and I defined the rehabilitation of the defective and weakened structures of the self as the goal of therapy, and stressed as an overall technical direction the therapist's effort in keeping narcissistic needs mobilized by demonstrating their link to the genetic matrix of selfobject relations. With the gradual lifting of repression, mobilized archaic needs are transformed into normal self-assertiveness and normal devotion to ideals. No education is needed, and, indeed, exhortative efforts, in contrast to analytic ones, are usually antitherapeutic.

My purpose in this paper is to discuss the treatment process in somewhat greater detail, with particular attention to disruptions of the selfobject transference. To this end, I should like to present the following case vignettes.

Mr. G., a lawyer in his early thirties, entered psychoanalytic treatment complaining of anxiety and depression that was at times so overwhelming that he could not concentrate on his work. He was aware of involvement with some of his clients to an extent inconsistent with his professional training and judgment. He had been the youngest of four children, and his father had been a successful corporation executive whose expectations the patient felt he had never been able to satisfy, particularly with respect to athletic performance. In fact, the patient had been a superior all-around student. His mother had apparently been an unreliable source of emotional support, sometimes too concerned and anxious, more often busy and distant. In the analysis his need for a constant and reliable relationship to a mirroring, confirming selfobject manifested itself, for example, in symptomatic reactions to even the most minor changes in his regular schedule of four appointments per week. Concomitantly, his intense need to idealize me was reflected in his gradual and mainly unconscious imitation of my style of dress and speech as well as in concern mixed with depressive affect when he imagined that some other patient had become my favorite and was thought by me to be more worthwhile than him.

In the following vignette from the fourth year of his analysis I hope to illustrate how a disruption of the transference evolved into a working-through episode. During the week preceding this sequence of sessions the patient had changed a Friday hour to the same time on a Tuesday. On the following Monday he talked at length about the struggle in his office to get rid of an unsatisfactory employee. Then he commented on how much more convenient the new Tuesday appointment was than the previous Friday session. While listening to these comments I picked up my appointment book and made a brief notation. Ordinarily I do not take notes during analytic sessions. The patient heard something, perhaps my motion or the scratching of the pen on the paper. At any rate, he fell silent suddenly and after a while I suggested that my writing had disturbed him. He was not sure, though he said he was aware of the noise and had become annoyed. But he doubted that his sudden silence was connected to this; he just felt he had nothing more to say.

On the next day he reported a surge of angry feelings after leaving my office. It made him furious to think that I was writing in my appointment book and not really listening to him. He felt he had been ignored and that he was helpless to do anything about it. Even though he reminded himself that my transgression had been relatively minor, he could not control his mounting tension and slept restlessly that night. In the morning he remembered a brief fragment of a dream. In the dream he was at the house of a friend with whom he was having an animated conversation when the friend's wife came in and both friend and wife walked into another room. We both agreed that in the dream he felt ignored and left out just as he had in the previous session. Further associations led directly to memories of his parents, particularly to instances in which his parents had been so caught up in their own interests that he felt shunted aside, ignored, and neglected. It became quite clear to both of us that the patient had reexperienced with me a set of feelings that were originally part of a repeated pattern of childhood events. My matter-of-fact acceptance of this, without either feeling or acting in an apologetic way for having precipitated the reexperiencing of this childhood constellation, helped the patient to lessen his own sense of blame and guilt over the disruption. Moreover, his memory of having felt overwhelmed by similar affects during his childhood augmented his beginning acceptance of his own genuine need for a different kind of response from his parents then, and from me now. Gradually he came to feel that my understanding and acceptance of his needs, even without my gratifying them, was legitimation enough of his self. The intense affect began to diminish and the tension between us began to fade. One might say that an intense quasi-infantile need for an archaic type of selfobject response had been transformed into an appropriate need for a reciprocal empathic resonance from the current selfobject.

I doubt there is anything new or very startling in this account of transference disruption and its restoration. Such disruptions occur innumerable times in any properly conducted psychoanalytic treatment. But our *conceptualizations* of these familiar occurrences can be very different. Thus, some colleagues, proceeding from a different set of assumptions, assumptions about the centrality of drives and defenses in the organization of personality, might have interpreted the same data in a different manner. As a part of this interpretation, they would have noted that during this phase of the treatment the patient was trying, in a half-hearted way, to comply with his wife's wish to become pregnant. At the same time he was actively exploring possible professional activities that his superiors might well have viewed as competitive with theirs. Thus, one might have concluded that, in the analytic situation with me, he was concealing his competitiveness under an apparent need for my positive responsiveness. And furthermore, that his initiative in changing the appointment schedule had been an unconscious act of aggression such as to call for retaliation on my part. The noise he perceived behind him when I began to write in my appointment book could then have provoked castration anxiety. The dream would show the wish that his mother protect him by taking the dangerous father away. Our subsequent transactions would have served to reassure him somewhat about the castration danger threatened in the transference.

I cannot say that this interpretation, or any of numerous other possible interpretations, would have been wrong. I *can* say, however, that in this particular young man, as well as in the majority of patients who present themselves for psychoanalytic treatment nowadays, the issues of drive and defense, while undoubtedly present, are peripheral to their most pressing concerns, to what brings them into treatment, peripheral, that is, to the central issue of maintaining an adequate measure of self-cohesion and achieving a somewhat satisfactory integration into their social surround.

In the following vignette my countertransference contribution to the disruption will be more obvious.

During the second year of her analysis Ms. C. was in a state of intense idealizing transference. She regarded me as a special kind of person, one who, in contrast to her three previous analysts, understood her completely. Her admiration found expression in excessively flattering comparisons of me with one of those previous analysts, a woman. She repeated with me the unbounded and erotically tinged adoration of her father that she clearly remembered as present from quite early in the oedipal phase; in fact, she recalled excitedly wrestling on a bed with her father and two-year-older brother. Father was the "good giant" in this game who protected her from the "bad giant" brother. These games went on for many months until the father left his wife and his family for another woman when the patient was about six years old.

During the brief episode to be reported in this vignette, my patient was depreciatingly critical of her husband, a successful professional who adored her and treated her with loving concern, as far as I could tell. Though she recognized his affection for her she was unable to respond to it, and experienced his attention, especially his sexual interest, as if she were being exploited merely as an object of masculine self-aggrandizement. Her symptoms included sexual coldness, dyspareunia, and various neuromuscular pains. She would reproach herself for being so unappreciative of her husband, of his kindness and generosity, and then, at times, reproach herself for being so sick, for being such a bad and unresponsive wife to him.

I did not recognize that she was repeating the archaic game of complaining about the "bad giant," now her husband, to me, the "good giant." I listened with silent acceptance as she derided her husband but did not grasp the plea for my intervention to protect her against the "bad giant" brother/husband. I did understand her subsequent self-reproaches as a plea to come to the aid of her crumbling self, which she experienced in the form of a mild depression and which led her to criticize herself as bad. It was at the end of a session in which she seemed to be feeling quite badly about herself that I said, "I wish we could have clarified some of these issues more so you would feel better." I thought I was communicating my empathic understanding of her depression and pain and my hope that sooner or later an appropriate understanding and explanation would be helpful. As it turned out, I was way off the mark, a not infrequent occurrence in treatment.

The next day she had difficulty talking and looked tense and fearful. She reported a restless night, was tired, achy, and had not felt like coming to the session at all. Long periods of silence characterized the next ten or twelve minutes. I called attention to her altered state and suggested that something might have happened during the previous day to precipitate this reaction. After some hesitation she confessed that after the session of the day before she feared that I was no longer interested in her, that I had given up on her, that I was disgusted with her because I had said I could not help her. Essentially, I replied: "Indeed, that's how I must have sounded to you and in the light of that experience we can understand your fears and hesitancy here today." In her subsequent associations she recalled how her father would sometimes get upset by the giant game with her and would suddenly stop. He would never allow her kisses to get near his mouth. When finally he left the family some months or maybe years later she blamed herself for having disappointed him too often, for having made him disgusted with her.

I was now able to recognize how my comment of the day before had repeated her father's turning away from her and his abandonment of the family. We could now talk about the re-enactment of the giant game within the analytic situation. The patient felt that I was again in touch with her feelings, that I again understood, so that the transference relationship to the idealized parental imago was restored. Without my having to say so explicitly, she knew that I had not left her the way her father had.

I might add that I also recognized a countertransference reaction that had interfered with my empathic perception of her. I had indeed become frustrated in my omniscient need to know and explain, and I do not doubt that my patient correctly perceived some tone of exasperation in my voice when I thought I was being empathic with her suffering.

In this vignette the drive-propelled erotic attachment to the idealized father and to his transference substitute in the analysis is clear. Still, it was not Ms. C.'s libidinal frustration that needed to be addressed and analyzed. Aside from the fact that these issues had been adequately dealt with in her previous analyses, the sudden surge of symptoms following my unempathic comment was not the result of heightened conflict over libidinal wishes but appeared in consequence of her imagined loss of a needed idealized selfobject. The disruption of the selfobject tie with me was experienced as the loss of a self-sustaining selfobject; her restlessness, fear, and somatizations were evidence of the beginning fragmentation of the self. When explanation and interpretation restored the selfobject tie by reestablishing an empathic resonance, the structural integrity of her self was also restored, with relief of the acute symptoms.

Though I have focused here primarily on the disruption of an idealizing transference, I wish to add that a more basic need for a mirroring selfobject response from the analyst—resulting from a faulty and unempathic selfobject tie with a depressed and harassed mother in infancy—became increasingly prominent in subsequent analytic work.

In my view, the kind of disruption I have described, with its attendant tension and emotionality, becomes the very centerpiece of the otherwise orderly and stepwise process by which the integrity of the self is restored. When a patient first comes into analysis—any patient, into any psychoanalysis—he will be both apprehensive and hopeful, and for a number of good reasons. The hope is for relief of symptoms, perhaps even for cure, and for the ever-elusive but dangerous closeness to others. The apprehension is born of numerous experiences in the past in which hopes and longings were disappointed, sometimes traumatically, with fearful damage to self and self-esteem. The new patient presents himself with a fragile, or even fragmented, self structure. Driven by fear, he dares hope he will be healed. Or, if one prefers more formal language, the fragile self, experiencing sometimes more, sometimes less fragmentation anxiety, comes in to search for those needed responses from mirroring and idealized selfobjects which will enhance its structural cohesion, its boundaries, its vigor. Strengthened by such an appropriately sustaining selfobject ambience, the self will begin to experience an amelioration of anxiety or of depression, and, perhaps, renewed energy for daily tasks.

Kohut (1977) argued that Freud's recommendations for evenly suspended attention require more than a mere negative suspension of conscious, goal-directed, logical thought processes. They also require the positive use of the analyst's prelogical modes of perceiving and thinking: "Evenly hovering attention, in other words, is the analyst's active empathic response to the analysand's free association" (1977, p. 251). To put this operationally, the analyst listens while at the same time attempting to sense and imagine what the analysand is experiencing, particularly his fears and his hopes. Empathy— vicarious introspection—guides the analyst to the analysand's own introspective experience. Psychoanalytic theory then leads the analyst to form tentative hypotheses about the conscious and, more importantly, unconscious meaning these introspective experiences might have. When he judges it to be timely, the analyst may state these hypotheses in the form of interpretations. The relevance and the truth value of these interpretations are then judged by observing their impact on the analytic process. Our interest is in moving the analysis forward, in deepening the emotional experience, in increasing the recall of recent and past events, and in facilitating the emergence of insight, by which I mean the recognition of patterns, especially repetitive patterns, where the here-and-now version of the transference makes sense as a repetition of an analogous pattern of the past, of the genetic matrix. To be more specific, an interpretation is not judged by the immediate "yes" or "no" of the patient, nor by an overall judgment that this has been a "good" hour or a "bad" one. It is the general course of the analysis, as observed over weeks and months, that becomes the final arbiter of the appropriateness of one's analytic posture and the correctness of one's analytic assessments.

All of these considerations cause us to be very careful and tentative. We wait a long time before making an interpretation and, in the meantime, restrict ourselves to letting the patient know that we are listening and that we are trying to grasp what it is that he is experiencing. Such an approach tends to avoid interfering with the unfolding of the transference, and, indeed, facilitates the emergence of intense archaic expectations for selfobject responsiveness from the analyst.

Conceptualizing this from the point of view of self psychology, the analysand's fragile or fragmented self experiences the analyst's interested listening and his attitude of trying to understand as a beginning response to a selfobject need so that, consequently, the self feels strengthened and more cohesive. Subjectively, the patient begins to feel better, and his symptoms as a rule become less painful. The analyst is being used as a selfobject because of his nonspecific interest as a helping professional. He has not "mirrored" the patient—he has not confirmed the patient's grandiosity. Nor has he held himself out to be admired by the patient. But the analyst has been experienced by the patient as sustaining the specific selfobject need which is required for strengthening the self. The exact nature of that selfobject need and its roots in the individual's personal history will become clear only as the analysis proceeds. Thus, any intervention which is not based on the patient's need, but, let us say, on the *analyst's* need to demonstrate his skill, competence, or theoretical sophistication, is likely to turn out to be inappropriate or premature, and will derail the spontaneous emergence of the selfobject transference, at least temporarily.

As for resistance, I have come to use the word less and less. Like it or not, it has acquired moral connotations that are inappropriate to psychoanalytic treatment. We may intend to make a neutral, matter-of-fact statement about what we discern about the patient's intrapsychic conflicts, but the patient hears an admonition, often a moralistic criticism, which is only partially a distortion determined by transference, for, in fact, we often do convey a sense of deep disapproval in our tone of voice or in some even more subtle way. I no longer believe that patients "resist" being analyzed. I believe they fear humiliation or rejection or some other form of depreciation and that this fear makes them sensitively cautious against revealing themselves candidly. In my "resistance interpretations" I make sure to point out that the analysand has good reasons to be on guard. The self always feels exposed to two potential traumas: the loss of a needed selfobject response, i.e., too much psychological distance from the selfobject, or intrusion of the selfobject across its boundaries into its own core, i.e., too little psychological distance from the selfobject. The more fragile the self structure, the more vulnerable the self and the more distorted the self's defensive maneuvers against the potential danger of being either too close or too far away from the selfobject. In analysis we are used to calling these defenses "resistances." But since in the self-psychological view these are not primarily directed against drives, but against selfobject failures which may fragment the self, I prefer to label these phenomena "measures of obligatory self protection."

To recapitulate, the analysand's fragile self has experienced the analytic ambience as a strengthening selfobject response. The patient's suffering has diminished and his archaic de-

mands have become focused on the analyst: A selfobject transference has become established. Sooner or later, however, this
apparently harmonious transference relationship becomes disrupted. I regard these disruptions and their analytic resolution
as the crux of the therapeutic process. This should not be taken
to mean that beneficial changes are *absent* during the often
prolonged periods of a relatively harmonious selfobject tie to
the analyst. During these calmer periods, the strengthened self
has at its command an increased functional capacity which enables it to experience self-satisfying achievements, which, in
turn, may further strengthen the self. These are not so-called
"transference cures" but solid and lasting accretions to self
structure. Patients with very highly structured defensive organizations—obsessive-compulsive patients, for example—may
go on for months or years before the slight tremor of disruption can be discerned by the analyst and become the focus of
the treatment. In other words, some patients need preparatory
work of this kind before they can gain enough strength to face
the affective storms unleashed by disruption.

On the other hand, there are borderline patients with fragmented selves who apparently never find sufficient inner tran-
quility to let themselves settle into a reliable selfobject transference. Perhaps they have good reasons not to trust others.
They may sense that affectively stormy disruptions may destroy
what little self structure they have established. For all but the
most unusually well-attuned analysts, attempts at psychoanalysis with these patients tend to become all disruption, without enough of the experience of reliable selfobject relationship.
But we should be careful to avoid the borderline label until
there have been trials of analysis by more than one or two
analysts.

What brings about the inevitable disruption to which I have
referred? From the patient's point of view, i.e., from the point
of view of the patient's *experience,* it is a feeling of not having
been listened to or of having been misunderstood or criticized,
or some other repetition of what it felt like as a child when,
inevitably, the parent could not be perfectly attuned to the
child. It is a genuine experience for the patient—it is real, not a
distortion. At that moment the analyst, in fact, does not under-

stand something. This something may be extremely trivial to the analyst, who is likely to have sensitivities different from the patient's. But it is not trivial to the patient. As far as I was concerned, I was only fleetingly and trivially distracted when I made the quick note in my appointment book. But the patient experienced my distraction as a meaningful reality, the reality of once again not being listened to while he was trying to communicate some very important and painful inner turmoil. His experience of my distraction was not a distortion of reality, but reality for him: The meaning of that reality was different for him than for me. A possible interpretation to the patient that his perception of reality was distorted would have added insult to injury. A proper interpretation, rather, acknowledges the patient's reality and tries to explain its meaning to him, usually in terms of his past experiences. A patient resists interpretation when it implies some fault on his part, e.g., that he wants to misread the analyst's intentions, or that his experience is not real, just transference from the past, or that, bad child that he was, he is just repeating past childish behavior in the here-and-now. An appropriate interpretation accepts that, as a child, the patient could hardly have felt differently under the circumstances and that the current happening inevitably has the same meaning to him. The reality of not being fully in tune with the analyst removes the latter as an available sustaining selfobject, thereby weakening the self, or even leading to its fragmentation. Resulting fragmentation anxiety mobilizes emergency measures to protect the self. These emergency measures may appear as symptoms or as acting out; sometimes there are no emergency measures, only surrender, and the patient's suffering is autoplastic, private.

Since the analyst is seen as the source of the threat that renders the self helpless, there may be narcissistic rage with the aim of wiping out the threat. Or there may be attempts to reconstitute some sort of self structure around an often prominent sexual fragment. Such a reconstituted self will view all experience as having sexual meaning. In other words, all relationships, including the transference, become sexualized. The analyst, who has in fact traumatized the self, may be perceived as a sexual object, and the self may attempt to regain the lost selfobject relationship by being seductive. I believe it is the sexualization consequent upon at least potential or partial fragmentation of the self which leads to the neurotic conflicts with which psychoanalysts have become so familiar.

Disruptions are brought to an end by interpretation and explanation. The selfobject relationship with the analyst is repaired and the self's integrity thereby restored. Both patient and analyst have gained greater insight into the vicissitudes of their relationship and its genetic antecedents. But has anything really been gained for the self? Has it become less fragile, less vulnerable, less needy, less demanding, less arrogant, less clinging?

I think so, though progress is often measured more in inches than in miles, as it were. Each disruption-restoration cycle increases the trust that one can be understood and that one can learn to understand others. The increasing trust in self and others represents the increasing strength of self structures. Clinically, we see fewer disruptions, decreasing intensity of affective storms when disruptions do occur, and greater tolerance for being out of tune with the needed selfobjects. This does not mean that selfobjects are no longer needed and that the millenium of autonomy, self sufficiency, and independence has arrived. It never will, for anybody. Kohut (1984) has described the essence of the process of strengthening the self as a replacement of archaic selfobject needs by an empathic resonance with the analyst. Sooner or later, the experience of empathic resonance with the analyst will lead the analysand to an increased ability to recognize potential sources of empathic resonance in his daily surround. Thus, the restored self becomes more skillful and less defensive in achieving a satisfactory integration into a self supportive social matrix. And, perhaps, belated maturation of the self's functional capacities allows the self to draw sustenance from the symbolic selfobject relations embedded in artistic, intellectual, and religious experiences.

Finally, I should like to stress that self psychology is not a *deviation* from the classical model. I hope I have been able to show that self psychology has not lost sight of either sexuality or aggression. Its proponents believe only that one cannot escape viewing psychological phenomena through the lens of the self, a proposition which does not remove self psychology from the mainstream of psychoanalysis but, rather, broadens that mainstream beyond its too narrow focus on biopsychological factors.

REFERENCES

Kohut, H. (1977). *The Restoration of the Self*. New York: International Universities Press.

———— (1984). *How Does Analysis Cure?*, eds. A. Goldberg & P. Stepansky. Chicago: University of Chicago Press (in press).

———— & Wolf, E. (1978). The disorders of the self and their treatment: An outline. *Internat. J. Psycho-Anal.*, 59:413–426.

10 Selfobjects, Development, and Psychotherapy

Michael Franz Basch, M.D.

WHAT IS PSYCHOTHERAPY? Literally translated it refers to the treatment of the psyche or mind, but what does that mean? We manage to avoid such questions in our training by busying ourselves with learning techniques that will let us help the patients whose problems confront and confuse us. We have neither time, interest, nor patience to deal with such questions as "What is mind?". We are practical people, and that is a philosophical issue we say and, furthermore, since even the philosophers disagree on the point, what good will it do us to concern ourselves with it? So, before we know it, we have become reasonably proficient at what we do without ever having really defined for ourselves what that might be. A strange situation indeed. What would we think of a cardiologist who could not describe the heart, or a dermatologist who didn't know what skin was? But then the mind is not an organ, or is it?

Even if they are not identified as such these issues become important when we are confronted by patients whose difficulties do not fit our particular frame of reference, or whose treatment does not proceed as we have come to expect. The more basic questions about our field of practice also come into focus when we try to compare the different schools of psychotherapy, combine a variety of techniques into a unitary whole, or weigh the merits of proposed new contributions to our field.

Often when answers are not forthcoming it is advisable to change the question. Rather than continuing to ask "What is mind?" I have found it more profitable to turn to everyday experience and ask what has happened when someone claims to have made up his mind? For example: "I am getting too heavy and have made up my mind not to eat lunch." A decision has been made. I think we will find that every time we use the word "mind" in an operational sense we can cash it in for the much less mysterious term "decision." What about the various functions we assign to the mind, like thinking, believing, concluding, considering, debating, remembering, and doubting, to name only a few? Here, too, I think, we will find that every one of these terms refers to the decision-making process. This also includes words in the affective realm like "feeling" or "mood" or "emotion" which indicate that a decision has been made regarding the dispositional significance of an experience. To love, to hate, to be angry at, to despair of, to fear, to be surprised by, and so on, all represent decisions based on information that has reached and been evaluated by our . . . our what?

There is today no doubt that the organ that carries out the decision-making process is the brain. Need we postulate a mind inside the brain, a noncorporeal organ, or higher-level homunculus, that directs the neurones to do their job? I think not. But this position, namely, that "mind" stands for no entity but for the decision-making process of the brain, must be further qualified. Information processing and decision making are not exclusively functions of the brain, indeed, they are capacities of all protoplasm. Nor are they limited to living matter; computers too are built so as to have a decision-making capacity. Any system so constructed that the effects of its behavior are fed back into it and influence its subsequent output, so-called negative or error-correcting feedback, constitutes a decision-making, goal-directed, or open system.

Since every living cell is programmed to exercise its function while maintaining its particular homeostatic state, and to transform environmental signals into information that it uses to achieve those ends, shall we attribute mind or thought to every cell or organized collection of cells? An argument could be made for that view, especially when one contemplates the sophisticated information-processing activity of an organ like the kidney, or that of the immune system, but at the same time we know that this is not what we mean by mind. Those are not the kinds of decision that we intend to include when in everyday usage we speak of making up our minds. Nor, for example, would failure of the immune system resulting in an allergic reaction be referred to as losing one's mind, even though an aspect of the body's decision-making process has gone seriously awry. So, not only do we locate mind in the brain, it is also limited to the brain. The brain is evolution's answer to the need for a supraordinate information-processing center, an ordering organ that can coordinate and control the decision-making activity of all the other organ systems. Shall we then equate brain with mind? Again the answer must be "no." Although the brain regulates the reproductive cycle, the blood's acid and base balance, assures the continuity of our heartbeat and our respiration, indeed, regulates all the vital functions of the body, these decisions being continuously made by the brain are not what we mean by "mind" or "mental activity." Maintaining homeostasis and adapting to the environment according to inherited feedback systems governed by physiological goals are not mental processes as we understand them. When we attempt to refine our concept of mind in this manner we realize that we reserve the term "mental" for activities designed to achieve endpoints that we impose on ourselves. In other words, decisions attributed to the mind involve symbolic rather than physiological, or at last purely physiological goals. When a child cries plaintively "I want to go home," we have no hesitation about calling that wish a product of mind, or mental, while a homing pigeon's flight across vast distances, amazing as it may seem, is not mental but instinctive behavior. It is the ability to conceptualize a "want," a "home," and, above all, an "I" that makes for a mental event.

These considerations, though not spelled out at the time, led the 17th-century philosopher Rene Descartes to declare "I think, therefore I am." In other words, the only reality we can be sure of is the self. But for Descartes mind, self, reason, and consciousness were all equivalent and interchangeable. Furthermore, the gift of reason, or mind, was a divine implant vouchsafed each human being, separate from the body and, unlike the body, not subject to further study or dissection. It was Freud who systematically demonstrated that unconscious thought is not a contradiction in terms, and that reason and consciousness are not equivalent.

What we today call psychoanalysis and insight-promoting psychotherapy is based on the recognition that thought need not be conscious. Though historically Freud was not the first to have taken this position, he discovered or rediscovered it for himself and, more important, systematically worked out its implications. What did not get resolved by Freud was the other assumption of the Cartesian position, so that, though we now speak of an unconscious mind, or mental apparatus, as Freud called it, the dichotomy between mind and body first formulated by Descartes remains intact. So firmly is it built into our everyday language—which essentially consists of two vocabularies, one used to describe the physical world, the other used to discuss the activities of the mind—that we find ourselves rebelling against the idea that the mind/body dichotomy is only that, an idea or belief, a philosophical position, and not an immutable fact of nature.

Today we can look at the brain differently than Freud and his contemporaries were able to do in the 19th and early part of the 20th centuries. Only since the Second World War, which saw the development of cybernetics or control theory based on the concept of information as a quantifiable form of power or intensity, have we been able to understand the brain as an information-generating and -processing organ rather than, as Freud saw it, an energy-dissipating organ (Basch, 1976a). The brain is the ordering organ that transforms the signals it receives from the rest of the body, from the environment, and, in the case of the activity we call thought, from itself into meaningful messages or information. That transformation from signal to meaningful message is accomplished by comparing the input with established patterns of organization to see if and how the input compares with what the brain has been programmed to expect, and, if the fit is not sufficiently exact, to generate muscular, glandular, or thought activity that will either lead to pattern matching, establish new adaptive patterns, or dismiss the input as being less than consequential. We no longer need to postulate mind as a substantive noun governing the unthinking brain. There is no need to predicate a homunculus that controls the activity of the brain in goal-directed fashion. The activity of the brain is explained by the activity of the brain, and mind describes one of those activities.

To study mind is not to become concerned in some way with an insubstantial entity, but to study an indirectly observable decision-making process governed and focused by a concept we call the "self." Infant observation and developmental psychology, made possible and inspired by Freud's original investigations of the significance of childhood experience, have gone far beyond the picture of development that Freud arrived at when he equated what he learned about the early development of conflict in the future neurotic with normal development generally (Basch, 1977). When we now ask, having exchanged "mind" for the decision-making processes related to the self, how this self develops and what its nature might be, we can get some answers.

Action, not reflection, governs infantile life. Though not as extensively as are other creatures, we come into the world programmed to react in specific ways to a range of specific stimuli. These genetically determined programs form the foundation for the development of affect and reason, which together make up the thought process.

Affect originates on the subcortical level, in the midbrain and the hindbrain which are set to respond automatically to the intensity and frequency of sensory stimuli regardless of their nature or origin. That is to say, affect is initially based on intensity patterns rather than on qualitative patterns. For each infant there is a range of intensity that represents an optimal level of stimulation. Stimulation in that optimal range recruits the baby's attention and leads him to track the stimulus. Stimulation above that range automatically leads to avoidance reactions and distress signals. When a heightened stimulus gradient is completely resolved it automatically produces a smile reaction, as when a child is tossed up and caught again by his father or mother, a game that always produces a cry of delight; when, however, heightened stimuli are inadequately resolved, there is confusion and loss of contact. Adultomorphizing the infant, and based on later transformations of these initially purely automatic behaviors, we call these reactions variously surprise, interest or excitement, distress, anger, fear, enjoyment, or shame (Basch, 1976b).

On the cortical level, the substrate for reason, the infant is preprogrammed to exhibit certain perceptual preferences. The physically comfortable and alert infant, placed in a semi-sitting position, prefers stimulation to absence of stimulation, prefers the unfamiliar to the familiar pattern, prefers sharp distinctions to monotony, prefers angles to straight lines, and, most important, prefers the human voice, face, and touch to any other stimulus. Together the inherited subcortical and cortical predispositions combine to lay down affectively toned patterns of experience that are remobilized when the occasion calls for it. For instance, a baby with a cleft palate for whom hunger is associated with overstimulation and ungratifying resolution will lay down a different pattern of expectation and therefore will show a different response to the nipple than a child who can satisfy his hunger comfortably when fed.

Inevitably the feeding experience and the affects associated with it will enter into the shaping of other experiences with the caregiver, and so on. These interlocking and evolving patterns of expectation generate a hierarchy of transactional experiences that, from the psychological point of view, forms the psychic structure we call the self.

In order to illustrate the importance of recognizing the variety of patterns of expectation from which the concept of self evolves, I should like to cite here a clinical vignette from a supervisory session. The patient had been talking for some weeks about some delicate negotiations he was conducting on whose outcome hinged his future with the company that employed him. In this particular hour the patient came in all aglow and opened with a statement to the effect that he had succeeded in bringing the matter to the hoped-for conclusion. He waited eagerly for the therapist's response. The therapist said nothing. The patient reacted with bitterness and drew an uncomplimentary parallel between the therapist's unresponsiveness and his mother's behavior. The rest of the hour was unproductive, the therapist repeatedly asking the patient what was on his mind, the patient either denying that he was thinking anything or bringing up trivia in a flat, distant tone.

I asked the supervisee what his purpose was in remaining silent at the point at which the patient reported his success. He told me that his silence was not purposeful, that he felt paralyzed and at a loss for what to do next. "What were you thinking while you sat there silently?" I asked. "I was wondering what the patient was trying to get away with," my student replied.

I bring up this incident not to discuss the pros and cons of what might have been said or whether silence was a reasonable response to the patient's implied request for acknowledgment, but because I think the supervisee's statement summarizes as well as anything I have read or heard the effect of what Stone (1981) calls the neoclassical position in psychoanalysis, the one based on the idea that whatever the patient does is at bottom an attempt to fulfill forbidden sexual and aggressive wishes, and it is the analyst's job for the good of the patient and the analysis to thwart him. My student was not clear about the nature of the theory that had given rise to his mental paralysis and left him at a loss for words and with the uncomfortable feeling that his patient was trying to put something over on him. But one does not have to be able to articulate the theory in order to be influenced by it. Indeed, the less one knows of the theory the more likely one is to be influenced by its unspoken presence in training programs, in the literature, and in case conferences. What we see here are the antitherapeutic constraints under which we work if our interventions are limited to only one group in the many patterns of expectations from which the concept of self evolves.

Kohut discovered that the symptoms of patients with narcissistic character disorder—for example, exquisite sensitivity to real or imaginary personal slights, while at the same time showing a total disregard of and insensitivity to the analyst as a person—are not resistances to the examination of deeper psychosexual conflicts, but the surface manifestations of a different transference potential, one which if activated leads to the formation and resolution of transferences other than oedipal, indeed, transferences of a deeper and earlier origin than the oedipal ones of the neurotic patient. This led to the elaboration of a clinical theory that resolves the dilemma of how one avoids direct gratification without practicing punitive deprivation. It is the concept of the so-called selfobject function that strikes me as basic for the liberating effect that Kohut's work has had for both theory and practice. Kohut learned in the analysis of narcissistic character disorders that the resistance his patients put up against emotional involvement with him was not resistance to acknowledging their longing for him as a person, but a matter of noncomprehension as to what he was after. It was like trying to explain the advantages of personal hygiene to a two-year-old who needs a diaper change—it won't stop crying. Therefore, the resistance of Miss F., for example, to Kohut's, as it turned out, incorrect interpretations, was not evidence of the patient's pathology but of her essential health (Kohut, 1971). She would not, as many patients have done, compromise herself and develop a false self, to use Winnicott's term, in order to maintain her relationship with the analyst, but continued to impose on the analyst the demand that he understand her needs to use him as an extension of herself who would echo her and find her acceptable. When Kohut, like Freud in his day, caught on, let the patient lead the way, and permitted the archaic transference to develop, he learned that the patient's grating, ill-tempered, literally depersonalizing demands of the analyst revealed a heretofore unsuspected frightened little child. The vicissitudes of that transference, once formed, could be dealt with by interpretation, and this time resulted in the patient's maturation through the development of a viable, that is, cohesive concept of self.

Freud once said that basic to human development were two biological facts, the biphasic onset of sexuality and the helplessness of the human infant. Freud explained the import and the vicissitudes of the first, Kohut was the first systematically and psychoanalytically to do the same for the second.

What Kohut reconstructed in the analysis of adults corresponded to what developmental psychologists were putting together from direct observations of and experiments with infants and children. As I pointed out earlier, the infant brain is perceptually prepared and eager for transactions with his environment, especially with the humans around him. Eager for stimulation, he has an affective armamentarium which automatically sends signals indicating his response to what is happening or not happening with and to him. Whether those signals—smiles, tears, frowns, babbling, eye movement, and so on—become meaningful messages depends on whether or not there is a receiver who can and will decode them and respond. The infant is helpless to help himself, not only in such matters as food, warmth, and shelter, but, equally important, in providing for the psychological nourishment, the human contact and stimulation, that, beginning with Spitz's work (1945, 1946), we know is required to assure life and continuity of maturation.

In cybernetic terms, the infant and his mother together form an error-correcting feedback system. An error-correcting feedback cycle consists of a goal, a pattern of behavior designed to reach that goal, a comparator, and an error signal which, when activated, indicates that the desired goal has not been achieved, i.e., that the pattern of expectation and the reality of the moment do not yet, or will not coincide, and that corrective activity must be instituted. The infant supplies a sophisticated array of error signals in the form of his automatic affective responses, and a basic but limited set of perceptual goals. The behavior for attaining those goals is for the most part beyond him and must be supplied by the empathic parent, that is, the parent attuned to his affective communications. Also, it is up to the parental portion of the infant-mother system to supply in acceptable and appropriate fashion the maturational goals that will activate the infant's potential as it emerges. Although the various feats made possible by coordination of gross and fine muscle movement with the senses—for instance, sucking, reaching, grasping, searching, walking, and talking—are instinctual, that is, genetically programmed capacities, these capacities do not develop without the necessary releasor provided by human contact and stimulation. That the same holds true for the maturation of human relationships was implied in Freud's work, but that aspect of development was not fully appreciated nor was a systematic operational approach worked out to deal with its pathological vicissitudes. Indeed, Freud's emphasis on the psy-

chosexual aspect of development had the inadvertent result of
making analysts positively unempathic with the manifestations
of the unresponded-to infant-child in their patients. Analysts
remained deaf to the error signals being sent out by their patients because they were considered to be *ipso facto* resistances,
resistances that had to be removed before the truly significant
material that needed to be worked on could emerge. Kohut's
clinical discoveries in the area of empathy and empathic failure
dovetailed with direct observations of parent-infant transactions and with the application of cybernetics and systems theory
to those findings.

The need for the function-fulfilling selfobject that Kohut
recognized in its most blatant form in patients with narcissistic
personality disorder reflects in adult life the empathic failure of
earlier years when the infant's or child's brain literally could not
function because its error signals went unheeded or were mis-
interpreted. Consequently, legitimate maturational goals were
either perverted or remained undeveloped in order to end the
discomfort engendered by the frustration of being misunderstood or not responded to. In later life the evidence of that
failure manifests itself in grandiose or idealizing transference
needs. These terms are, of course, based on psychoanalytic
observation and are therefore adultomorphic. The infant is
neither grandiose nor idealizing. The affective error signal—
the cry of distress, anger, or fear, for example—that is set off
when the infant brain tries to fulfill its ordering function and is
unable to execute those motor movements that would complete
the feedback cycle, serves as a communication to the parent
who, if empathic and capable, understands what is needed and
provides the motoric power and coordination required for
mastery. In later life, when an adult insists that others cease to
be individuals and submit to being used as tools, it strikes us as
unpleasantly and unjustifiably imperial, and Kohut used the
word grandiose to describe the impression such patients made
on him. Similarly, when the immature brain proves incapable
of dealing with the nature and quantity of stimuli impinging
upon it, and the cry of distress is generated, the empathic parent will soothe the child, holding and rocking it, for example.
The parent will shut out distraction, minimize extraneous in-

put, and through bodily union restore an earlier quiet, rhythmic, and less tumultous state. In adult patients this manifests itself in a longing for union with the admired analyst so as to be symbolically reabsorbed and reassured as one once was when held by the parent. Kohut called this the need for establishing an idealizing transference.

In the beginning there is only, as Kohut called it, a virtual self. The infant as an individual exists in the mind of the parents, that is, in the conceptualization of the parents. At about 18 to 24 months his own capacity for conceptualization matures and the infant demonstrates that he is beginning to organize individual experiences in terms of general categories of his own making. Furthermore, he is beginning to reflect on his activities as such. The capacities for generalization and reflection together make possible the so-called symbolic function. It is not long before the brain activity of ordering experience through generalizing and reflecting becomes itself an object of generalization and reflection, is reified and labeled "self." As Buckminster Fuller so aptly said, "I seem to be a verb."

Maturation continuously poses new tasks. Throughout life, when mastery does not seem feasible and when external reality and/or the fantasy products of our own symbolic activity threaten to disorganize us and call for soothing, we seek and need the intervention of appropriate selfobjects. Failure in this area generates the array of functional psychopathology that is dealt with in psychoanalysis and psychotherapy.

As Kohut (1977) clarified, oedipal conflict as the causative factor in the psychoneuroses is one dramatic and instructive example of a particular selfobject failure associated with instinctual disinhibition, one that transforms what should be a normal maturational phase into a cul-de-sac from which the patient cannot extricate himself until the analyst, as empathic selfobject, first lets him reenact the conflict in the transference and then, through interpretation, helps him to find a more satisfactory solution for the formerly repressed conflict. This step then permits maturation to continue from the point at which it had previously been arrested. But the oedipal conflict is only one such instance of selfobject failure and cannot serve as the ordering framework for all we see in our practices.

The lack of relevance of psychoanalytic instinct theory for the majority of problems encountered in a general psychotherapy practice (Basch, 1983) has led to the establishment of other so-called schools of psychotherapy that address the various issues presented by patients with non-neurotic pathology. To name a few: Patients with what we would now call merger needs stimulated Rogers to develop client-centered therapy with the emphasis on acceptance of the patient-as-he-is as the *sine qua non* of treatment. Patients for whom inadequate information processing rather than a conflict of goals was central for pathology led to the formulation of cognitive therapy. Various emotive-cathartic procedures have been developed to deal with those patients whose affective development is distorted. Behavior therapy is directed at patients in whom not the goal, but the behavior to reach the goal is deficient, inadequate, or otherwise problematic, and so on.

Although each form of nonanalytic therapy had validity in that it arose out of clinical need and could show results with particular groups of patients for whom traditional psychoanalysis and psychoanalytically oriented insight psychotherapy had failed, these schools threw out the baby with the bathwater. The bathwater being the centrality of the Oedipus complex for all pathology, the baby being the psychoanalyst's emphasis on the transference and the dynamic unconscious.

Kohut's formulation of the selfobject transferences—the expansion of the concept of transference to include all aspects of unconscious motivation—frees us to enter the frustrating, counterproductive, or self-destructuve decision-making process of our patients at any level of maturation, and lets us help a patient to gain insight into and correct whatever portion of the feedback cycle is affected.

Kohut, through the use of Freud's method of introspection and empathy, has given us, for the first time, a clinical theory that explains the results obtained by all the various schools of therapy and potentially permits them to be reunited with insight psychotherapy. The selfobject concept makes possible the unification of relevant findings from academic developmental psychology, child observation, and adult analysis. It is the key to the unitary theory that has so long been sought; it could do for psychology what the theory of the cell has done for the biological sciences. To bring that potential to fruition is, I believe, the task that faces us as psychotherapists in the coming years.

REFERENCES

Basch, M. F. (1976a). Psychoanalysis and communication science. *The Annual of Psychoanalysis*, 4:385–421.

——— (1976b). The concept of affect: A re-examination. *J. Amer. Psychoanal. Assn.*, 24:759–777.

——— (1977). Developmental psychology and explanatory theory in psychoanalysis. *The Annual of Psychoanalysis*, 5:229–263.

——— (1983). The significance of self psychology for a theory of psychotherapy. In *Reflections on the Self*, eds. J. Lichtenberg & S. Kaplan. Hillsdale, N.J.: The Analytic Press.

Kohut, H. (1971). *The Analysis of the Self.* New York: International Universities Press.

——— (1977). *The Restoration of the Self.* New York: International Universities Press.

Spitz, R. A. (1945). Diacritic and coenesthetic organizations; the psychiatric significance of a functional division of the nervous system into a sensory and emotive part. *Psychoanal. Rev.*, 33: 146–162.

——— (1946). Hospitalism: A follow-up report on investigation described in Volume 1, 1945. *The Psychoanalytic Study of the Child*, 2:113–118.

Stone, L. (1981). Notes on the noninterpretative elements in the psychoanalytic situation and process. *J. Amer. Psychoanal. Assn.*, 29:89–118.

11 Psychoanalytic Psychotherapy: A Contemporary Perspective

Anna Ornstein, M.D.

IN ORDER TO DEMONSTRATE in a concrete way some of the influences that self psychology has had on the practice of psychoanalytic psychotherapy, I should like to begin my discussion with a clinical vignette. My patient was a 32-year-old clinical psychologist who had recently gotten married to a woman with whom he believed himself to be in love, but toward whom he could not freely express his love. Rather, he said, he found himself to be just as "selfish" as he thought he had always been. He had always been preoccupied with his own needs and concerns and had always placed these ahead of other people's desires. Thus, he and his wife would go to restaurants of his own choosing; he could not share his belongings with her; he insisted that she should do things in the house his way. Now he thought this "petty" and "compulsive" and wanted to change. Moreover, he believed this problem to be part of a larger difficulty involving an inability to experience affects, especially loving ones and to express these spontaneously. In their physical relationship, for example, he was distressed when he found himself at times withdrawing from his wife's embraces or from a simple touch. He spoke little about their sexual relationship other than to mention, rather casually, that at times he suffered from premature ejaculation.

The patient worried that his difficulties had been of such long standing and so pervasive as not to be amenable to once-a-week psychotherapy. But since this was the only form of treatment he could afford, and because he was in acute distress, we proceeded on the once-a-week basis.

I have deliberately chosen to discuss the treatment of a mental health professional because I believe that this patient's idea of how psychotherapy worked was consistent with a traditional view of therapy generally held by mental health professionals, one based on the hydraulic model of the mind. Conflicts and poorly managed affects (anger, rivalry, sexual passion) lurk within the dark and seething cauldron of the unconscious; once recognized and brought to awareness, these affects are expected to lose their power, with cure the result.

Thus the patient expected the therapist to read his unconscious mind in his dreams and fantasies, and directly translate his symptoms into "well-known" dynamic-genetic formulations. He would frequently express disappointment that the therapist had not confronted him with her understanding, forcing him to accept some "awful truth" about himself. He was convinced that this was what he needed in order to overcome his difficulties.

It is not surprising in the light of these treatment goals that the patient was very cooperative. From the beginning, he reported his fantasies faithfully, emphasizing those he considered to indicate "resistances." An outstanding fantasy was one he frequently had while sitting in the waiting room: He imagined that the therapist would be late and that, once in her office, she would do something that would indicate that she was bored and uninvolved with him; he would then become angry, savor his rage for a while, eventually insult her and storm out of the office.

To some this fantasy would indicate the presence of a great deal of anger which the patient needed to express: He was setting up a situation in his mind that would permit the expression of his anger. If the anger was defensive, nevertheless—or maybe because of it—its interpretation should have been the first order of business in his treatment. Some would go even further and say that the analysis of this fantasy could have provided hints as to the patient's diagnosis. The fantasy, it could be argued, reveals a primitive personality organized around oral rage, which would then explain his narcissistic attitude toward people. To put it in another way: The patient's "selfish" behavior, and his inability to experience and express love, could be considered a narcissistic defense against oral envy and rage; this, in turn, would be responsible for his fear of intimacy and for his fantasies of having an angry exchange with the therapist. On the basis of this formulation, then, the therapist would be urged to accede to the patient's wish for confrontation because such confrontation—informed by the new understanding—could potentially be curative.

The therapist did not interpret the fantasy. Not because the theory that would have explained the fantasy to her satisfaction differed from the one just described, but because any *explanation* offered to the patient in relation to a single fantasy or dream or symptom—no matter how detailed and thorough— would not facilitate the evolution of a therapeutic process. Indeed, the opposite would be true: The "dynamic explanations" of the fantasy, dream, or symptom would fragment the therapeutic experience and carry the treatment into experience-distant terrains. I am not suggesting that any of the patient's communications should be dismissed. Rather, that they be considered as only one aspect of an evolving therapeutic process. The therapist did not share the patient's conception of the treatment process; she did not concern herself with "removing" his "resistances" in order to expose affects that would tell him the truth about himself.

The patient himself interpreted the fantasy as still another evidence of his resistance; he thought that he needed to create a situation in his mind in which the therapist would be responsible for his failure to face his unacceptable feelings. Rather than addressing the content of the fantasy, the therapist told him that his concern over his "resistances" helped her appreciate his hope and expectation that she would force the door open that kept his unconscious thoughts and feelings hidden. Could this concern with his "resistances" be related to their meeting only once weekly, and to his fear that they may not accomplish their goals unless she applied some force to help him reveal the hidden part of his psyche? "Yes", said the patient. "One of us has to tip the bucket. . . . if you don't question and challenge me, I will never do it on my own. . . ."

At this time the therapist had not yet understood the specific, idiosyncratic meaning of the patient's concern with what he called his "resistances." Nor had she understood that in this metaphor he was expressing an expectation that the therapist recognize even those of his feelings that he himself could not be aware of and therefore could not articulate.

Before describing the particular hour in which the therapist understood and interpreted the meaning of this expectation, I should like briefly to cite some pertinent data regarding the patient's background.

He came from a once well-to-do, upper-middle-class European family. His father had been a highly respected businessman in the relatively small community in which they lived. The patient recalled that he had experienced the townspeople's respect for his father in the form of "reflected glory." He was proud of his father, though personally he had little to do with him. The family lived in a very traditional manner: The father was always somewhat at a distance, feared and respected. The children (two older sisters and the patient) were raised by nurses, though the mother rarely left the home; she kept busy with the many social obligations that the father's position demanded. The patient felt particularly close to his older sister, ten years his senior. One of the "secrets" that he hoped held the key to the solution of his problems was that, as a little boy, he had had sexual fantasies about this sister. Exploring this possibility, he spoke in a rather intellectual manner of how he could have displaced onto his wife his incestuous wishes for his sister.

But the childhood memories that appeared to be the most disturbing to the patient related to his early adolescence: At age eleven he had been sent to a boarding school at a considerable distance from home. He had the feeling now that his parents had had no idea as to how he had felt about this. It had been done for the sake of his education. At the school he had felt very lonely and unhappy. During his stay, his father died suddenly, but the patient did not recall grieving his loss or feeling any sadness on hearing the news. Thus, the possibility that unfinished grief was at the bottom of his difficulties was also explored in his treatment.

Indeed, the subject of his father's death brought on the strongest and most painful affects in treatment. He recalled for example, coming upon a newspaper article about his father that had indicated that his business deals may not all have been above board; he could still feel the devastation that this news had created in him.

I shall now focus on the hour in which the therapist came to understand the meaning of the patient's wish that she actively search out feelings that he himself was unaware of; an hour in which she was able to interpret this in a way that fully resonated with the patient's self experiences. (In paying close attention to the therapist's interventions and the manner in which they promoted the deepening of the therapeutic process, I am elaborating on a more detailed discussion that appeared in a previous publication. There the opinion was expressed that psychoanalytic psychotherapy can be considered on a continuum with psychoanalysis as long as the therapist's interventions are not manipulative (supportive or reassuring) but, rather, fairly consistently interpretive [Ornstein and Ornstein, 1977].)

In the hour under review, the patient entered the office visibly irritated. As he sat down he said: "I challenged you. . . . I have been trying to find fault so that I can get some action. . . . It seems to me that we continue to deal with the obvious. . . . I have this fantasy that if I could only scream and yell, call you names, that all my inhibitions would be gone." He thought for a moment and then added: ". . . but I am no longer sure that this is what I really want. . . . there is something else . . . but how will we get that door open?" The therapist said that clearly some doubt had crept into his previously held conviction that what he really needed was to scream and yell and engage her in some kind of fight in order to get well. "Could it be," she asked, "that for you to be able to scream and yell would be the *result* of a cure rather than the means to achieve it?"

This interpretive comment (significantly, put in the form of a question) expressed the therapist's own theory of the treatment process. In essence, she implied that the patient would be able to scream and yell once he experienced himself to be, in relationship to the therapist, safe with all his feelings. The therapist's position relative to the process of treatment can be expressed as follows: Affects cannot forcibly be "liberated" from repression by means of confrontations. Rather, to experience and express affects is a capacity that requires a well-consolidated self that is not threatened by feelings of any kind, loving and tender, as well as angry and destructive.

The therapist's somewhat ambiguous "interpretation" was followed by a brief silence, after which she continued with a tentative offer of a more comprehensive understanding of the patient's communications. She said that his persistent demand that she "open the door" or "tip the bucket" so that the "truth" about him could be revealed, made her think that what might be most disturbing to him was that she did not fully understand him, and that he wished she would. Yes, he wished that the therapist had some magical powers to understand him. And, yes, that was more important than *what* it was she would see inside of him. The therapist then continued: "Just like you wished your parents understood what it felt like for you to go to the boarding school, to leave your family and friends—all the things that were important to you and that you were familiar with. You couldn't tell them then how you felt, but you wished they would have known anyway and not sent you away. You wish now that I could understand everything about you— wishes and feelings that you are not aware of. If I knew about them, you could feel secure in my presence; it is then that you could scream and yell."[1] It was at this time—well into the hour—that the patient recalled a dream from the night before. In the dream, the therapist came over and stood beside him. She stood in the small triangle that was created by his chair, the wall, and the desk. He was not sure if she said anything or not, but he cried aloud in his dream and thought that he could

[1]This memory was as a screen memory, one that contained earlier wishes to be heard or "read" in a way that could have made him feel safe or complete. The use of the memory in this interpretation ought not be viewed as an attempt to reconstruct a traumatic experience that was responsible for the patient's current difficulties.

never do that in her actual presence. After a brief silence the therapist asked him what he made of the dream. He said that the crying brought him a sense of relief and happiness that he could do it. The therapist added to this that apparently there was a precondition to his ability to cry: He had the therapist stand right next to him, kind of trapped in the small area between his chair, the wall, and the desk. Did he have any thoughts about that? To him, the patient said, it meant that he still resisted closeness. This interpretation, in light of the actual content of the dream, in which the patient had had the therapist as close to him as possible, needed further exploration. Thus, the therapist wondered whether or not the dream might indicate that, at least in his sleep, he had overcome the fear of closeness, and that, as a matter of fact, he was able to experience her presence so close to him precisely because, in the past, she had not responded to his invitations to do battle with him, which would have reinforced his fear of closeness. Could it be, she said, that what made it possible for him to cry was the safety that he could now feel because, rather than being engaged in a battle, the two of them were able to understand where the persistent wish that she know everything he thought and felt came from? As the therapist spoke, the patient's face darkened, and it became obvious that he was trying to hold back tears. Neither of them spoke and the tears eventually began to flow down his cheeks. It took him some time to reach for a tissue; when he did, he looked up at the therapist. She then said that her way of understanding his dream must have been experienced by him as if she had just come over "to his side." Very quickly and quietly he said "yes," and after another brief silence, with the end of the hour, he left the office.

REFLECTIONS ON THE CLINICAL EPISODE— THE INTERPRETIVE PROCESS

The first task of the therapist whose therapeutic attitude and mode of interpretation are informed by self psychology is to ascertain the patient's affective and cognitive state and, correlatively, the way in which the therapist is being experienced by the patient so as to understand the effect of that experience, in turn, on the patient's state (Schwaber, 1982). This task can only be achieved in an ongoing dialogue in which the therapist offers her understanding *tentatively* as to what goes on in the patient's mind. It is the patient who has to help the therapist grasp the nuances of his self experiences—the momentary experiences as well as those the patient describes from the past. On this level of communication, the therapist may not yet be ready to give meaning to the patient's self experiences; she is merely checking whether or not she has understood what the patient has intended to say. The therapist's tentativeness is indicated by the way in which she makes her statements. In the treatment described above, the therapist said: "What I hear you say is that you are hoping I would, in a very active way, interact with you, so that in this once-a-week therapy, you can be assured that we will be able to 'unearth' the feelings that are hidden from you." This kind of communication aims at establishing a therapeutic dialogue which, even though it has a therapeutic effect in its own right, is only the beginning of a more comprehensive interpretive process. Articulating her understanding on this level, the therapist was only restating what the patient was conscious of. What about the unconscious affects? Don't they have to be exposed exactly in the manner in which the patient wanted them exposed, by removing the repression barrier and the other defenses that keep them hidden in the unconscious? Articulating the patient's experiences in such a way that the patient is able to confirm them would be considered by many, as it was by the patient, "saying only the obvious."

Schwaber (1977), in her discussion of the paper to which I referred earlier, asked the following pertinent questions regarding empathic communication: "When we say we are being empathic with our patients—empathic to what and at what level? Is it to what the patient is revealing or to what he is concealing; to what is consciously or preconsciously put forward or to what is being repressed; to his infantile yearnings or to the adult side of him that wishes to master these; and if our empathy is directed toward the infantile ones, along which axis, the narcissistic or the object-related; and to which elements

within him—the babe, the toddler, the schoolboy; to the curative wish he proposes or to what *we* think he should get from his
therapy?" (p. 365).

Schwaber's observation is an important one. It raises the
question as to how the empathic mode of listening and interpretation can encompass that aspect of the psyche with
which the patient cannot resonate at that moment because it is
split off or repressed. I would respond by saying that clinical
experiences such as my patient's recall of a dream at a particular moment in the hour indicate that empathic understanding
creates an increase in self-cohesion which enhances mental
functioning and makes defensive operations less necessary. In
the treatment reported in the vignette, the increase in self-
cohesion was the result, I would suggest, of a silent merger
transference that had become established in the course of the
therapeutic dialogue, as the therapist succeeded in communicating her progressively more comprehensive understanding
to the patient. It was on the heels of an interpretation expressing this more comprehensive understanding that the patient
was able to recall a dream the content of which indicated that
such a transference was indeed in existence—more specifically,
that having the therapist "on his side" was a precondition for
his ability to cry. This increase in the consolidation of the self
appears to enable patients to experience and explore affects
they could not tolerate previously, either because of their intensity or because of their particular content: jealousy, rivalry,
hostility, love, sadness, guilt, shame. The exploration of these
affects—and their gradual acceptance by patients as their
own—constitutes the second part of the interpretive process:
the exploration and acceptance of the repressed and split-off
part of the psyche.

I shall now indicate, though only in a tentative way, how the
part of the treatment described above facilitated the understanding of my patient's presenting complaints, and how his
childhood memories contributed to this understanding.

As a child, the patient had been a "good boy." When, at age
eleven, he was sent away to a boarding school, he did not cry or
express disappointment. By then, he had become successful in
isolating his affects. That isolation of affect, among other de-

fenses, prevented him from mourning his father's loss. In his treatment, he wanted to overcome this sense of isolation; he entered therapy with a curative fantasy representing his wish for "a new beginning" and an activation of his "thwarted need to grow": The fantasy that the therapist would know all of his hidden feelings and thoughts and that this would protect him from her acting toward him in a way that could be painful to him. Thorough understanding of this fantasy helped the patient overcome the sense of isolation he had experienced in his childhood. The memory of his wish that his parents had known how he had felt when he was sent off to boarding school served as a screen for his feeling that, in a more general way, they had been indifferent to his emotions.

SUMMARY

I have discussed a short segment of a treatment process to demonstrate some aspects of the contribution of self psychology to psychoanalytic psychotherapy. The clinical episode illustrates that the empathic listening position and the interpretive mode of intervention were increasingly able to explore deeper layers of the patient's psychopathology.

I have also offered a tentative explanation of the manner in which the deepening of the therapeutic experience occurred in spite of the fact that empathic interpretations could not directly articulate the repressed and otherwise split-off parts of the psyche. Clinical observation supports the proposition that the patient's experience of the therapist as a selfobject results in a temporary increase in the patient's self-cohesion, one that makes defensive operations less necessary. Under these circumstances, the patient is able to experience affects which he had previously repressed and/or disavowed because of their threat to his self-cohesion.

This explanation, though offered from a very different theoretical perspective, is similar to Kris's explanation of "the good analytic hour" (1950). In Kris's view, the therapist's interpretations do not "provide insight." Rather, it is the patient's own preconscious mental processes that mediate and integrate the analyst's interpretations in the process of achieving insight. The essential aspect of the therapeutic work is therefore done silently, outside of the analyst's awareness in the patient's own preconscious thought processes.

My patient's use of the therapist as a selfobject similarly occurred silently, permitting him to experience affects that had been warded off before. This view of the treatment process would thus suggest a very different meaning to the waiting-room fantasy from the one that I suggested earlier. Rather than interpreting the fantasy as one in which the patient "buys himself the license" to express his dammed-up aggression and hostility, we can now recognize in the fantasy an effort on the patient's part to respond to the therapist's dreaded indifference and noninvolvement in a way in which he could not respond to his environment as a child. The waiting-room fantasy was an aspect of his curative fantasy: He hoped that in his treatment experience his anger and indignation would force the therapist to recognize his feelings and break through the sense of isolation he had experienced within himself as well as in relationship to his immediate emotional environment.

REFERENCES

Kris, E. (1950). On preconscious mental processes. *Psychoanal. Quart.*, 19:540–560.

Ornstein, P. & Ornstein, A. (1977). On the continuing evolution of psychoanalytic psychotherapy: Reflections and predictions. *The Annual of Psychoanalysis*, 5:329–370.

Schwaber, E. (1977). Discussion of "On the Continuing Evolution of Psychoanalytic Psychotherapy: Reflections and Predictions," by P. Ornstein & A. Ornstein. *The Annual of Psychoanalysis*, 5:329–370.

_____ (1982). Psychoanalytic listening and psychic reality (unpublished manuscript).

12

Self Psychology and Psychotherapy

Discussion of "Selfobjects, Development, and Psychotherapy," by Michael Franz Basch, and "Psychoanalytic Psychotherapy: A Contemporary Perspective," by Anna Ornstein

Frank M. Lachmann, Ph.D.

THE TWO PAPERS under discussion have addressed certain aspects of the distinction between psychotherapy and psychoanalysis. Dr. Ornstein has reiterated an argument which she and Paul Ornstein advanced in a previous paper (1977) in which they placed psychoanalysis, psychotherapy, and focal psychotherapy on a continuum. A decisive characteristic of these treatment modalities, according to the Ornsteins, is the essentially interpretive nature of the communications to the patient. In contrast stand the non-psychoanalytic psychotherapies in which, as Dr. Basch has suggested, the "baby is thrown out with the bathwater." What remains in the tub are manipulative techniques, support, reassurance, direction, and advice. I should like here to consider the relationship between psychotherapy and psychoanalysis and the role of interpretation in the treatment process in the light of the recent contributions of self psychology.

The therapist's selfobject function, and the use of the empathic mode, are by now well-recognized features of the self-psychological method. Explicating these issues in the context of Dr. Ornstein's vignette may help to clarify some of the practical clinical applications of self psychology to psychotherapy.

The extent to which Ornstein's patient presented himself as a "guilty man" is striking. He confesses his crimes—his present-day selfishness, his "resistance" in treatment, his childhood sexual fantasies about his older sister. His expectation that treatment will be based on his sense of guilt coincides, as Ornstein points out, with a view of psychopathology prevalent in the mental health community. But from the vantage point of self psychology, Ornstein's patient may have been using his sexual fantasies, and indeed his sense of guilt, to organize his self experience (Stolorow and Lachmann, 1980, especially Chapter 8). He may thus have been able to sustain certain idealizations of his parents (or mask his disillusionment with them) so as to maintain self-cohesion in the face of the devastating abandonment fears that surfaced later in the treatment and that were telescoped in the memory of the "tragic" event of his being sent to boarding school. By not committing herself prematurely to the patient's view of himself as guilty, Ornstein enabled the deeper issue to emerge. Thus, when the patient stated his belief that the waiting-room fantasy was evidence of his resistance, Ornstein responded by saying that his concern over his resistance had "helped her appreciate his hope and expectation. . . ."

In effect, Ornstein conveys to her patient that she sees him as more than simply a "resister." She sees him as a person who has hopes and expectations. She thereby offers him a broader perspective within which he might view himself. Later, when the patient reports a dream and again interprets it in terms of his resistance, Ornstein interprets it differently, as evidence of his progress in overcoming his fear of closeness. In both cases, she acknowledges developmental strivings and advances rather than concurring with the patient's narrow view of himself (see Lachmann and Stolorow, 1980).

These dramatic interchanges embody the essence of the self-psychological perspective on human nature. In neither intervention did Ornstein simply reflect back to the patient what he had consciously presented to her. Rather, she held and presented to her patient a somewhat more organized, somewhat more cohesive, somewhat more positively colored, somewhat more articulated view of himself than he had presented. It was a view not so experience-distant that he could not resonate with it but just far enough ahead so that he could move to accept it and, in so doing, alter his self perception and self experience. The empathic mode of listening to and understanding the patient enabled Ornstein to frame her interventions at this optimal level.

The aspects of the therapeutic process in which the patient experienced Ornstein as performing a vital selfobject function can be conceptualized as follows:

(1) The therapist held up to the patient a slightly more organized view of himself than the patient held of himself at that moment. The parallel to the mother-infant relationship should be apparent. Basch refers to Kohut's (1977) concept of the infant's "virtual self"—the infant as an individual as he exists in the mind of his parents. The slightly more organized view of the child or patient as held by the parent or therapist provides a requisite impetus for maturation and/or structuralization (see also Loewald, 1980).

(2) The use of the empathic mode enabled Ornstein to understand and address her patient's concern over his "resistiveness" as evidence of his developmental strivings rather than as evidence of his wrongdoing and guilt. The patient was understood as a "tragic man" rather than a "guilty man."

Have psychotherapists implicitly treated their patients according to the tenets of self psychology? They probably have. If parents are able intuitively to further their infants' development by holding a slightly more organized view of them, we should expect no less of the intuition of therapists. Spelling out the link between the therapist's and the parent's selfobject functions should place our treatment on a firmer scientific basis, though the research on infant development, so far as I know, has not yet provided us with the necessary carefully controlled observations in support of this hypothesized link. Such research *does* offer compelling evidence that the infant is indeed capable of taking his parent as a selfobject. Recent findings point undeniably to the conclusion that the infant is capable of entering into complex transactions at an earlier age than had previously been postulated. Whereas Freud's "narcissistic" infant had to give way to Mahler's "symbiotic" infant, the latter now has to give way to the infant "prepared and eager for transactions with his environment," as Basch puts it.

To return to Ornstein's paper, had she not identified her vignette as having been drawn from a once-a-week psychotherapy, and had not this very issue of frequency appeared specifically in the content of one of the sessions, I believe it would have been difficult to infer from the material and her way of working with it that the patient was indeed seen but once a week. This suggests, I think, a basic truth which self psychology has to offer about the nature of psychoanalysis and psychoanalytically oriented insight therapy. These forms of treatment cannot be distinguished from nonanalytic therapies on the mechanical basis of frequency, nor solely on the technical bases of interpretation, abstinence, and so on. What self psychology tells us is that it is the therapist's *stance* vis-á-vis the patient that determines the analytic or nonanalytic nature of the treatment. Indeed, I would classify Ornstein's responses to her patient not as interpretations in the narrow sense but as "unifications" (Gedo and Goldberg, 1973). That is, the patient was dominated by a self fragment of "resistiveness" or "guiltiness" for which the therapist provided a broader context, a more benign and complex model of his self organization, thereby promoting a developmental advance. And I believe that this was the appropriate therapeutic response whether the patient was seen once a week or five times a week. It should also be apparent that the response to the patient's archaic selfobject transference required more of the therapist than noninterference with its establishment and maintenance. Legitimate noninterpretive activity cuts across the psychotherapy-psychoanalysis boundaries when selfobject functions are addressed.

As Basch's vignette illustrates, analysts have traditionally considered the gratification of infantile wishes a central danger to be avoided in the therapeutic setting. This danger must now be balanced against the equal danger of frustrating developmental strivings and inadequately acknowledging developmental advances. Traditional technique carries with it the danger of inadvertently repeating in the analysis the traumata that precipitated the patient's pathology—that is, when developmentally arrested configurations are misunderstood as structural conflict. The treatments of Miss F. and of Ornstein's patient illustrate that careful attention to the patient can provide the analyst with a grasp of the clinical material that makes it possible to avoid this danger.

One often-cited difference between psychotherapy and psychoanalysis is that supportive and educative comments are supposed to be more characteristic of psychotherapy. In turn, it is believed that such comments can confound the transference and thus preclude a genuine analysis. But such "manipulative" comments are not an intrinsic aspect of psychotherapy, as Ornstein's case shows. Moreover, such comments *do* occur in analyses, though their occurrence may not always be reported in the analytic literature. When they occur, they can be explored with respect to their meaning to the patient and their effect on the treatment. Certainly, the less frequent visits of the therapy patient as compared with the analysand may affect the transference and the other material that emerges. Less frequent visits often make it more difficult for the therapist to grasp the nature of the transference and its historical roots. The analyst is often in a better position to grasp the crucial childhood events that underly the patient's conflicts. This distinction, however, is only quantitative, affecting the content to which attention is most often directed. The stance of the clinician and his functions vis-á-vis the patient remain unchanged.

Drs. Basch and Ornstein have described the contributions of self psychology to the practice of psychotherapy from very different vantage points, and yet without contradicting each other. One might almost say that the more analysts learn about self psychology and about their function as selfobjects in treatment, the better they will be at practicing psychotherapy. To the analyst's role of interpretation we must add other therapeutic functions of which the selfobject function is perhaps the most crucial. The use of the analyst as a selfobject by patients at various levels of psychic organization has roots in earliest infancy as a releasor of maturational progressions. It thus transcends the role of interpretations, a point with important implications for the future of our methods of treatment.

REFERENCES

Gedo, J., & Goldberg, A. (1973). *Models of the Mind.* Chicago: University of Chicago Press.

Kohut, H. (1977). *The Restoration of the Self.* New York: International Universities Press.

Lachmann, F., & Stolorow, R. (1980). The developmental significance of affective states: Implications for psychoanalytic treatment. *The Annual of Psychoanalysis,* 8:215–229.

Loewald, H. (1980). *Papers on Psychoanalysis.* New Haven: Yale University Press.

Ornstein, P., & Ornstein, A. (1977). On the continuing evolution of psychoanalytic psychotherapy: Reflections and predictions. *The Annual of Psychoanalysis,* 5:329–370.

Stolorow, R., & Lachmann, F. (1980). *Psychoanalysis of Developmental Arrests: Theory and Treatment.* New York: International Universities Press.

IV SELF-PSYCHOLOGICAL APPLICATIONS: DIRECTIONS FOR FUTURE RESEARCH

13

Self Psychology: A New Conceptualization For the Understanding of Learning-Disabled Children

Estelle Shane, Ph.D.

I FIRST BECAME INTERESTED in learning-disabled children several years ago when, on reviewing the case histories of such children, I was struck by the number of early developmental difficulties and/or traumatic experiences in the population. All of the children had exhibited some emotional distress. Most came from homes disrupted by divorce or death of a parent, several had psychotic mothers or fathers, and some had histories of serious illness requiring hospitalization.

The learning problems of children with emotional difficulties have been studied in the past using traditional psychoanalytic formulations (e.g., Abrams, 1980). I shall focus here on the contribution of self psychology to our understanding of the learning process, and, in particular, on how self psychology illuminates data derived from empirically based psychological and educational research regarding the learning-disabled child. Such an undertaking is important if only because it is relatively rare in educational circles to investigate the social and emotional problems of the learning-disabled youngster. Once a child is diagnosed as having a learning disability, psychological and sociological aspects tend to be overlooked, perhaps because of the urgency of the need to correct the failed learning process. And yet, parents and educators alike believe that emotional issues are central to learning. In a survey I conducted among parents and teachers, self-esteem—a consistent and dependable regard for and pride in oneself—ranked first in a field of twenty-five cognitive and affective attainments as that deemed most important to the learning process. Self psychology has much to say about self-esteem and self-esteem regulation, and if only for that reason should be worth exploring in terms of its application to learning difficulties.

Attentional capacities, too, are obviously important to the ability to learn. It is my contention here that such capacities are integrally related to the development of the self, attributable in large measure to the adequacy of the mother-child relationship. The mother who elicits and sustains the child's attention and who joins the child in his activities is fostering, in a most vital way, the child's skills and abilities in this regard. Self psychology's focus on the mother-child unit is thus relevant here as well.

In most basic outline, self psychology posits a "nuclear self," the earliest form of which is expressed in a characteristic form of behavior: The infant places himself squarely in the middle of his world. His mother is mainly viewed as within his self orbit, a satellite serving his needs—an archaic "selfobject," perceived by the young child as without a separate locus of intentionality. The child at this stage of development is said to possess a "grandiose self," not only because he sees himself as the center of the universe, but also because he is, in his own view, all-powerful in controlling that universe. Parental responses of pride and admiration "mirror" the child's grandiosity, and cause him to feel loved. Parents unconsciously encourage the development of those aspects of the child's personality in which they can feel genuine pride, and ignore, even discourage, other aspects for which they can feel no such genuine admiration. On the basis of their general attitude, one aspect of the child's self—his goals and ambitions—develops.

It is also important during this phase of development that parents provide the necessary strength and security to sustain and soothe the child. To this end, and in support of the development of a second aspect of the child's self—his ideals and standards—parents allow themselves to be idealized for their qualities of omnipotence and omniscience. In this way, they function as "idealized parental imagos." In a slow, well-timed process called "optimal disillusionment," the child gradually disabuses himself of his notions of parental omnipotence and omniscience, and comes to be able to do for himself what his parents must inevitably fail to be able to do for him. He learns to comfort himself when his parents are absent. He learns to believe in his own ability when his parents have not provided him with sufficient emotional support. These capacities are borrowed from the parents by means of "transmuting internalizations": Self structures are transformed in response to optimal (non-traumatic) frustration. Thus, as the child slowly becomes disillusioned of his parents' omnipotence, he replaces it with his own competence. By such means, structure is built and functions previously supplied by the parents are gradually internalized to become the ideals, ambitions, and skills of the nuclear self.

Self psychology thus proposes a "bipolar" model of the self: at one pole ambitions, at the other ideals, and mediating between the two skills and talents. When the self possesses the talents and skills necessary to satisfy its ideals by achieving its ambitions, self-esteem is maintained. Conversely, when the self lacks such talents and skills, and its ambitions are not achieved, shame and humiliation result, often globally described as loss of self-esteem.

Of course, ambitions are both innate and learned. A healthy curiosity and fascination with novelty is found in every normally developing infant. Ideals, too, develop from the beginning of life, with the experience of the ideal state of satiation and comfort, and with the beginning sense of omnipotence. Skills and talents are obviously inherent to an extent. But environment, especially the parental environment, modifies these primitive ambitions, ideals, and talents, and instills new ones. The more empathic the parent, moreover, the more smoothly will ambitions, ideals, and talents interdigitate, maintaining an optimal balance among them. Ambitions, thus, will not be so pressing in the child that they are consistently unsatisfied, ideals will not be set so unrealistically high that no performance can satisfy. On the contrary, ambitions will be matched with skills and talents that permit the attainment of reasonably demanding ideals. A parent in good empathic contact with the child can sense when he can achieve for himself, and when he needs just the right amount of help. The child thus learns when it is reasonable to expect to accomplish on his own, and when it is appropriate, without a sense of shame or humiliation, to ask for and expect help from others. He is capable of functioning without his mother's physical presence. He is self-confident, ambitious, reasonably tolerant of himself and of his occasional need for help, able to expect success and to endure failure. He is, in short, a child with adequate self-esteem and adequate capacity to attend to the learning process.

What goes on to produce a different kind of child, prone to learning difficulties? It goes without saying that for some children innate factors play the largest part. The development of certain skills and talents depends heavily on innate endowment (perceptual development, language acquisition, gross and fine motor coordination, etc.). These capacities are all dependent upon neurological adequacy for their optimal development. But even where there is neurological adequacy, children may fail to acquire the skills necessary for the achievement of ambitions and ideals. In large part, I believe, this can be attributed to failures of transmuting internalization.

A child who has been neither empathically mirrored nor optimally disillusioned may seek continuously for gratification of his grandiosity. Archaically self-centered, he does not appreciate, in an age-appropriate way, the competing needs and rights of others. He cannot take another's point of view or exercise even minimal empathy. Once in school, he may persist in a grandiose fantasy in which he omnipotently attains his ambitions without acquiring the skills that would allow realistic success. He appears to expect to achieve without work, and to receive praise from the teacher for minimal effort and achievements, just as praise was carelessly given or denied at home, praise unrelated to real accomplishment. At school he experiences the pain of loss of self-esteem when his grandiose fantasies are deflated. He seems arrested in the development of that pole of the self encompassing goals and ambitions.

Similarly, a child with unrealistically high ideals may unconsciously set standards for himself so unreasonable that he experiences a chronic sense of failure. Such children are often precocious in their development. Their skills and talents may be above average, but their standards and ideals always exceed them. They worry a great deal and are nagged with doubts and fears of failure. They will try nothing until they are certain of success, and take little pleasure in learning. From the point of view of the casual observer, self-esteem in these children is unaccountably low. Most likely they have had parents who, because of their own low self-esteem, have narcissistically disparaged them. These children, too, are unready for school and suffer shame and humiliation from failure to live up to the ideals of the nuclear self.

Empirical studies have shown significant correlations between self-esteem, "learning motivation," and "learning achievement." In one study, Lefcourt (1976) applied "attribution theory" to an investigation of the perception of causality in youngsters—judgements on the part of the learner as to why a particular action resulted in success or failure. Attribution of causality was shown to be related to subsequent behavior. Depending upon whether a child placed the locus of control inside or outside himself, he was prone either to strive to achieve or to allow failure (inevitably) to occur. In a related set of studies, Bryan and Bryan (1981) have demonstrated that children judged to have low self-esteem viewed their own efforts as having little influence on outcome; chance or luck ruled in their eyes. Children with high self-esteem, on the other hand, attributed the outcome of an event to their own efforts and abilities. Chance or luck did not figure into their attribution of causality. In a third set of studies, Ruble and Boggiano (1980) investigated the attitudes of students described as having high achievement motivation—or desire to succeed. These students, like those described as having high self-esteem, attributed their success in an activity to their own ability and/or effort. Failures on their part were perceived as due to their own lack of effort. Students low in achievement motivation, on the other hand, just like those with low self-esteem, attributed their success in an activity to good luck, ease of task, or another's relative stupidity. Such differences in achievement motivation are apparently determined by causal attributions. To the extent that a child feels he can affect the outcome of an event by his own efforts or abilities, to that extent he is motivated to achieve; when outcome is attributed to chance or circumstance, motivation to achieve is lacking. What occurs in the latter group of children is termed, in educational circles, "learned helplessness" (Seligman, 1975). These youngsters become increasingly convinced that they are victims of circumstance. When left to choose their own tasks, they choose those either too easy or too difficult. By contrast, those with high motivation are likely to initiate achievement activities; that is, they work with greater intensity, persist longer in the face of failure, and choose more tasks of moderate difficulty, so that success is assured, gratification achieved, and attribution of control in themselves confirmed.

A child who attributes his performance to luck can perhaps best be understood as one whose sense of self is not cohesive. He does not see himself as the possessor of his own skills and talents, does not experience his ambitions as predictably attainable, and cannot reward himself for living up to his ideals. We might say that this child's attribution of success or failure to luck is a reflection of the experience of capricious parental support, that which encouraged and rewarded arbitrarily or inconstantly. Thus, the mother who lacks empathy with her child cannot consistently mirror his developing grandiosity with her own pride in him and what he does, and provide timely support, encouragement, and reward for his later performance; and cannot consistently afford to the child appropriate opportunities to idealize her so that, through optimal disillusionment, he can acquire appropriate ideals for himself. The child's shaky, or even fragmented, sense of self then leads him to attribute control and order to the outside world. Effort on his part becomes pointless. His conviction that all order and control exists outside himself is inevitably reflected in, and subsequently confirmed by, his school performance.

Recent empirical educational research has also focused on the social and emotional side of learning disabilities. Educators have always had difficulty in distinguishing between children with learning difficulties and those with emotional difficulties.

Once a child is designated learning disabled, as opposed to emotionally disturbed, the emotional and social difficulties experienced by the youngster are often ignored, both in the educational literature and in the classroom. A recent surge of interest in the social and emotional side of the learning-disabled child, however, has yielded some interesting data. Investigators (e.g., Bryan and Bryan, 1981) have listed the difficulties of such children as including, in addition to academic failure, a remarkably consistent cluster: rejection by classmates, rejection by teachers, and difficulty in interpreting the nonverbal social communications of others. Some of these investigators have attempted to study why the learning-disabled child should be so universally rejected, and why he should be unable to infer meaning from the behavior of his peers.

Bryan's studies (1974, 1977), based on observations of interactions between the learning-disabled child and his peers and teachers, reveal that children with learning difficulties consistently say socially insensitive things. Bryan concludes that the learning-disabled child has as much trouble reading people as he does books, and that this may be the reason behind the notable dislike which people of all ages appear to have for the educationally handicapped youngster.

Again we can turn to self-psychological formulations for an explanation of the apparent insensitivity of these children to others. Earlier I referred to the normal development of the self through a stage of archaic grandiosity in which the child views himself at the center of the universe. At this stage others do not have needs or rights of their own, and it is impossible for the child to take their points of view or to empathize with their feelings. It may be that the learning-disabled child is arrested, in part, at this early stage of development, and cannot see his teachers or peers as existing for any reason other than to help and support him, at all times and exclusively. In self-psychological terms, he is incapable of mature selfobject relationships. He is arrested at the level of archaic selfobjects. Thus, he says things to others which have the effect of hurting them because he disregards completely their separateness and individuality. Indeed, the responses of classmates and teachers to the learn-

ing-disabled child are remarkably similar to those of psychotherapists to patients who suffer from such disorders of the
self. In Bryan's studies, teachers and children report feeling
ignored and disrespected—in effect, as if their existence were
of no consequence to the child. The ordinary human response
to one who engenders such feelings is boredom, irritation, and
emotional withdrawal. Bryan and Bryan (1981) have suggested
that the dislike of the teacher for the educationally handicapped child should not be denied by the teacher, but rather be
used as a means of differential diagnosis, to help in the handicapped learner's identification. All of this is virtually identical
with what Kohut (1971, 1977) has described as the experience
of the therapist in working with patients who have disorders of
the self, and with his suggestions for utilizing countertransference responses for differential diagnosis. Therapists who
work with patients arrested at levels of archaic grandiosity find
themselves unreasonably angry and rejecting of such patients
for unearthing their own frustrated grandiose wishes. Having
rejected these wishes in themselves, they unconsciously reject
them in their patients. Once the countertransference response
has been understood and mastered by the therapist, he is then
in a position to help the patient express, understand, and master what would otherwise be the cause of the patient's rejection
by others. Teachers, too, might benefit from the same kind of
self-understanding to work more effectively with learning-disabled children.

Kohut elaborated two types of transferences formed in the
therapeutic situation by individuals suffering from disorders of
the self. In the "mirror transference," the analyst is viewed by
the patient not as a person in his own right, but instead as an
archaic selfobject whose function is but to mirror the grandiosity of his patient. When the therapist fails in this function,
as inevitably he must from time to time, he is met with narcissistic rage or with arrogant withdrawal. His countertransference
response to such a patient—which response is used as a diagnostic tool—is that of irritation and even anger at being treated
as if he did not exist outside the patient's orbit.

The second category of transference is that of the "idealized
parental imago." The therapist is viewed as an omnipotent and

omniscient protective figure to be utilized by the patient as a source of calmness, comfort, and organization. The countertransference response on the part of the therapist is one of anxiety and uneasiness. He does not wish to be so idealized, since this idealization is at variance with his own more realistic self-assessment. If the therapist has not come to terms with his own grandiosity, he may find such adulation unduly exciting and may try to correct the patient's view of him, thereby bringing the idealization to a premature closure. Awareness of the temptation to correct the patient's misperception becomes a diagnostic tool, pointing to the nature of the transference involved.

A knowledge of these transference and countertransference configurations might be useful in dealing with the learning-disabled child. Knowledge of transference in general has been helpful to educators. Alpert (1959) described corrective object relationships whereby developmental arrests of children were dealt with not by reliving in the transference of the therapeutic situation, but in the context of the child's living with a surrogate parent. The teacher-parent surrogate provided what had been missing in the child's life—love, attention, direction, etc. Although the method did not involve interpretation of the transference, it did require an understanding of the transference needs of the child and their judicious gratification in the nontherapeutic setting. Psychoeducators, too, utilizing psychoanalytic understanding, have provided parental functions for children who needed it in special school settings.

It seems not unreasonable to me to consider applying the special transference configurations delineated by self psychology to work with the learning disabled. An educator could well expect to be placed in the role of a mirroring selfobject by such a child, just as a therapist is by his patient. Rather than react with anger and rejection, he might be able not only to tolerate but utilize his special role to facilitate the child's development. In other words, I am suggesting that knowledge of this special role not only be used for diagnosis, but consciously for meliorative purposes. The teacher might thereby provide the empathic mirroring respones so necessary for the development of self-esteem in these children.

There is an extensive literature in educational psychology devoted to the role of the teacher in determining the success or failure of the child. Such studies have sought to demonstrate the power of self-fulfilling prophecy. Ever since Rosenthal and Jacobson published *Pygmalion in the Classroom* (1968), describing an experiment in which teachers were advised that randomly selected students could be expected to achieve because of very high I.Q.'s and then those students *did* achieve as if that were so, the literature has been replete with subsequent studies questioning, refuting, replicating, and validating the self-fulfilling-prophecy thesis. Whatever the ultimate verdict, teachers' attitudes toward children must clearly be important to some degree in determining children's performances in the present, and even, to some extent, in the future. The effective teacher, I would suggest, becomes a selfobject for the child, providing him with a mirroring experience. By enhancing the child's grandiosity in this manner, he allows the child to work with greater vigor, self-confidence, and with higher self-esteem than he would have otherwise. Conversely, a teacher who looks down upon a student undermines his grandiosity, diminishing his self-confidence and self-esteem.

Finally, while it is not so obviously reported in the literature of psychological and educational research, it is even more common for the teacher to become an idealized parental imago for the child. That is, the teacher is perceived by the child as embodying ideals and standards the child thinks of as his own, though he recognizes, at least partially, that they are actually embodied in the other. A teacher who too quickly disillusions the child, not permitting the idealization to blossom, destroys what might otherwise have become a helpful relationship, one which might have led to the student's acquiring, through transmuting internalization, ideals and standards truly his own. Kohut has demonstrated that such selfobject relationships remain important right into adult life, for it is through such relationships that a healthy self continues to develop.

REFERENCES

Abrams, J. C. (1980). A psychodynamic understanding of the emotional aspects of learning disability. In *Advances in Special Education:*

Perspectives on Applications, Vol. 2, ed. B. K. Keogh. Greenwich, Conn.: J.A.I. Press.

Alpert, A. (1959). Reversibility of pathological fixations associated with maternal deprivation in infancy. *The Psychoanalytic Study of the Child,* 14:169–185.

Bryan, T. H. (1974). An observational analysis of classroom behaviors of children with learning disabilities. *J. Learn.Dis.,* 7:26–34.

_____ (1977). Learning disabled children: Comprehension of nonverbal communication. *J. Learn. Dis.,* 10:501–506.

_____ & Bryan, J. H. (1981). Some personal and social experiences of learning disabled children. In *Advances in Special Education: Socialization Influences on Exceptionalities,* Vol. 3., ed. E. K. Keogh. Greenwich, Conn.: J.A.I. Press.

Kohut, H. (1971). *The Analysis of the Self.* New York: International Universities Press.

_____ (1977). *The Restoration of the Self.* New York: International Universities Press.

Lefcourt, H. M. (1976). *Locus of Control: Current Trends in Theory and Research.* Hillsdale, N.J.: Erlbaum.

Rosenthal, R. & Jacobson, L. (1968). *Pygmalion in the Classroom: Teacher Expectation and Pupils' Intellectual Development.* New York: Holt, Rinehart & Winston.

Ruble, D. N. & Boggiano, A. K. (1980). Optimizing motivation in an achievement context. In *Advances in Special Education: Basic Constructs and Theoretical Orientations,* Vol. 1, ed. B. K. Keogh. Greenwich, Conn.: J.A.I. Press.

Seligman, M. E. P. (1975). *Helplessness: On Depression, Development, and Death.* San Francisco: Freeman.

14

The Self in a Small Group: A Comparison of the Theories of Bion and Kohut

Lars B. Lofgren, M.D.

THE "TAVISTOCK" SMALL group, or study group, inspired by the work of Wilfred R. Bion, has been described extensively in recent literature (e.g., Bion, 1959; Rice, 1965; Rioch, 1970a, b, 1971; O'Connor, 1971). Bion was an officer in the British army during the Second World War assigned to a hospital treating cases of various "war neuroses." Since the hospital was under-staffed, Bion developed the idea of using the organization itself as a therapeutic modality. The results were convincing enough to make him interested in continuing to work with groups and in trying to understand the psychological dynamics of the groups in which he was the professional member. According to Bion (personal communication), the therapeutic rationale for such groups was that they allowed members to work through anxieties created by relations to part objects. As a group phenomenon, such part object relations were mainly expressed as "Basic Assumptions," to which I shall return later. Bion's thinking deeply influenced professionals at the Tavistock Centre for Applied Social Research, especially Rice. He and his co-workers were responsible for developing the Tavistock group, mainly as part of a residential conference designed to serve as a working model for organizational consultation. During this process the groups came to lose their former aspect as therapy groups. Instead, they were seen as singularly effective didactic devices, designed to illustrate in a convincing way the obstacles that make efficient work in groups and organizations so difficult. The groups came to be described by some members as "a crash course in the unconscious." Therapeutic intention was denied and therapeutic result regarded as purely accidental. The group came to be thought of as especially suitable for the study of a certain type of group process in that it represented a situation that in several important respects is fairly standardized.

The typical group consists of twelve members and the task of the group is to study its own behavior in the *here and now* with the aid of a consultant. The members are usually professionals who desire to learn something about Tavistock groups. They are chosen to maximize heterogeneity as far as profession, sex, age, etc., are concerned. The consultant is specially trained, and guided in his behavior by rigid instructions. He is not allowed to do anything that in his opinion does not facilitate the learning that takes place around the task of the group. In keeping with this limited role, he rarely answers questions, avoids eye contact with the members, is absolutely punctual, and does not announce his arrival and departure in a verbal way. He tries to locate himself cognitively and emotionally at a point equidistant to all the members, thus trying to evaluate the role of the silent as well as the talkative members. He addresses himself only to group processes, seeing personal action in terms of what it represents for the group and not in terms of individual motivation.

Although this definition of the consultant's role is clearly derived from psychoanalytic technique, his behavior is even more rigidly defined than that of the analyst. The almost laboratory strictness of the definition leads to a situation in which certain events occur with great regularity in different groups with different consultants. As part of a total conference experience, the Tavistock study group meets for seven to fifteen sessions over a period of three to eight days. (Attempts have been made to arrange study group meetings weekly over an extended period of time but the dynamics of such groups have turned out not to be easy to understand.)

At the beginning of the first session, members are usually quite anxious and try various ways of dealing with the new situation. They introduce themselves to each other and then try to get the consultant to assume a position of leadership, locating in him all authority to perform the work. When this does not succeed, periods of desultory and confused actions follow. At times the group behaves in a more uniform fashion and certain patterns of action can be discerned. Thus, when all members join in an effort to get the consultant to lead the work, all may respond to their failure and to the surrender of their own competence with abject dependence. They then cast about for a member on whom to depend. Or they might unite in feelings of rage and try to destroy the task of the group, fight with the consultant, or fantasize about fleeing to the outside. Sometimes they try to encourage two members to join together in symbolic sexual union so as to provide a messianic solution for the future. These behaviors are periodically interrupted by an attempt to perform the work—that is, to study the behavior of the group. In the beginning these attempts are shortlived, and only increase toward the end of the study. Another way to avoid the strain of the group situation is to negate all individual differences in the group and enjoy a *unio mystica*, a thoughtless, problem-free bliss.

Bion (1959), after observing that these phenomena occurred with considerable regularity, made the first attempt to provide an explanation for them. He argued that even if a group has agreed to the assumption that they are coming together to do work, covert processes will tend to invalidate the overt assumption. Instead, the group manifests behavior similar to that described above. It lapses into dependency, rages about the task or tries to flee from it, and sometimes looks for a messianic leader. Bion pointed out that the group members behave as if they actually had met *to* depend on somebody, *to* fight or *to* flee, or *to* set up a pair to provide a future solution. Bion called these "Basic Assumptions" and described the three states that reflect them: "Basic Assumption Dependency," "Basic Assumption Fight-Flight," and "Basic Assumption Pairing." Basic Assumption Dependency is the state in which group members surrender their own competence and try to endow one person with the competence to carry out the task, with themselves as passive followers or spectators. Basic Assumption Fight-Flight describes a state wherein members look for leadership either to destroy the task or flee from it. Finally, Basic Assumption Pairing indicates a process whereby two members are especially endowed with the hope that they will produce a messianic leader or a solution in the future. Bion emphasized that all of the Basic Assumption Groups have an intense need for a leader—a leader designed to provide comfort and succor as in the dependency state, an action leader as in the fight-flight state, or a pair carrying the hope for the future as in the pairing state. It is characteristic of the Basic Assumptions that they appear only one at a time. When one of them is in ascendancy, they make the Work Group difficult or impossible. Sometimes they are partially manifested as when the Work Group is suffused by emotions generated by one of the Basic Assumptions. Further characteristics of Basic Assumption Groups include total resistance to development and lack of a time sense—that is, the Basic Assumption groups are in a certain sense always in session.

Bion saw these Basic Assumptions as originating from certain "protomental" states common to all persons. He visualized them as forming a matrix in which physical and mental are undifferentiated, and from which emotions flow to create the Basic Assumption Groups. According to Bion, the three Basic Assumption modes seem to represent aggregates of individuals who share between them qualities of one partner in the oedipal situation (the early Kleinian oedipal situation rather than the oedipal situation of classical psychoanalysis). The group is thought to stimulate in the minds of the participants a reexperiencing of the primitive primal scene, and the mechanisms of splitting and projective identification are used extensively in the process.

At least to a non-Kleinian, phantasies about the content of the mother's body seem to play little part in ordinary life, and most human interaction can hardly be described as a reenactment of the primitive primal scene. What then *are* the peculiar processes that cause these motivational factors to emerge in such groups?

It has already been observed that self psychology may be applicable to the understanding of group processes and may aid the therapist in formulating therapeutic strategies. Meyers

(1978) agrues that group therapy is an excellent vehicle for treating patients with self pathology who are otherwise not analyzable. He summarizes three distinct phases in the development of the therapeutic group process:

(1) The establishment of a cohesive group self by working through the resistances among group members to the loss of individual archaic grandiosity and/or to the fear of merger. This allows for the inherent push in groups to idealize the leader and the group.

(2) The establishment of the idealizing transference and the working through of the transference by transmuting internalization. The maturation and exposure to reality of the grandiose self occurs in this phase.

(3) The termination phase, which is crucial for solidifying structural change by the internalization of the idealized parental imago embodied by the therapist and the group.

Stone and Whitman (1977) point out how many group processes can be understood in the light of self psychology. They identify the way in which the need for mirroring appears in the group and leads to different manifestations of mirror transferences, including twinship and merger phenomena. Stressing the need to idealize the leader, Stone and Whitman cite the rage generated in a Tavistock training group when the leader did not live up to the idealizing expectations of the group members.

Gehrie (1980) points out how important it is that an individual receive phase-appropriate mirroring from a culturally cohesive ideology and have the opportunity to establish an idealized attachment to such a set of values. If this is lacking, the person may well experience a sense of rejection and isolation. Such processes should be considered in the context of both the small group and the therapy group, though at this stage their significance to such groups remains hypothetical.

KOHUT'S WORK

Kohut (1971) has pointed out that the self exposed to regressive pressures in the form of narcissistic injuries is liable to fragmentation. This fragmentation can be of various degrees, corresponding to the solidity of the self. Thus there are certain selves that even under strong pressure remain essentially cohesive and other selves that fragment even under relatively mild pressure; most selves occupy a position between these extremes. Especially conducive to narcissistic injury is the experience of lack of empathy. The experiential correlates to fragmentation are drops in self-esteem (sometimes covered over by grandiosity), narcissistic rage, disappearance of ambition, and hypochondriacal preoccupations, to mention some of the more important ones. Which features of a Tavistock group are conducive to regression and the experience of narcissistic injury because of a perceived lack of empathy?

Several factors can be pointed to in this respect. Most members come to the group with considerable fear of what is going to happen because most of them have been told gruesome stories by gleeful former participants. The task of studying its own behavior is difficult for the group to grasp, especially under these conditions. Members who have built part of their identity on laboriously achieved skills and who may enjoy quite some professional recognition feel that these skills are worth nothing in the present situation. Since the consultant does not respond to the desire for comfort and soothing, the only feedback is from members with similar experiences. A feedback situation is created that intensifies the discomfort and leads to increasing feelings of strangeness and vagueness. All these factors contribute to maintain an intense regressive pressure. Another important factor—perhaps the most important one—is located in the behavior of the consultant. As has been indicated, the consultant tries to locate himself at a point equidistant to the members of the group, and makes his interpretations from this vantage point, so that, in effect, *all* members will experience his interventions as profoundly unempathic. It is reasonable to assume that even in professional people (the usual members of a Tavistock group) the self contains both defensive and compensatory structures that are still not totally firmly entrenched. Thus the condition for regression of the self is present.

Kohut (1971) states that pressures on persons with narcissistic personality disorders can lead to a feeling of fragmentation "consisting specifically of a sense of separation of their self

experience from their various physical and mental functions"
(p. 97). This aptly describes the experience of the majority of
people in a small study group, although there is an occasional
individual who seems able to hold his personality together.
Thus, either the regressive pressure of the situation is unusually strong, or professional persons in general have enough
narcissistic difficulties to make such experiences possible. Both
are probably factors.

COMPARISON TO BION'S FORMULATIONS

Basic Assumption Dependency is a state in which group members feel helpless, incompetent, unskilled, and worthless. In
this situation they look for a leader to make things right again.
According to Bion (1959), the group tends to turn to the "sick-
est" person, preferably a hysterical psychopath. The state of the
members can be regarded as stemming from the narcissistic
injury experienced in the group and from a movement in the
direction of fragmentation of the selves involved, creating a
feeling of low self-esteem and an intense hunger for a selfobject
to restore cohesiveness to the self. The consultant is not available because of his limited role definition. In almost every
group, however, there is at least one member who in these
conditions can muster some overt grandiosity, even if he is not
quite a hysterical psychopath. This person becomes the leader
of the Basic Assumption Dependency Group. As he creates a
temporary feeling of cohesiveness, the members rally to some
extent. The grandiosity of the leader can seem quite promising.
Soon, however, the essential hollowness of his leadership becomes apparent. Disappointment and rage set in and the leader
is deposed. The group will then either look for a new leader or
switch to another Basic Assumption mode. It is interesting to
note how Kohut's vertical-horizontal split between overt and
covert grandiosity and a weak reality self is represented in the
group. In the group these aspects of the narcissistic personality
take on the quality of *social roles*. The consultant represents the
reality ego or self, but in a weak way because he is temporarily
discounted as not having magical powers. His attempts to de-

scribe what goes on from a realistic point of view fall on deaf ears.

In the Basic Assumption Fight-Flight Group, the members are filled with rage and a desire for action. The rage is narcissistic, emanating from an injury seen to be caused by the consultant, who is viewed as cold and unempathic, or by the task, which is viewed as an intolerable burden. The solution is to destroy the consultant or the task, or flee. Although a leader can usually be found to assist the group in these strivings, the regression is less profound than it is in the dependency group. Since a certain amount of grandiosity is shared by the members and their leader, ambition is present to a considerable extent. This ambition, however, is not directed by any viable ideal, mainly because the disappointment with the consultant is so intense. This state thus represents the breakdown of the idealized parental imago. The consultant has been tried and been found wanting. Rage wells up, ambition looks for action but, in the absence of ideals, can find only destructiveness or flight.

The Basic Assumption Pairing Group is that in which the group looks for a messianic solution created by a sexual act between two of the members. In my experience, it is less common than the two others, and never occurs in groups of psychotic or severely borderline patients who function mainly on a preoedipal level.

Kohut (1971) has described how a first line of defense of the fragmenting self is sexualization. Idealization (directed toward a whole person) is replaced by voyeurism, and grandiosity is expressed in sexual exhibitionism. Kohut (1971) described how the weak self resorts to stimulation of sexual ideals and goals in the Oedipal phase, whereas the well-developed self does not need such intense stimulation.

The pairing group represents a situation in which the members feel themselves moving in the direction of fragmentation but regression is still not particularly intense. In this situation the group turns to voyeuristic or exhibitionistic activities. Two members of the same or opposite sex start an interaction the sexual nature of which is manifested in various ways. Sometimes sexual allusions are overt, sometimes it is only the quality of interaction that impresses the observer as sexual. The other members are awed and silent witnesses of this performance, as the following example illustrates.

In the late nineteen-sixties a Tavistock group began with some members expressing considerable anger because there were no black female participants. The rage subsided after a time, but the mood was desultory. Two protagonists then emerged, a white male and a black male. As the rest of the group became silent observers, the interaction between the pair took on an increasingly exalted and intensely emotional quality. Finally the consultant pointed out that by this interaction the pair was trying to create a black female that would thus solve the group's initial problem. The interaction between the pair subsided and after a while the group began to function in a dependency mode.

Finally, there is the Work Group. According to Bion, the tools of the Work Group are organization and structure. This aspect of group functioning can be seen in the state in which, with or without consultative help, the regressive pulls have been overcome and the cohesive selves of the participants have been restored, indicating a return to the maintenance of individuality and a movement from "drive-regulated" to task-oriented behavior. Now the need for an idealized leader disappears. Instead, leadership will be exercised in dynamic fashion by whichever person can best address the task at a given moment. In this climate the need for a selfobject is minimal; each member remains responsible for all aspects of his personality. As a rule, the group shifts into a work mode toward the end of group life, maintaining it for increasingly long periods.When this happens, members often have a sense that important learning has taken place, though it is difficult to describe in concrete terms. Some members may also feel a therapeutic effect, a conviction that they have changed and that these changes will last. The explanation of this phenomenon may be sought in the vicissitudes of idealization. A few leaders, including the consultant, have been idealized and found wanting. The group has also been idealized as such, as an enormously powerful structure, one moment malevolent, the next moment benevolent. The idealization is broken down with the discovery that the "group" after all does not exist, that it is merely a congregation of individuals with a common task. This revision of idealized structures or objects leads to what Kohut (1971) has called *transmuting internalization,* essentially a product of reality testing. The process may briefly be described as the breaking down of an idealized object and the internalization of its depersonalized parts in the form of competence. (Thus members regain their skills when the leader of the dependency group is no longer viewed as magically potent.) The second important process is the internalization of idealizing strivings that then attach themselves to the superego. Thus, while the restoration of the competence of the members, in combination with their improved processing of group events, leads to a sense of learning and achievement, the idealization of the superego, especially of the part which values knowledge (already prominent in most professionals), leads to a feeling that the pain of learning was worthwhile, and also a belief that one is somehow, to some extent, protected against regression in the future. Finally, an increase in the narcissistic idealization of the superego leads to greater stability, probably subjectively experienced as a therapeutic result, a personal "improvement." The cohesiveness of the self has increased, making it more able to fulfill its role as organizer of ego activities (Kohut 1971).

An interesting and not altogether rare aspect of the Work Group is the appearance of creativity. This may take the form of new formulations as to what is going on, formulations of poetic myths, and so on. Much of this remains on an action-thought level (Kohut, 1977). Kohut (1976) has pointed out that during the creative process the creation itself is enormously invested with narcissistic energy, leading to a more or less severe depletion of the self. Under these conditions the creative person tends to ally himself with an idealized other who is viewed as protecting the enfeebled self. A well-known example of this, of course, is the relationship between Freud and Fliess during the writing of *The Interpretation of Dreams.* It appears that during such periods of creativity the group functions as an idealized protector. This seems to be a different kind of idealization than that described before insofar as destructive forces are maintained within the participants and not projected onto the idealized group.

Thus it can be said that the study of the functioning of the cohesive self and its functions can satisfactorily explain the events that take place in a small study group of the Tavistock type. While it is true that such groups are based on well-defined, almost laboratory-strict requirements, we should not be surprised if self psychology also illuminates other types of groups and what is usually called "group dynamics."

REFERENCES

Bion, W. R. (1959). *Experiences in Groups.* New York: Basic Books.

Gehrie, M. (1980). The self and the group. In *Advances in Self Psychology,* ed. A. Goldberg. New York: International Universities Press.

Kohut, H. (1971). *The Analysis of the Self.* New York: International Universities Press.

_____ (1976). Creativeness, charisma and group psychotherapy: Reflections on Freud's self-analysis. In *Freud: The Fusion of Science and Humanism,* ed. J. Gedo & G. H. Pollock. *Psychological Issues,* Monograph 34–35. New York: International Universities Press.

_____ (1977). *The Restoration of the Self.* New York: International Universities Press.

Meyers, S. J. (1978). The disorders of the self: Developmental and clinical considerations. *Group,* 2:131–140.

O'Connor, G. (1971). The Tavistock method of group study. *Science and Psychoanalysis,* 18:100–115.

Rice, A. K. (1965). *Learning for Leadership. Interpersonal and Intergroup Relations.* London: Tavistock.

Rioch, M. J. (1970a). Group relations: Rationale and techniques. *Internat. J. Group Psychother.,* 20:340–355.

_____ (1970b). The work of Wilfred R. Bion on groups. *Psychiatry,* 33:56–66.

_____ (1971). "All We Like Sheep" (Isaiah 53:6); Followers and leaders. *Psychiatry,* 34:258–273.

Stone, W. N. & Whitman, R. M. (1977). Contributions of the psychology of the self to group process and group therapy. *Int. J. Group Psychother.,* 27:343–359.

15 Shakespeare and the Psychology of the Self: The Case of Othello

Hyman L. Mulsin, M.D.

THE MARRIAGE OF self psychology to Shakespeare is, I should say, a marriage, or perhaps a merger, made in heaven. Shakespeare's heroes and heroines are all involved with self-realization, self-aggrandizement, self-deficits, and the need for a responsive surround to assist in their unfolding development or during crises of self-cohesion. When one attends to the manifest concerns of Othello, Hamlet, Lear, or Macbeth, they are revealed to be self-concerns, differing in each of the protagonists in terms of their specific situations. From the outset of *Hamlet,* the hero experiences himself as immersed in sorrow and inept, a configuration which, from the first soliloquy on, he connects to his relationship with his mother. He is inept, of course, in the sense that he lacks the vigor to do what any red-blooded prince would do under similar circumstances. (By contrast, note Laertes' responses when he is informed of his father's death: He storms the castle with fire in his eyes and is prepared to kill Claudius in vengeance for Polonius' death.) King Lear is manifestly disorganized after the last of the many insults thrown at him so that the old man who rushes into the tempest is overtly psychotic and hallucinates a trial in which he brings his evil daughters to the bar of justice. Shakespeare now shows his appreciation of the need for the selfobject's ministrations when he describes the thinking processes of Lear returned to normal under Cordelia's soothing care.

An approach to the dramas which utilizes the self and its selfobjects attempts to answer the question, What is Hamlet's pervasive experience of himself in relation to Gertrude, Claudius, and King Hamlet? It attempts to understand the nature of Hamlet's bonds with the significant people in his surround. It makes these judgments through the use of empathic cognition, i.e., vicarious introspection. The classical drive-defense orientation would, in contrast, have as its operational enquiry, What oedipal and preoedipal conflicts are described in *Hamlet*? Hamlet's anxious inaction in the face of his need to avenge his father's murder would thus reveal a man seemingly caught up in endless repetition of an oedipal fixation, so that to kill the usurper Claudius for a deed which he could also have performed himself is, as Freud (1900) would have it, a form of killing himself. Gertrude would then be the oedipal mother for whom Hamlet longs. Destroying Claudius would thus bring Hamlet victory over all his fathers, the prospect of which causes him intense castration anxiety.

In short, whereas the classical psychoanalytic approach would understand the data of literature in terms of preexisting paradigms of oedipal and preoedipal conflict, the self-psychological approach requires the observer to view the protagonist with empathy. This perspective enables us to appreciate the protagonist's current self needs, whether it be longing for periodic merging with an archaic selfobject during a time of crisis or whether it be a perpetual striving to fill out a self defective in soothing functions. An observer using the self-psychological approaches, given sufficient data, will be able to observe modal self/selfobject patterns of the hero he is studying. Of course this is not equivalent to the transference data obtained in psychoanalysis, but it does give an understanding of the self needs revealed in the dyads the hero commonly structures. In describing these self/selfobject patterns, the observer can also begin, if the data permits, to enter into the mental life of the protagonist so as to understand the strengths and the vulnerabilities of the self under study. This line of investigation may lead to a definition of the bipolar self of the hero and demonstrate the presence or absence of a program of action. Finally, one may be able to discern, not only the specific deficits and strengths of the self, but its potential for repair. At times, one can witness repair processes already instituted.

A hero as complex as Hamlet will invite a variety of psychoanalytic investigative approaches. One can view his inaction in terms of Kohut's Tragic Man, whose principal problem involves the realization of his vision of ideal action, or as typical of Freud's Guilty Man, who is ambivalent and conflicted in the face of repressed oedipal longings. In the matter of choosing between these, I am guided by Kohut's (1959) statement: "Only a phenomenon that we can attempt to observe by introspection or by empathy with another's introspection may be called psychological" (p. 308). I believe we must resist the temptation to impose predetermined patterns on literary characters as much as we must do so with living patients.

OTHELLO: TRAGEDY AS SELF DEMISE

Shakespeare's *Othello* has been approached by many psychoanalytic and literary scholars as either a case history of Iago's psychopathology (Wangh, 1950; Smith, 1959) or a study of Iago's villainy (Bradley, 1950; Fiedler, 1973). When Coleridge referred to Iago's character as "the motive hunting of motiveless malignity" (1884, p. 388), he summarized the prevalent view of *Othello* as a play in which Iago's attacks on his master and his master's lady embody the major theme of the tragedy (see Feldman, 1952–1953; Levin, 1976; Reid, 1968; Asimov, 1978). In this essay, I will advance a different thesis: That Othello's decompensation, culminating in his murder of his beloved Desdemona and his suicide, represents an understandable outcome of self demise, the collapse of a weakened self aided and abetted in its decompensation by the treachery of Othello's "honest" and trusted aide Iago. Since I am concerned only with the psychology of Othello, I will attempt neither to illuminate the self of Iago, nor to discern the motives underlying his villainy toward his master. I would stress, however, that Othello's psychic disarray should in no respect be adjudged a measure of Iago's power.

Othello is first revealed to us through the commentaries of his aide Iago and Iago's comrade-in-hatred Roderigo. They describe the Moorish general as an arrogant adventurer who has managed to capture the heart of the fair Desdemona, the daughter of a prominent Venetian senator. When Othello is told that he is in danger—Desdemona's father is about to confront him with a band of vigilantes seeking to retrieve his daughter—his speeches reveal a dignified, self-assured veteran of hostile encounters:

> Oth.   Let him do his spite.
> My services which I have done the signiory
> Shall out-tongue his complaints. 'Tis yet to know—
> Which, when I know that boasting is an honor,
> I shall promulgate—I fetch my life and being
> From men of royal siege: and my demerits
> May speak (unbonneted) to as proud a fortune
> As this that I have reached. For know, Iago,
> But that I love the gentle Desdemona,
> I would not my unhoused free condition
> Put into circumscription and confine
> For the sea's worth.
> [Act I, Sc. II, lines 19–30]

Now, as Othello, his spouse Desdemona, and others of his retinue receive orders from the Duke and his council to sail to Cyprus, he speaks once again in a manner befitting a seasoned warrior who places duty to the state above all other considerations:

> Oth.   The tyrant custom, most grave senators,
> Hath made the flinty and steel couch of war
> My thrice-driven bed of down. I do agonize
> a natural and prompt alacrity
> I find in hardness; and to undertake
> These present wars against the Ottomites.
> Most humbly, therefore, bending to your state.
> [Act I. Sc. III, lines 248–254]

Speaking of his wife's wish to join him he says:

> Oth.   Let her have your voice.
> Vouch with me heaven, I therefore beg it not
> To please the palate of my appetite,
> Nor to comply with heat, the young affects
> In my defunct and proper satisfaction;
> But to be free and bounteous to her mind.
> And heaven defend your good souls that you think
> I will your serious and great business scant
> For she is with me. No, when light-winged toys
> Of feathered Cupid seel with wanton dullness
> My speculative and officed instruments,
> That my disports corrupt and taint my business,
> Let housewives make a skillet of my helm,
> And all indign and base adversities
> Make head against my estimation!
> [Act I. Sc. III, lines 282–296]

Othello and the Venetians are victorious over the Turks. He is exuberant as he rejoins his wife who has come to Cyprus along with her maid Emily, the wife of Iago.

> Oth.   It gives me wonder great as my content
> To see you here before me. O my soul's joy!
> If after every tempest come such calms,
> May the winds blow till they have wakened death!
> And let the laboring bark climb hills of seas
> Olympus-high, and duck again as low
> As Hell's from heaven! If it were now to die,
> 'Twere now to be most happy; for I fear
> My soul hath her content so absolute
> That not another comfort like to this
> Succeeds in unknown fate.
> [Act II. Sc. I, lines 212–222]

It is precisely at this moment that Iago begins to plot. He first causes Lieutenant Cassio to lose face in a drunken misdemeanor. He then plants the idea in Cassio's mind to ask Desdemona to become his petitioner with Othello. Next he begins insinuating to Othello that Desdemona and Cassio are involved in an amatory relationship.

Othello's reaction to Iago is at first to dismiss the insinuations of wrongdoing between his trusted lieutenant and his wife:

> 'Tis not to make me jealous
> To say my wife is fair, feeds well, loves company,
> Is free of speech, sings, plays, and dances well.
> Where virtue is, these are more virtuous.
> Nor from mine own weak merits will I draw
> The smallest fear or doubt of her revolt,
> For she had eyes, and chose me. No, Iago;
> I'll see before I doubt; when I doubt, prove;
> And on the proof there is no more but this—
> Away at once with love or jealousy!
> [Act III, Sc. III, lines 210–219]

Shortly thereafter, however, he begins to doubt his wife's fidelity and his capacity to maintain her devotion. First he says:

> Oth.   Why did I marry? This honest creature doubtless
> Sees and knows more, much more, than he unfolds.
> [Act III. Sc. III, lines 276–277]

Then he proclaims:

> Haply, for I am black
> And have not those soft parts of conversation
> That chamberers have, or for I am declined
> Into the vale of years (yet that's not much),
> She's gone. I am abused, and my relief
> Must be to loathe her. O curse of marriage,
> That we can call these delicate creatures ours,
> And not their appetites! I had rather be a toad
> And live upon the vapor of a dungeon
> Than keep a corner in the thing I love
> For others' uses.
> [Act III. Sc. III, lines 298–307]

With Iago's repeated innuendoes of wrongdoing, Othello is in a state of disarray as he proclaims to him:

Avaunt! be gone! Thous hast set me on the rack.
I swear 'tis better to be much abused
Than but to know't a little.
[Act III. Sc. III, lines 379–381]

Following this declaration, he cries out in anguish:

Oth.   What sense had I her stol'n hours of lust?
I saw't not, thought it not, it harmed not me.
I slept the next night well, was free and merry;
I found not Cassio's kisses on her lips.
He that is robbed, not wanting what is stol'n,
Let him not know't, and he's not robbed at all.

Iago.   I am sorry to hear this.

Oth.   I had been happy if the general camp,
Pioneers and all, had tasted her sweet body,
So I had nothing known. O, now for ever
Farewell the tranquil mind! farewell content!
Farewell the plumed troop, and the big wars
That make ambition virtue! O, farewell!
Farewell the neighing steed and the shrill trump,
The spirit-stirring drum, th' ear-piercing fife,
The royal banner, and all quality,
Pride, pomp, and circumstance of glorious war!
And O ye mortal engines whose rude throats
Th' immortal Jove's dread clamors counterfeit,
Farewell! Othello's occupation's gone!
[Act III. Sc. III, lines 383–402]

He now shifts his allegiance to Iago, making him lieutenant and consorting with him on plans to kill the putative lovers, Desdemona and Cassio. Iago further incites Othello by planting a handkerchief of Desdemona's—a gift from Othello—in Cassio's room, which he promptly produces as evidence of the liaison. Next he tells Othello that Cassio has stated that he did indeed "lie" with Desdemona, which story causes Othello to fragment and fall into a trance:

> Oth.   Lie with her! lie on her!—We say lie on her when
> They belie her.—Lie with her! Zounds, that's fulsome.
> —Handkerchief—confessions—handkerchief!—To confess,
> and be hanged for his labor—first to be hanged, and
> then to confess! I tremble at it. Nature would not invest
> herself in such shadowing passion without some instruction.
> It is not words that shakes me thus.—Pish! Noses,
> ears, and lips? Is't possible?—Confess?—handerkerchief?
> O devil!
> [Act IV. Sc. I, lines 44–52]

Iago now begins to mock his leader without restraint. He is to set up an interview with Cassio that Othello will observe, at which they will discus Cassio's conquest of Desdemona. Iago says:

> Good sir, be a man.
> Think every bearded fellow that's but yoked
> May draw with you. There's millions now alive
> That nightly lie in those unproper beds
> Which they dare swear peculiar. Your case is better.
> O, 'tis the spire of hell, the fiend's arch-mock,
> To lip a wanton in a secure couch,
> And to suppose her chaste! No, let me know;
> And knowing what I am, I know what she shall be.
> [Act IV. Sc. I, lines 78–86]

And somewhat later:

> Do but encave yourself
> And mark the fleers, the gibes, and notable scorns
> That dwell in every region of his face;
> For I will make him tell the tale anew—
> Where, how, how oft, how long ago, and when
> He hath, and is again to cope your wife.
> I say, but mark his festure. Marry, patience!

Or I shall say you are all in all in spleen,
And nothing of a man.

   Oth.   Dost thou hear, Iago?
I will be found most cunning in my patience;
But (dost thou hear?) most bloody.
[Act IV. Sc. I, lines 95–106]

At this point in the drama we witness a radical transformation in the self of Othello. The former restraints and elegance of manner are gone as he confronts his wife with accusations of infidelity. He strikes her in public, seemingly without provocation. This latter scene occurs directly after a visitor from Venice brings orders from the council that Othello is to return to Venice leaving Cassio in charge. Suddenly Othello, without regard for his visitor, begins to discharge his pent-up rage against his wife:

     O devil, devil!
If that the earth could teem with woman's tears,
Each drop she falls would prove a crocodile.
Out of my sight!
[Act IV. Sc. I, lines 267–270]

From this point on, Othello's deterioration proceeds rapidly. In a frenzy now, he accuses his wife's maid of conspiring with his wife to arrange sexual encounters with Cassio. Next he orders his wife to their chambers and after hearing that his imagined rival has been accosted and apparently killed by Iago, proceeds to suffocate and then strangle her.

When the truth of her fidelity becomes apparent, Othello, in despair, takes his own life. Just prior to his suicide, he utters his last words, which reinstitute the self of the forthright general vexed beyond endurance:

   Oth.   Soft you! a word or two before you go.
I have done the state some service, and they know't—
No more of that. I pray you, in your letters,

When you shall these unlucky deeds relate,
Speak of me as I am. Nothing extenuate,
Nor set down aught in malice. Then must you speak
Of one that loved not wisely, but, being wrought,
Perplexed in the extreme; of one whose hand
(Like the base Indian) threw a pearl away
Richer than all his tribe; of one whose subdued eyes,
Albeit unused to the melting mood,
Drop tears as fast as the Arabian trees
Their med'cinable gum. Set you down this;
And say besides that in Aleppo once,
Where a malignant and a turbaned Turk
Beat a Venetian and traduced the state,
I took by the throat the circumcised dog
And smote him—thus. [He stabs himself]
[Act V. Sc. II, lines 392–410]

DISCUSSION

It is my contention that *Othello* is not simply a tragedy of one man's victimization by another, as various psychoanalytic and literary scholars would have it (Wangh, 1950; Smith, 1959; Levin, 1976; Asimov, 1978). According to this view, Iago's need for vengeance after having been passed over by Othello for the post of lieutenant unleashed a volcano of uncontainable anger, or what we might call chronic narcissistic rage.[1]

Other critics have concluded that Othello's decompensation was, as Coleridge put it, what "any man would and must feel who had believed of Iago as Othello" (1884, p. 125). Coleridge went on to describe Iago's machinations as "the motive-hunting of motiveless malignity" (p. 49).

---

[1]Iago's uncontrollable needs for revenge have been evoked by a disturbance in his relationship with Othello. Othello by his choice of Desdemona to be his wife and Cassio to be his lieutenant has disrupted a self/selfobject relationship. Thus Iago's narcissistic rage, the result of the ruptured relationship, becomes the dominant and pervasive motivation in his life.

Whereas the tragedy of Othello to Coleridge is the tragedy of the enormity of human deception and the blunders of the spirit, especially the blunders of the noble in spirit, to Bradley (1950), Othello's character was "comparatively simple" (p. 106). Othello was, as he himself described, indisposed to jealousy but unusually open to deception. But once stirred up to an intensity of passion, he would act without delay.

My view of the tragedy departs from the "innocent victim" version of Othello, the noble spirit duped by a masterful villain. Othello is indeed victimized but not primarily by his ensign. He is rather the victim of his own experience of himself as black, aging, inarticulate, a foreigner who fears that his capacity to keep his young Venetian wife is limited. These are the words he uses to reveal his anxieties:

> Haply, for I am black
> And have not those soft parts of conversation
> That chamberers have, or for I am declined
> Into the vale of years (yet that's not much),
> She's gone.

Thus, when Iago reminds Othello of the deviousness of Venetian wives and of the deviousness of Desdemona in marrying Othello without her father's knowledge, it is *Othello's* reaction that is remarkable, namely, the heroic general fully accepts his aide's comments about his wife's capacity for deception:

> Oth.   Why did I marry? This honest creature doubtless
> Sees and knows more, much more, than he unfolds.

Suddenly the speech and posture of a man once of surpassing self-control and elegance, even in the face of his enemies, is transformed. Note how quickly Othello moves away from the words ". . . I'll see before I doubt; when I doubt, prove; And on the proof there is nor more but this—Away at once with love or jealousy," to:

> O curse of marriage,
> That we can call these delicate creatures ours,
> And not their appetites! I had rather be a toad

And live upon the vapor of a dungeon
Than keep a corner in the thing I love
For others' uses.

In a word, his decompensation has quickly taken the form of
the fragmentation manifest in this speech:

Oth.   Avaunt! be gone! Thou hast set me on the rack.
I swear 'tis better to be much abused
Than but to know't a little.

My argument centers on the following: It does not seem
possible that a lowly ensign could have so powerful an impact
on the self of a successful general as to cause him so readily to
conclude that his wife had turned against him. It matters not
that Iago was widely regarded as honest, as Othello says over
and over:

This fellow's of exceeding honesty,
And knows all qualities, with a learned spirit
Of human dealings.
[Act III. Sc. III, lines 293–295]

Honest or not, Iago should not have been able, by his own
devices, to intrude on Othello's trust of Desdemona. Something
else would be required, namely, Othello's self-doubt, a self-
doubt so extreme that Iago's innuendos and unproven suggestions could be accepted with a minimum of challenge.

We might say that Othello saw his wife as an idealized figure,
not only Caucasian but a Senator's daughter, and himself as
being no match for her. Iago's innuendoes would then have
confirmed his own sense of inferiority so that the noble general
could suddenly become the depreciated general whose wife—a
wife he never deserved—wanted to be rid of him.

On the surface, of course, Othello's life was proceeding quite
well. There was the victory at Cyprus and the reunion with his
wife, an event he celebrated with great joy:

Oth.   It gives me wonder great as my content
To see you here before me. O my soul's joy!

If after every tempest come such calms,
May the winds blow till they have wakened death!
And let the laboring bark climb hills of seas
Olympus-high, and duck again as low
As hell's from heaven! If it were now to die,
"Twere now to be most happy; for I fear
My soul hath her content so absolute
That not another comfort like to this
Succeeds in unknown fate.

And yet, shortly after Desdemona has rejoined him in
Cyprus, his vulnerability becomes manifest. Is it not odd that,
after so great a victory and on the very first night of his reunion
with his wife, he should react to Cassio's drunkenness with so
little generosity and with what we can only call an excess of
punitiveness, immediately demoting his faithful lieutenant?
Does he not stand on his authority? Significantly, it is shortly
after this episode that he begins to react to Iago's innuendoes.
My point is that Othello stands on his authority in the matter of
Cassio's drunkenness because his reunion with his beautiful
young bride has apparently brought on a resurgence of his
feelings of inferiority. His sense of diminished self-worth is
nowhere better shown than in his quickness to conclude, "She's
gone," even before he has been presented with Iago's fabri-
cated evidence.

In sum, Othello has experienced a transference reaction to
his spouse that entails a form of self-regression. From this point
on, he is vulnerable to any real or imagined manifestation of his
inferiority.

The next parts of the play, I believe, involve attempts to
effect a self-repair. The attempts at self-repair come about in
the special relationship Othello structures with Iago, not the
other way about, as is commonly described. It is Othello who
seeks out Iago, psychologically speaking, and who begins to
relate to him as an idealized figure to whom he submits and
whom he indeed blindly follows. Through this process, Othello
actually regains some degree of psychic peace.

Directly after Iago offers his first innuendoes of evil, Othello
begins to credit him with a kind of power over himself:

". . . thou hast set me on the rack." From this point on, Othello's elevation of Iago to the status of an archaic idealized selfobject takes place rapidly. He becomes passive. He waits for Iago to present him with the inevitable evidence. He allows Iago to poke fun at him:

> O grace! O heaven forgive me!
> Are you a man? Have you a soul or sense?
> [Act III. Sc. III, lines 420–421]

At this stage of their transformed relationship, Iago is clearly in charge, and indeed, Shakespeare has the two characters celebrate their new self/selfobject union in a ritual not unlike a marriage. Iago speaks of being in Othello's service where the obverse is true. As Othello kneels and vows revenge on Cassio and Desdemona, Iago says:

> Do not rise yet. [Iago kneels.]
>
>   Oth.   And will upon the instant put thee th't.
> Within these three days let me hear thee say
> That Cassio's not alive.
>
>   Iago.   My friend is dead; 'tis done at your request.
> But let her live.
>
>   Oth.   Damn her, lewd minx! O, damn her!
> Come, go with me apart. I will withdraw
> To furnish me with some swift means of death
> For the fair devil. Now art thou my lieutenant.
>
>   Iago.   I am your own for ever.
> [Act III. Sc. III, lines 528–539]

Such is his control over his former master that Iago now throws caution to the winds and, lying again, tells Othello that Cassio has informed him that he has had a sexual liaison with Desdemona. Othello's distress leads to self-fragmentation with disruption of his mentational processes—he falls into a "trance." Iago, continuing to exert his will over Othello, now punishes him further by having him witness an interview in which Othello believes that Cassio and Iago are discussing Desdemona, when in fact they are discussing (with great jollity) Bianca, Cassio's mistress. When Othello attempts to defend Desdemona's virtues, Iago now without hesitation orders his "apprentice," Othello, to kill her. Iago tells Othello that he will himself be Cassio's "undertaker." This scene is remarkable in the way it shows the complete reversal of the relationship between the general and his ensign:

> Othello.   But yet the pity of it, Iago! O
> Iago, the pity of it. Iago!
> [Act IV. Sc. I, lines 210–211]

To which Iago says, in what is clearly a sarcastic tone:

> If you are so fond over her iniquity, give her
> patent to offend; for if it touch not you, it comes near
> nobody.
> [Act IV. Sc. I, lines 212–214]

Othello follows his lead and the dialogue continues:

> I will chop her into messes! Cuckold me!
>
> Iago.   O, 'tis foul in her.
>
> Oth.   With mine officer!
>
> Iago.   That's fouler.
>
> Oth.   Get me some poison, Iago, this night. I'll not expostulate with her, lest her body and beauty unprovide
> my mind again. This night, Iago!
>
> Iago.   Do it not with poison. Strangle her in her bed,
> Even the bed she hath contaminated.
>
> Oth.   Good, good! The justice of it pleases. Very Good!
>
> Iago.   And for Cassio, let me be his undertaker. You
> shall hear more by midnight.
>
> Oth.   Excellent good!
> [Act IV. Sc. I, lines 215–227]

Thus Shakespeare has described with remarkable clarity what is perhaps the most significant aspect of the drama, the transformation of the relationship between the general and his aide. Iago has become the selfobject whom Othello follows without challenge. They have merged in an archaic self/selfobject bond in which Iago functions for Othello as the idealized parent imago whose evil directions are followed in a reflexive way.

As the play comes to an end, Othello no longer exhibits his former traits. He is no longer the high-minded, unflappable Moor whom the Venetian Senate relies on to fight their wars. He strikes his wife in public, and accuses her of whoring with Cassio. As the emissary from Venice remarks, seeing him in this state of disarray:

> Lod.   Is this the noble Moor whom our full senate
> Call all in all sufficient? Is this the nature
> Whom passion could not shake? whose solid virtue
> The shot of accident nor dart of chance
> Could neither graze nor pierce?
> [Act IV. Sc. I, lines 290–294]

In sum, *Othello* portrays an archaic selfobject bond in which the self of Othello becomes merged with the idealized parent so as to compensate for a fragmenting self. By virtue of this compensation, Othello is able to act—he kills Desdemona. But his self-repair is illusory. When he ultimately recognizes the evil of his selfobject, he takes his own life, with all the dignity of his former nature—a nature both strong and imperfect.

REFERENCES

Asimov, I. (1978). *Guide to Shakespeare*. New York: Avenal.

Bradley, A. C. (1950). *Shakespearean Tragedy*. London: Macmillan.

Coleridge, S. T. (1884). *Lectures and Notes on Shakespeare and Other English Poets*. London: Bell.

Feldman, A. B. (1952–1953). Othello's obsession. *Amer. Imago*, 9:147–163.

Fiedler, L. A. (1973). *The Stranger in Shakespeare.* New York: Stein & Ray.

Freud, S. (1900). The interpretation of dreams. *S. E.,* 4 & 5.

Kohut, H. (1959). Introspection, empathy and psychoanalysis. In *The Search for the Self,* ed. P. Ornstein. New York: International Universities Press, 1978.

Levin, H. (1976). *Shakespeare and the Revolution of the Times.* Oxford: Oxford University Press.

Reid, S. (1968). Othello's jealousy. *Amer. Imago,* 25:274–293.

Smith, G. R. (1959). Iago the paranoiac. *Amer. Imago,* 16:155–167.

Wangh, M. (1950). Othello: The tragedy of Iago. *Psychoanal. Quart.,* 19:202–212.

16 The Self and the Creative Process

Kurt A. Schlesinger, M.D.

DEVELOPMENTS IN SELF PSYCHOLOGY have widespread ramifications extending into areas beyond the clinical psychoanalytic realm. One such area is the problem of creativity, which I shall attempt to examine in this paper.[1] The object of scrutiny is going to be a poem I wrote two years ago which I shall set in the context of my personal history and psychology. Thus, the distance between creator, creation, and reader should be significantly reduced, a problem perhaps as much as an opportunity.

From this juxtaposition of poem and self analysis of the poet, I shall attempt to support some specific and general propositions about creativity and its relationship to self psychology. Several questions should immediately come to mind in connection with such a project.

Can a poem that has not been recognized as having literary merit serve as a takeoff point for a discussion of the creative

---

[1]Since I shall not review the literature here, I should at least like to make a downpayment on my intellectual indebtedness by listing the names of those workers in the field of creativity to whom I am beholden: Margaret Brenman-Gibson, Phyllis Greenacre, Erik Erikson, Heinz Kohut, Arthur Koestler, Ernst Kris, and the members of the Colloquium on Psychoanalysis and Art of the San Francisco Psychoanalytic Institute under the leadership of Stanley Steinberg.

process? Since I hold with a non-euphemistic definition of the creative product, that it is not *ipso facto* a good, beautiful, or true thing, then any mental construct could serve as my example. For at bottom it is the human proclivity for forming constructs that underlies creativity. These constructs may range from integrated conceptual wholes to fragmentary gleanings. The basic creative process is the construction of self, the establishment of a coherent, continuing sense of self, a *construct*, with positive affective coloration (self-esteem). In the ongoing life-long activity of self creation and renewal there are generated a wide range of activities and products. When these have more universal appeal, we consider them art. But if my definition is accepted, then the creative process subsumes *both* artistic and non-artistic creativity. Or, put another way, artistic achievement and less recognized creative endeavor have similar functions in self creation, renewal, and repair, and possess analogous dynamics.

The reader might also ask how an analytic procedure and particularly a self-analytic one can avoid distortions arising from the personal myth, that is, the manner in which we construe our own experience to accord with our need to maintain a coherent and positive sense of self. Perhaps it is enough to say that awareness of the myth is the best safeguard against the distortions arising from it. But this is too defensive an answer and inconsistent with the very thesis of my presentation. For in my view the construction of self is the universal motivational act which shapes and focuses how we construct—how we *construe*—our experience. Our construction of our experiential world will then, in turn, feed back on and shape our self construct, and so on.

Finally, I should note that it is a rather ideally coherent sense of self which I have considered thus far in relation to creativity. But creativity may also reflect a less stable, incoherent, discontinuous, and ambivalent sense of self with negative affective coloration. Thus symptomatic, destructive, and maladaptive activity can all be subsumed under the rubric of creativity. The creative self may be so distorted that efforts at expression, maintenance, and repair are grossly maladaptive, personally and socially, thus validating and perpetuating a malformed self. Creativity is not a palliative. It encompasses the entire range of human activities that are motivated by the search for coherence and the creation of meaning.

Let me now present the poem to which I have referred. One July day, two years ago, I wrote the following lines:

MORNING PRAYER

". . . all Jews will report to the
New Market Place at 0500 hours on
September 23, 1942, for transport
and resettlement.
WORK BRINGS FREEDOM."

S.S. Major Degenhardt
Polizeichef Tchenstochau
Heil Hitler

Thousands of remnants of the Jewish problem
thronged into the marketplace of Czestochowa
awaiting the freightcars like Texas yearlings
on their way to the Kansas City stockyards.

In obedience to the summons they came
to that marketplace where Leja
mother of my mother purveyed mountains
of blood oranges from legendary Capri
piled higher than my childish grasp
could reach. They came uncountable
as the golden pyramid of my vanished past.

The Black Madonna, the compassionate mother, gazed
from Yasna Gora Monastery hill, impassively
as she had with tranquil benevolence
on a thousand years of pogroms.

Of those summoned Avrum Laib
appeared crowned in his fur hat and wrapped
from head to foot in his prayer shawl.
Amidst the gray and black shapes of the frightened

milling throng his fringed striped white shawl
was a pillar of light in the predawn dark
radiating a familiar order to those nearest
who turned toward him forming a clustering
circle in the gray bewildered chaos
of hapless fear.

Avrum Laib swayed and intoned the morning prayer.
Those nearby rocked and joined the sing-song chant
imploring heaven's gates to open for the dawning day.

The ancient chant rose above the timorous babble
to the slategray sky.

But did the gates of heaven open that day?

Jew! yelled the captain out of the grayness
hand on holster—while grandfather prayed on
white center of a dark-spoked wheel

Accursed Jew! screamed the black-cloaked captain
gun-butting aside the dark human knot
forcing his way toward the swaying central whiteness
of Avrum Laib.

Goddamn Jew croaked the blackbooted one as the
parting dark mass brought him face to face with
the talith-wrapped praying swaying Avrum Laib.

With his gun against Avrum's chest he barked
Shut up Jew!
Hat off Jew!
Shawl off Jew!
Avrum replied
        "German! That's how I dress
        to pray and to die."

Then die filthy Jew dog
screamed the German and fired.
Avrum fell.
A slowly enlarging bloodstain
formed on the white prayer shawl
now become his shroud.

At 0700 hours the transport left
on schedule and none remained
to perform the final office
for the last Jew of Czestochowa.
From the all-merciful, Holy Mother of Czestochowa
still no sign only eternal, inscrutable silence.
Did the sun rise that day? Did the gates of heaven open?

In the place of the golden orange mountain
of my childhood, lay my grandfather's body
on the sunless marketplace
and my man's reach falls as short
as the helpless grasp of my childhood.

As I wake in the gray dawns
I still wonder, did
the gates of heaven open
that day for Avrum the Lion's morning prayer?

The poet's story—the story that is my story—begins in
Czestochowa, Poland, where I was born as the First World War
was ending. Within six months of my birth, my family—that is,
two older brothers, my mother, father, and myself—moved to
Germany, where I grew up. When I was two and a half, my
younger brother was born.

When every summer for the first eleven years of my life my
mother went back to Poland to visit, I was for the eight to twelve
weeks of the trip her travelling companion. First as a babe-in-
arms, later as a sturdily trudging three-year-old, then as a
schoolboy and preadolescent. The landmarks of my growing
up are epitomized in a series of memories of the train change at
Katowicze where, in my earliest years, I was carried half asleep
from train to train, where later I walked amidst the hissing
locomotives and the milling crowd, clutching my blanket and
my mother's hand, where later still but now without blanket, I
walked hand in my mother's hand, where finally I walked with
the suitcases, by myself.

At last we would arrive in Czestochowa—as I remember it,
usually at night. My grandmother's porter with his horse and
wagon would be there, and my uncle Laibel, and they would

take us safe and sound to Ulicza Ogrodowa Number Nine where my maternal grandmother Leja lived and where my mother had grown up.

There would be excited greetings and exchanges and comments about how I had grown, although I never could see much change in my size—I was small. My grandmother, Bobbe Leja, had been widowed many years before I was born, and when my grandfather Shulim died, she raised her nine children and carried on the family business by herself. This business consisted of a store and warehouse from which oranges, apples, and other fruits were sold to local stores in the surrounding communities, and an open-air market stand where the region's peasants would come to do their weekly shopping. On market day Bobbe Leja would be up at dawn and off to oversee everything and set things up. I would be brought along later, into the market-day bustle. I watched her haggle, make deals, order the porter around, maintaining an air of control throughout, but taking time to butter a hot bagel for me bought from an itinerant peddler who carried them impaled on a long cane and sold then before they cooled.

When I was younger the huge pile of oranges towered above me. This presented me with a curious conundrum—a conundrum of my own creation. For I knew that the only safe place from which to take an orange would be the top of the heap, but I could only reach the lower portion, and only on tiptoes at that. Thus if I grasped within my reach the entire pyramid would collapse. It was my grandmother who gave me oranges, and to this day the blood-colored sweet orange is, in my mind's eye and in my taste, memory. Like other beautiful memories, this one became tinged with horror in a retrospective change of meaning. But I suppose the sense of precariousness was already contained in the original, untainted picture.

All morning on market day assorted aunts, uncles, cousins, and family friends would come by and identify me as the "*einikel*" from "Deutschland" (the grandchild from Germany), Hendel and Schloimeh's son. I would be pinched on the cheek, kissed, fondled, and given assorted things to eat, and various messages for my mother and father. Since both my mother's and father's parents lived in Czestochowa, and since each had eight siblings and many friends and acquaintences, there was much pinching on the cheeks and many kisses and things to eat.

Every day during my stay I would spend some hours with my paternal grandparents, Bobbe Chayo and Saide Avrum. I would be taken by my mother or someone she delegated to Alejah Number One, where they lived on the main thoroughfare. Later I found my own way. There was a heavy wooden gate, a central courtyard, grandfather's furniture workshop, and the upstairs living quarters where my father and his eight siblings had grown up. I knew grandfather as Saide but saw early that everyone else had a unique name for him. He was addressed as Avrum Laib by my grandmother and by intimates, Reb Schlesinger by Jews, Pan Schlesinger by Poles, Tatte by my mother and father. I was in awe of him. If I arrived early enough he would still be upstairs in his prayer shawl and phylacterics chanting his morning prayer. He would place his index finger on his lips to enjoin conversation and finish his devotions. As he folded his shawl and put away his phylacterics in a small velvet bag embroidered with Hebrew letters, he would talk to me. He called me Yankele. He asked about my brothers and father, he asked about Germany, but always, most importantly, he asked if I had learned to read yet. The summer I turned six I was primed for this question, since in the eight months before I had gotten a good start on reading, though it was not German that I had learned to read, nor was the reading of German the object of my grandfather's inquiry. When my grandfather asked me if I had learned to read yet, he meant Hebrew, and that is what I had learned. I may have been too young to go to the German public school, but the local rabbi in Wiesbaden had had no compunctions about teaching me Hebrew, even at the age of five. So I learned to read Hebrew a year before I learned to read German.

Eagerly awaiting my grandfather's annual inquiry, then, I answered everything else according to protocol. "Yankele, have you learned to read yet?" "Yes, grandfather!" I answered. His eyebrows moved up and toward each other and he smiled, palming his beard. He pulled a book from the shelf and opened it, pointing to a passage. It turned out to be Genesis and a passage I had already gotten to with Rabbi Ansbacher. I read in

Hebrew and translated into Yiddish a phrase about how God spoke to Avrum and told him to leave his father's house in Ur-Chaldea and go to a promised land which would be his and his descendants. Phrase by phrase I read the Hebrew and gave the Yiddish translation and as I came to the bottom of the page, my granfather said, "Well done, Yankele, well done."

Avrum Laib in my mind stands for the indestructible one, the fierce guardian. The name Laib is the Yiddish word for lion. He lived on the main thoroughfare of the town, a tree-lined boulevard which led uphill to Yasna Gora monastery in which is housed an 11th-century icon painted on ebony known as the Black Madonna. She is the Holy Mother of Czestochowa, and the patron saint of Poland. She heals the sick who come from all over the country to receive her miraculous bene-factions.

When the wooden gate of the courtyard was open, I would watch, with fascination and fear, the pilgrims as they ascended the sloping hill on the last mile of their journey. Some ascended on their knees. Some flagellated themselves as they stopped periodically to chant a mysterious prayer. Some came in groups with banners, singing and dressed in colorful costumes. All of it inspired fear in me. It was the "other," that which we were not part of and which was strange. It was not discussed. And the summer was the height of this activity. Although I saw it as an alien, separate thing—over there "them"—I had also heard enough and inferred enough to know that the exotic proces-sion could turn into a rampaging mob that came after "us." So I eyed the wooden gate which seemed so huge and strong to me. I had also felt this otherness in Germany where anti-Semitic insults, some Nazi-inspired, others belonging to a thousand-year tradition dating back to the Crusades but become part of the secular culture over time, kept me aware of the feeling of "us" and "them." It was terribly humiliating to walk down a Wiesbaden street as a five-year-old child with my hand in my mother's hand and have someone yell insults about the god-damn Jews, Christ-killers, and be helpless to do anything but ignore the taunts and keep on walking.

Inside the courtyard, my grandparents' house was shut off by the gate from the unending stream of devout pilgrims. That gate shut out the fearful world and made courtyard, furniture workshop, and living quarters safe haven in a dangerous world. There no anti-Semitic taunts entered and there Grandfather Avrum in prayer shawl and phylacterics chanted the morning prayer.

Avrum the Lion's image has superimposed on it, in a kind of montage, the image of his father, who was in his nineties and whom I visited in his small booklined room in the house in the town near Czestochowa where he lived. He sat with a volume in his hands, with a hanging, ticking, chiming clock on the wall. He would prop the book on the study table before him, pat me on the head, ask about his grandson Shloimeh—my father— and of course the inevitable question about what I was studying. I knew from my experience with his son that my great grandfather meant Jewish studies and when I told him Genesis, he allowed that that was a fine book for starters. The Nazis killed him some nine years later (some three years before they killed his son) when he was over a hundred years old, but I still cherish the magical fantasy that he would be sitting there poring over his Talmud if I could visit him. And he would ask me, "Yankele, what are you studying?"

Although my mother's father, Saide Shulim, died many years before my birth, he is also part of my inner cast and his role is epitomized in the following story I was told about him. He was a follower of the Radomsker Rebbe, who arrived in Czestochowa one day in 1904. His followers in the town had prepared a gala welcome for him at the railroad station and Saide Shulim, prominent fruit importer, was there holding an elaborate basket of fruit as part of the presentation. The train arrived. The Radomsker and his entourage debarked into the joyously singing, hand-clapping group of local Chassidic devotees. Grandfather rushed forward holding out his fruit offering to his beloved teacher and suddenly collapsed and died right there. This happened years before I was born. In my child's mind I embellished the story. I saw then and can still see the oranges rolling all over the station platform as joy is followed by horror.

So these are images of the poet's childhood, their existence a necessary but not sufficient condition for the writing of the poem. For these images and their elaborations had been with me for years before I wrote the poem, dormant most of the time, sometimes heightened and brought forward by the mnemonic pull of current events. In fact, I must exercise some restraint here, where the potential for spinning an interminable associative analytic web is all too evident.

But however partial the picture I have drawn, I think it conveys the sense of helplessness and vulnerability, the sense of outsidedness, that informed my childhood, the knowledge that the grandparents whom I held in awe suffered from the same fears and vulnerability that I did. Then, too, there was the sense of specialness to my mother and in being Jewish with the ambivalence they entailed. Compounding all this, finally, was the curious double life I led growing up as an outsider in Germany. I was the only Jewish boy in my grades in the first four years of public school. And I wasn't even one of *their* Jews. I was an outsider, from Poland. Sandwiched between these slabs of Germany, as it were, were the summer slices of Czestochowa with their special flavor.

Then came the move to America. I was eleven. My father had moved there five years before so that my grandfather, his father, had become his surrogate. Transported from Wiesbaden to the West Side of Chicago, I suffered from culture shock, despite my previous experiences of feeling peripheral in alien cultures. I didn't know to call it culture shock then. I just felt very badly.

Paradoxically, then, for all the sense of vulnerability and outsidedness I had felt in Europe, I missed Wiesbaden and the order and peace and cleanliness I now associated with Germany. By contrast, this new version of Germany, the West Side of Chicago, was the Midwest equivalent of Hell's Kitchen. The roughness, the violence frightened me. I had learned to read English, and avid reader that I was, read the *Chicago Tribune* word for word. I read of the St. Valentine's Day Massacre in which members of Capone's gang had machine-gunned members of a rival gang just a mile away from where I lived and just a month before we arrived. In those days, the Leopold and Loeb case was in the final stages of appeal with Clarence Darrow as defense attorney. I pored over the newspaper account of how the two Chicago youths—Jews, no less—had cold-blood-edly killed a third one, also Jewish. That even Jews could be infected by such epidemic violence was beyond my understand-ing. In my head then echoed a Talmudic teaching on the commandment "Thou shalt not kill." The rabbis say: "If the choice is to slay or be slain, let yourself be slain." A newspaper reporter was killed in a murder with a gangland tie. I told my father I wanted to go back to peaceful, violence-free Germany. I could live with friends in Wiesbaden and finish school there. My father said I should wait and see how I felt in three months. My depression soon abated and my campaign to return to Germany went into limbo.

Let me now shift to a time thirteen or fourteen years later. I am in the midst of the Second World War, on a ship anchored at the port of Augusta in Sicily waiting for orders to sail up the western Italian coast to back up the drive to push the Germans out of Italy. The USO has shipped some magazines, and I have selected a *Readers Digest*, which I preferred to news magazines which only rehashed what I had already heard the week before on the BBC short wave. Suddenly I was reading a story re-counting the rumors filtering out of Nazi-occupied Europe about the death camps—what had already happened and what was still going on. I felt completely devastated. My sense of total helplessness was translated onto the physical plane. My pulse went up to 160 and I believed I was dying of a heart attack. The magazine article had demolished a piece of denial compounded by ignorance for an instant, like a lightning bolt brilliantly out-lines a blacked-out scene before there is darkness again.

Shattered now was the romantic myth of how we were going to win the war and be reunited with grandparents, uncles, cous-ins, and hear of their hardships and suffering and share with them their joyous liberation and relief. Visions of reestablished family ties, of letters and visits, all collapsed as I saw in that brief flash the small heap of corpses that made up my family group—an infinitesimal fraction of the larger whole of the twin mountains of six million Jews and six million others that would become part of our psychological landscape when the blackout ended at war's end. The soap-bubble, pipe-dream fantasy of how I would make my way across Europe to Czestochowa where I would see Bobbe Leja and Bobbe Chayo and Saide Avrum Laib and everyone else in a grand reunion with Yankele, Shloimeh and Hendel's son from America—returned to the scenes of the summers of his childhood—that fantasy collapsed with an acute traumatic neurotic reaction, a severe anxiety attack, experienced as a heart attack. In retrospect, I think that I felt a devastating sense of helplessness and at some level guilt for surviving and for not doing more. A normal electrocardiogram administered by a reassuring physician and a return to shipboard duty that same night contained the attack.

The campaign for the liberation of Italy continued. The invasion of Southern France. Commitment to duty, wartime discipline, the participation in the actions and power of the larger group, ten-million Americans under arms, allied with millions of others, Europeans, Asians, Africans, in a fight for freedom, enabled me, through my connection with such emotionally powerful strands as these, to defend against and push aside the devastating feelings of helplessness of that night when I saw clearly and could not bear what I saw. My own helplessness was part of the vision I could not bear. It is clear to me now that my idea to become a physician and a psychiatrist first crystallized shortly after the night of my attack. It expressed my need not to be vulnerable and to defend myself against the self-contempt of helplessness.

Other activity, other campaigns, marriage, family, training, career, and 35 more years follow. Fifty years after Wiesbaden and Czestochowa, two summers ago, I am visiting my 93-year-old mother, and I have taken her and my aunt out to dinner. My aunt is in her eighties and is my late father's youngest sibling. As often occurs on these occasions, we get into a discussion of the past and of family.

My aunt, who has never spoken directly of the Nazi horror, unexpectedly tells of how, in 1942, her father, Avrum Laib, died. I had assumed all these years that he had gone to Auschwitz with the more than one hundred of my other relatives who had perished there, but mine had been a vague notion of mass horror the very vagueness and multiplicity of which served as a distancing device to diminish the intensity of the experienced affect.

Her description of his death had a sledgehammer effect on me. There is no simple way to convey my feelings—helplessness comes closest, and it barely conveys the degree of vulnerability, sadness, self-accusation, and rage that overwhelmed me. I was flooded with affect-charged memories, the affects going back, back, back to Sicily, to Czestochowa, back to Wiesbaden, back to Chicago. The following three weeks I functioned in a depressed haze. I felt old. My body felt weighted down. Every movement took great effort. Periodically I would remember scenes from my childhood and again and again these would impress me with my helplessness, my failure and humiliation.

After three weeks I sat down one day and wrote the poem. The essential facts are stated there, set into my memories of Czestochowa.

After I wrote the poem I felt great sadness, but the charged memories which had tumbled over each other and had felt so overwhelming now seemed ordered and manageable. The depressive, old, heavy feeling abated, and I was no longer flooded with the sense of helplessness that had so suffused me. My sense of myself no longer had that utterly vulnerable feeling of fragile aging which had made my bodily movements and thinking feel like excruciating efforts.

Presented with the news of the Holocaust horror in a generalized description, I had reacted and could only react with an aversive anxiety reaction. It is not that I subsequently pushed the matter out of my awareness. I dealt with it as most of us do, with sadness, pain, guilt, but also with a continuing gnawing sense that I should have been able to do more and that what had gone before had made me complicit in special ways. I had been there. When I could invoke more specific images and commit them to paper, my feelings altered.

The imagery of the non-interceding Madonna refers in understated form to my experience that Catholic Poland and anti-Semitic Poland are one. My memories of childhood stories of the Polish form of anti-Semitism—the club-wielding, randomly cruel Jew-hating of religious peasants and bourgeois—antedate my later, less visceral understanding of the Nazi form of efficient and orderly extermination by the secular S.S. and its hundreds of Major Degenhardts.

As I read the poem I am brought up short by the cattle image. It is not based on my personal experience unless I count a single schoolboy visit to the stockyards of Chicago. I owe it to James Agee's short story "The Yearling," which tells of a steer who tries to warn the cattle being shipped to slaughter that the myth of their being sent to some paradisiacal grazing ground is false. He is not believed.

The epigraph sounds so stereotypical. We have heard its like so many times that we no longer experience affect with it. It is the German text translated into English of the actual summons by which the Jews of my birthplace, including my grandfather and a hundred other relatives, were summoned that day, the day after Yom Kippur. Major Degenhardt of the S.S. is not a creature of my imagination. That is the name affixed to the order for "resettlement" which brought mass death to the community into which I was born. Czestochowa is some 40 miles north of Auschwitz. Why do I mention this banal fact of geography? Because it means that the ultimate horror is close by, tangible, not something vague, general, far away. I was born a 45-minute drive from Auschwitz. And the Nazis were not just a movement led by infamous monsters whose names echo down the corridors of history; they were thousands of tangible, unsung Major Degenhardts doing their jobs as careerists at their desks in the S.S., signing orders for transport and resettlement and repeating the motto *Arbeit macht frei!* while sending people to their deaths with a minimum of mess or fuss, cleanly and in good order. That is also a form of creativity—to dispatch six million people. First to imagine it and then to translate the fantasy into the everyday organization to achieve it. It implies a certain sense of self that finds such a thing fulfilling.

So, in the poem, I could embody and order the vague and shadowy images floating in my head. Although I had argued for years against the canard that the Jews had been docile in the face of their destruction and thereby complicit, it was not given to me to imagine my grandfather acting as he did until I was told that he did. I should have known that he would have insisted that whether you have five minutes to live or 50 years, how you define yourself determines how you can act, what choices you see as possible. Such choices are ultimately the meaningful definition of self.

A pseudo heart attack, a depressive reaction, a professional career, and a poem are such choices, with differing implications for the self, but all playing a role in self formation and maintenance.

The specific image of my 82-year-old grandfather, acting as he saw fit, beholden to no earthly power in the final moments of his life, crystallized an awareness for me that I had been striving to achieve all my life. It took me 50 years plus three weeks to fully take it in. Judging by my initial reaction to the image of his death, I treated it as another narcissistic blow, another loss of self-esteem, another affirmation of my guilt, vulnerability, and helplessness and of my membership in a group that was characterized by guilt, vulnerability, and help-lessness. As Freud tells us in his work on mourning, the loss of a loved one is first experienced as a loss of part of the self, as a blow to narcissistic integrity, and as a failure, with accusations toward self and others, and then is gradually transformed in such a way that the lost person becomes a part of the self. The creation of the poem capped the process in which my loss of self-esteem and my guilt at my rejection of my grandfather's and father's values were transmuted into something self-en-hancing. The realization that helplessness and vulnerability are primarily subjective states can be liberating, and the kind of mastery that can then assuage anxiety is the mastery stated through the poem rather than the mastery of overt actions, of military campaigns, of achievement.

Let me give another example of how I have used the poetic form as an expression of the striving for self mastery, and of how significant a theme in my life has been the struggle with helplessness—how much the expectation of not being able to act and its frustration has been accompanied by shame and guilt.

Seventeen years ago on a visit to New York I went to a small dinner party with colleagues. Jean and Milton Rosenbaum were there and the late Robert Bak. At some point in the conversation the question went round the table: Of what in our lives were we most ashamed? I remembered an episode in Wiesbaden during recess as a second-grader. I told it. I do not remember what the others told. But the episode had been running around in my mind since its occurrence. I had analyzed it. It continued with me. As I was preparing this paper and as the themes of shame and vulnerability came up again, I wrote it down in the form of an embryonic poem. Again, setting it on paper brought some sense of mastery, an awareness that I could be different from the other, without denial of him. For I could not deny him without denying part of myself.

RECESS

He suddenly appeared at recess
clothed in black caftan with long earlocks
and skull cap precariously perched on his head.
I in *lederhosen,* in a short-sleeved shirt
with no headcovering
like a proper Wiesbaden second-grader,
he a beardless miniature replica of
my grandfather in faroff Czestochowa.
I spoke to him and he answered in a
sing-song, awakening echoes of a past.
I must have been ashamed for him and for myself
and he looked past me at something I could not see.
Suddenly swooping down, a Hans or a Horst
grabbed his headcovering and laughingly
tossed it to a receptive comrade.
The new boy put both hands on his head
and ran after his cap uttering some
plea for its return. When he came within
a few feet of its possessor, it was tossed teasingly
to another (and so it went for the 15 minutes
of recess). Making plaintive, pleading sounds
he ran, hands on head, from Hans to Fritz to
Horst, to Erich to Karl and back again.

And I just stood there and did nothing. I was
ashamed and afraid. When the bell rang the skull
cap was dropped on the playground where he retrieved it.
No blood was shed that day.
But when he had looked past me had he seen something?
Had he seen something that I (the brightest of the
second-graders) could not see?

Wherein lies the mastery? Not just in setting the episode down, not alone in the confession of my fear. Mastery lies in the concomitant recognition, as such things are recounted, that in current analogues to the childhood confrontation there is a chance of restitution, of acting more like my grandfather had. Not to be silent and passively endure, but to see choices and exercise them. My grandfather was not alone. In the *Encyclopedia Judaica* there is the following entry under Czestochowa: "The Jewish fighting organization tried to organize guerrilla units in the nearby forests . . . but . . . they were murdered by Polish terrorists of the *National Armed Forces*." So the socialist Jewish underground fighters and my Orthodox grandfather had died in the same cause, even while, in their lives, they had been bitterly opposed to each other.

All this touches on the paradoxical ambivalences with which my childhood images of Jewishness are endowed. As a result of these ambivalences, I had been drawn in adolescence and young manhood to radical politics, which held out for me a Marxist solution to the power dominance and bigotry of the society I grew up in. So my action solution was first political action, before my choice of career. But I never fully resolved the inner doubt about helplessness. Helpless fear, self-contempt, and shameful humiliation are as much a part of my Jewish identity as are pride and wonder at Jewish survival and feelings of belonging to a community with origins stretching far into the past. I have to reconcile my admiration for my Orthodox grandfather's martyrdom and the self-enhancement which I derive therefrom with the fact that I long ago stopped believing in God.

The poem expresses my belief that there is no external supraordinate power, no higher appeal. That whatever order we impose on the cosmos is human. My depression was an expression of a threat to the coherence of my sense of self, the stripping away of my relative sense of self that had been built on a current and a past sense of competence, of having things under control. Now I had to confront the vulnerability coupled with humiliating shame which belonged to an earlier time of my life. I had felt helplessness before. I had countered it with a sense of competence, experiencing myself as able to act on the world, impose order on it, so as not to feel overwhelmed. I had experienced hatred and denigration before and countered it with the sense of a loved self derived from closeness to my mother, and from the early self experience of being part of an extended family with my mother's mother and my father's father as large and looming figures in a sea of emotional support. I had established a sense of myself as a loyal, courageous person and was confronted with a picture of myself as treacherous and cowardly for having denied those closest to me, a picture which I had submerged.

There had indeed been a degree of emotional withdrawal from family and Jewish community, a way of looking at them and my connection with them with some detachment, a sense of separation. I had viewed this as a positive thing, self-enhancing, as fostering my independence, my maturity, as my getting away from weakness and shame. Now, on reinterpretation, this shift looked to be part and parcel of my treachery and cowardice, already presaged in the German schoolyard, when I watched a fellow Jew being teased.

My intelligence, my study and understanding of things, had been as far back as I could remember a source of a subjective sense of power which worked against the vulnerabilities of childhood and which enabled me to cultivate an intellectual detachment from the family side by side with my involvement with them. This very detachment had been undermined by my aunt's graphic account, just as that same account had shaken severely the balance between my vulnerability and helplessness and the offsetting feelings of competence. I suffered a great letdown in my pride of being bright. I could not use it to feel powerful or lovable when it was so lamentably inadequate, and long-recessed memories of childhood failures, those which had been defended against by being the brightest, emerged.

Now I could have my identification with my grandfather without feeling the need to have it take the forms of religious belief and ritual observances, and without needing grandiosely to feel that I should have been able to save him. In his last moments he had given me something which I could make my own and which could function as the expression of a true self, all the while that it did not require me to deny my relative helplessness.

Strength lies in our ability to look out on the vast cosmos and its turning lights, finding no clues, only masterless night. To own our minds and acknowledge our finiteness and vulnerability, to obtain mastery from the fact that this acknowledgment is coupled with our continuing efforts to function, to love, to seek, to struggle against disorder, to be human, this is what I mean by strength.

The question of my great grandfather and grandfather, "What are you studying, Yankele?" had set me on a course that brought knowledge that eventually separated me from them. But in form I was still identified with them and with the "book." That is the solution to my sense of having betrayed them.

The maintenance of my sense of self is a process that goes back nearly as far as I do. It is a continuing process of staving off certain meanings placed on being and loss and viewing them instead in terms that allow life to go on, with the understanding that what one has been is as much a part of oneself as what one is and will be, without needing to deny any of it or put it into any true-versus-false self conflict. One cannot build a coherent sense of self on a negation, on a reaction formation self.

At the heart of creativity lies the human capacity to construe. This faculty plays the key role in the development of the self. The subjective sense of self is in itself a construct which is determined by early relationships and their constructions and meanings, as the capacities of the self function in feedback fashion to construe relationships to the other even as the self is molded by them.

Human beings endow their inner and outer experiences with meanings, organizing such meanings into various patterns, more or less enduring. When these patterns persist, they have a determining role in the construction of further experience.

The constructs are syntheses of cognitive-affective patterns which, *in vivo,* are not separable into their cognitive and affective components. For the infant (as well as the adult) there are no neutral cognitive experiences. To extend Sanders's description of the infant as "a hypothesis generator," I would add that both the infant and the adult are very passionate about their hypotheses.

The development of the construing self is not a linear unfolding. A series of antithetical polarities or incongruences need to be resolved in the process of developing a self concept. Such a resolution is dynamic. That is, the self concept is born of conflict and continuously functions with intensities arising out of the clash of meanings: the needs of the self to feel whole as against the fear of fragmentation; to feel safe rather than vulnerable; to feel individually related to others as against the fear of isolation on the one side and the fear of being taken over on the other; to feel effective rather than helpless; to feel chosen and affirmed rather than bypassed. There are countless creative possibilities in the construal of these conflicts, and my list cannot be exhaustive any more than there can be an exhaustive list of metaphors or, for that matter, concepts.

Author Index

Italics denote pages with bibliographic information.

A

Abelin, E. L., 64, *68*
Abraham, K., 95, *114*
Abrams, J. C., 191, *200*
Adler, G., 117, 119, 122, 125, 126, 128, 130, *133, 134*
Alport, A., 199, *201*
Anderson, O., 9, *17*
Arnold, M. B., 33, *39*
Asimov, I., 217, 224, *230*
Atwood, G., 16, *19*, 94, 100, *115*

B

Basch, M. F., 7, 12, 13, *17*, 23, 25, 28, 29, 30, 31, 34, 38, *39*, 160, 161, 162, 168, *169*
Bergman, A., 51, 64, *69*
Bergmann, A., 36, *40*, 51, 64, *69*, 108, *114*
Bettelheim, B., 67, *68*
Bibring, E., 85, *89*
Bion, W. R., 47, *49*, 203, 205, 209, *213*
Boggiano, A. K., 195, *201*
Bowlby, J., 34, 36, *39*
Bradley, A. C., 217, 225, *230*
Brandchaft, B., 47, 48, *49*, 94, 98, 100, 101, 105, *114, 115*

Brandchaft, G., 117, *134*
Bryan, J. H., 195, 197, 198, *201*
Bryan, T. H., 195, 197, 198, *201*
Buie, D. H., 117, 122, 128, *133, 134*
Burnham, D. G., 121, *134*

C

Capra, F., 65, *68*
Chodorow, N., 65, 67, *68*
Coleridge, S. T., 217, 224, *230*

D

Dinnerstein, D., 65, 67, *68*

E

Ehrhardt, A. A., 53, *69*

F

Feldman, A. B., 217, *230*
Fiedler, L. A., 217, *231*
Fraiberg, S., 123, *134*
Freedman, D. A., 34, 35, *39*
Freud, S., 4, 13, 14, *17*, 31, *40*, 45, *49*, 72, *89*, 120, *134*, 216, *231*

Subject Index

as primary motivational drive, 61–63
shame experience and, 82–84
in Work Groups, 211–12
Self demise of Othello, 217–24
Self-esteem
in learning-disabled children, 194–95
learning process and, 192
Self-fulfilling-prophecy thesis, 200
Self-mastery, creative process and
striving for, 247–52
Selfobject
bond, archaic, 228–30
concept, 21–29, 164, 168–69
experience, varieties of, 43–50
function
gender and, 52, 54
idealization, 59, 63, 65, 67, 111–12
mirroring, 59, 60, 63, 65–67
of parents, 35–36, 63–68, 185–86
in therapeutic process, 130, 164,
185
need for, 27, 28, 166–167
responses of, 46, 59
theory of development, 108–9
theory of motivation, 15–17
use of analyst as, 187
Selfobject transference
of borderline patient, 109–11, 121–22
archaic, 47–48
defined, 25
disruptions in, 143–56
analytic ambience and, 150–52
case vignettes, 144–50
countertransference, 147–49
as crux of therapeutic process, 153
patient's experience of, 153–55
results of, 155
holding and soothing qualities of,
129–30
idealizing, 25, 110, 147–50, 167, 207
mirroring, 25, 76, 110, 198–200, 207
parent–child relationship and, 26–
28, 35–37
theoretical implications of, 21–41
instinct theory and, 25, 29–33
narcissistic personality disorders
and, 21–25
Oedipus complex and, 26–27, 167
tension reduction theory and, 33
use of term, 37–38, 46–48
Self-preservation instinct, 31, 33, 34

Self psychology
basic principles of, 143–44
contributions of, 37
countertransference and, 125–27
development of, 22–23
use of term, 38–39, 48–49
Separateness, need for, 121, 137. See
also Selfobject transference
Separation and individuation, 36–37,
67
Separation anxiety, 123
Sexism, 58. See also Feminine self, psychology of
Sexuality, 6–11, 33, 55
Sexualization
of Basic Assumption Pairing Group,
210–11
of selfobject relationship, 154–55
Shakespeare, self psychological approach to, 215–31
classical psychoanalytic approach vs.,
216–17
Othello, 217–30
self demise as tragedy in, 217–24
Shame, 71–90
creative process and, 248–50
depression and, 85–87
exhibitionism and, 74–75
failure of compensatory structure
and, 83–85
in Kohut's early writings, 74–76
motivation in, 87
"nameless," 81
palliation of, 80
psychoanalytic treatment of, 86–87
rage and, 87–88
related phenomena, 71–73
in The Restoration of the Self, 81–86
self-cohesion and, 82–84
Small group, self in, 203–13
Bion's work on, 203–6
consultant and, 204–5, 208, 209–10
Kohut's work and, 207–9
comparison to Bion's, 209–13
phases in development of, 207
regular dynamics, 204–6
transmuting internalization in, 207,
212
Split, therapeutic, 22–23, 24
Splitting, defensive, 107–8, 111
Stereotyping, gender, 60